ENDOR

Carma Naylor was a lifelong Mormon, a devoted follower of their teachings until the Lord opened her eyes to the truth. In her books, *A Mormon's Unexpected Journey*, she reveals many of the hidden truths and facts of this religion and is a must read for any who have wondered what Mormonism is all about.

—**Pastor Chuck Smith** (now deceased), Founder of the Calvary Chapel movement with over 2,000 affiliated churches worldwide, author of many books and still heard nationwide on the radio program Word for Today

I highly recommend Carma Naylor's magnificent two-volume book called *A Mormon's Unexpected Journey* (*Finding the Grace I Never Knew*). It is a powerful and inspiring account of Sister Carma's uncompromising search for truth after having dedicated forty years of faithful service to the LDS church. It is, hands down, the best book ever written on this subject of coming out of Mormonism and into biblical Christianity— and I've read everything!

—**Dr. John B. Wallace**, practicing Dentist, Lecturer, Bible Teacher, and Author of *Starting at the Finish Line* (*The Gospel of Grace for Mormons*)

Carma's books are so helpful for the person who is seeking to know the truth regarding Mormonism. Although they are filled with good sound biblical doctrine and theology, that is not the main thrust. The primary emphasis is love. Carma's love for the truth, for who God is, and for her family resonates throughout. The love of God for fallen man fills the pages. Anyone genuinely searching for the truth and asking for meaning to this life will find their questions answered in these books.

I wholeheartedly recommend *A Mormon's Unexpected Journey*.

—**Pastor Tony Magana**, Calvary Chapel Yakima Valley, WA

Carma Naylor loves Mormons. I have sat with her on several occasions as the tears of love have dropped from her eyes as she talks about those for whom she cares so deeply. These pages are stained with those tears. Her greatest desire is for each one to hear the truth and to know the Eternal Son of God, the Lord Jesus Christ, God come in the flesh.

Her story is intriguing. Her message is clear. You will be blessed by reading.

> —**Dr. Walter Price**, Baptist Pastor
> Fellowship in the Pass, Beaumont, CA
> (recently retired), and the author of *God Focus*

I have known no one more passionate or sincere about the truth of God's grace than Carma Naylor. Her love for Scripture, her love for Mormons, and the depth of her studies are clearly evidenced in this incredible, true story. The book is an invaluable resource for those who want to know more about Mormonism—or contrast it with biblical Christianity—from a compassionate woman who has experienced it firsthand.

Highly recommended!

> —**Kelly Pinkham**, Freelance Writer and Editor

There is nothing as powerful as the personal testimony of someone whose life has been changed by the Lord. Carma shares her experiences in such a way that no one can doubt the hand of God intervening in her life and the life of her family.

> —**Pastor Stacy Smith**, Baptist Pastor
> Valley Baptist Fellowship, Yucaipa, CA

A
MORMON'S
UNEXPECTED JOURNEY

CHP. 8 - The Book of Mormon
v. The Bible

VOLUME I

A MORMON'S

UNEXPECTED JOURNEY

Finding the

Grace

I Never Knew

CARMA NAYLOR

Thy word is a lamp
unto my feet,
and a light
unto my path.

Psalm 119:105

TABLE OF CONTENTS

NOTE TO THE READER

When I started writing years ago, I had no intentions of writing a book. I simply wanted to write my testimony for my family and friends who could not understand me. Since discussing my changed beliefs was often a closed door, or strained at best, I was compelled to write; believing that someday those I love would read and understand. As my journey kept going, I kept writing. I ended up with so much material that I decided to divide it into two books.

While I have written these books to anyone seeking truth, I pray that those who have become disillusioned with religion, as well as the devout religious person, will read my story to the end so that you can find God's grace and the answers much faster than I did. To my reader who has already found God's love and grace, may this book help you grow in grace and share it with a friend.

Sincerely,

Carma

FOREWORD

A **Mormon's Unexpected Journey** is a riveting testimony of Carma Naylor's search for the truth that would set her free. Carma's transparency about her inner struggles, her rejection by family and friends, and her heartaches as a mother will captivate your heart and enable you to relate to the reality of life's trials. A Mormon's Unexpected Journey is a concise theological treatise that walks you, step-by-step, through Mormon doctrines and challenges each one with the truth of Scripture. It will equip the new believer as well as the seasoned theologian with insights into the Mormon's head and heart in order to share the truth and love of God with them. These two books are written for the Mormon to read as well. If you have ever struggled with how to share your faith with a Mormon friend, Carma's writings will show you the way in a simple and loving manner.

I have had the privilege of being a part of her journey and actively ministering to this family in many of these situations and trials. Her story will encourage you. The Truth in these pages will set you free. This is not just another book about Mormonism; it is a must-read for every Christian.

—Dr. Bruce Edwards, Pastor
Hope Fellowship
Branson West, Missouri

ACKNOWLEDGEMENTS

Throughout my journey, the Lord put the right person in my path at the right time to lead me in His truths. I wasn't sure what I would do with my manuscript when I was finished writing, but I knew that the Lord would lead me to the right people, as He had done all along; and He did. He brought interested, qualified people into my life that read my manuscript and were the first to offer me encouragement with their positive feedback. I have chosen not to mention their names for fear of leaving someone out, but it was through their words of encouragement that I started gaining confidence that my writings may become a book someday. I am grateful to each of them.

Of course, there are other very special people, who I want to acknowledge and thank. First and foremost, my deepest gratitude goes to my family, without whose support and encouragement this book would have never been completed. Words are not sufficient to express my thanks for their believing in this project and giving me encouragement when I needed it. Most of all, I am grateful for their prayers and the spiritual strength I have received from each of them at various times over the years while this book was in the making. My heartfelt, special thanks goes to my best friend, my husband, for his patient, loving support.

Special recognition and appreciation is due our daughter-in-law Kara Naylor, for sharing one of her many talents and helping to design the front cover. She also drew the illustration and the map of Central America in volume two.

I am especially indebted to the wonderful staff at Oak Glen Christian Conference Center for their spiritual influence on my family and for providing a beautiful, peaceful haven away from the chaos and demands of life where I could hear my Shepherd's voice and write.

I am grateful to Ronda Steele, God's most recent gift to me in the final stages of this book. She selflessly gave of her time reviewing my manuscript and provided valuable input.

I want to express my thanks to Susan Bramlette for all her valuable work. She was not only my editor, but also a spiritual mentor and friend.

Most importantly, I want to thank my Father in Heaven, and my Lord and Savior, Jesus Christ, for my journey with them and for helping me write that journey. All the credit and glory go to "Him that is able to do exceeding abundantly above all that we ask or think." (Ephesians 3:20)

INTRODUCTION

The Church of Jesus Christ of Latter-day Saints is one of the fastest-growing churches in the world today—and with good reason. Who would not want to join a church that promises a happier, more solid family life now and, even better, a family that will last through all eternity? Who would not want to avail himself of the outstanding Family Home Evening program or the many exciting youth programs designed to produce clean, upright, moral young people who will shine as lights in the midst of this perverse world? Who would not want to belong to an organization of which Jesus Christ is the Head, who speaks to a living prophet today, as He did to Moses and other prophets of Israel?

What a secure feeling to know that if you follow the prophet you won't be led astray by Satan's deceptions. Surely every good person would want to belong to an organization with a vital social structure of high standards with a membership of clean-living, happy people that love each other and take care of one another's needs (not to mention a welfare program that feeds the poor among them).

Should not every Christian want to be part of an organization that claims to be the only religion with the authority to act for God—the Holy Priesthood? Surely anybody that has heard the Mormon Tabernacle Choir sing or attended an all-church dance festival at the Rose Bowl, or visited a Mormon temple cannot help but be impressed with the quality and splendor of this fast-growing, wealthy church.

Yes, the attractiveness and appeal of a faith that promises to satisfy the needs of human nature is indeed apparent in the Mormon Church. What, then, could be wrong with an organization that appears to offer the answers to today's troubled world? Why would anybody leave such an effective church, at the risk of losing his family and friends? Why would anybody want to point out anything negative about such a choice organization that claims to give to the world goodness, truth, and the only way back to Father in Heaven?

This book seeks to answer these and other questions you may have as I tell my true story of leaving the Mormon Church after forty years of loving, living and believing in, and giving my life to it. I am writing my story because I believe God wants me to share my experience with the many Mormons that He loves and that I love. I pray that you will read it with an open, prayerful mind and understand the spirit in which it is written.

My purpose in writing this book is not to tear down or destroy something good, as some may suppose. Instead, my desire is to help Mormons (and others in any religion) who are struggling to make themselves "good enough" or "worthy" of Jesus to understand that the gospel is not a message of what we have to do to make ourselves right with God, it is the message of what God has already done to make us right with Him. I want them to find the true gospel of grace that Christ's Apostles wrote about in the New Testament. Yes, this book does expose many fallacies within the Mormon Church and you may ask, "Why would you want to be negative about a good thing?" I would ask the same question of Mormons: "Why would you send thousands of young missionaries out into the world every year to bring people out of their Christian religions and into Mormonism? Aren't you doing it because you believe you have something better that they need to know about?"

That is the same reason I give for writing this book. I have found something better, and I want to share it with those I love in the Mormon Church. I have discovered the pure, simple gospel of Jesus Christ and set aside the added doctrines that changed it. I have found His peace, His love, and His grace—that for which I'd always hungered, despite my religious efforts.

As a devout Latter-day Saint, I thought I had the best; but there was something missing. I longed to hear Jesus say, "Well done thou good and faithful servant." Even though I was a faithful member of the church, I never knew if I had done enough and if I was worthy to stand before the Lord. Today I am ready. I have an assurance that He has accepted me and I belong to Him. Not because of my righteous acts, but because of what my Lord and Savior, Jesus Christ, has done for me.

If you recognize that something is missing in your life, if you have a longing to fill that void with the love and grace offered to you by Jesus, if you desire to find His easy yoke, or desire to help others find God's grace, then keep reading—this book is for you!

CHAPTER 1

AN HONORABLE HERITAGE

*"Trust in the LORD with all thine heart; and lean not
unto thine own understanding. In all thy ways
acknowledge him, and he shall direct thy paths."*
—Proverbs 3:5–6

On April 6, 1830, six men met in Fayette, New York, and organized a church. This church has grown into an organization with a worldwide membership of more than fourteen million in just one hundred eighty years. April sixth was always a very important day in my life, also. Not only was it the day my church—The Church of Jesus Christ of Latter-day Saints—was organized, but I was also taught that it was the true birthday of Jesus Christ and that for this reason the church was established on that date.

In addition to these great events, the day had another significant meaning to me: it was my own birthday. I was made to feel special being born on such an important day. The annual General Conference of the church was always held on this date. It was a time when the Saints gathered in Salt Lake City at the historic tabernacle located on Temple Square for three days of inspiration and direction from the leaders of the church and the twelve apostles who were prophets, seers, and revelators.

These conference sessions were broadcast over the radio throughout Utah so that everyone could listen to them (now they are broadcast *worldwide* via satellite.)

My birthday, therefore, was always marked with the virtue of hearing the familiar voices of these beloved "general authorities" fill our home. I could recognize most of them by their voices, and I eagerly anticipated the message of the Prophet, hoping he would give some indication that Christ's return—an event I looked forward to, even as a child—would be soon.

These conference sessions and the tabernacle broadcast every Sunday were so meaningful to me as a child and youth that they became an integral part of my life. I loved the strains of the tabernacle choir, which permeated our home with a peaceful and holy sound every Sunday morning.

My Mormon Roots

I not only felt special as a child because my birthday was on April sixth, but also because I was blessed to have been born into a Mormon family with wonderful, devout parents. My youthful memories include the inviting aroma of fresh, hot cinnamon rolls baked every Saturday morning and hot bread every other day. My mother was an excellent cook, seamstress, and a hard-working and thrifty homemaker who taught her skills in the home to her four daughters. We learned to grow our gardens, can fruit, sew our own clothes, crochet, and make quilts.

Excellence was a part of my Mormon culture, as well as industry and personal accomplishment. I loved this culture. I loved earning the personal achievement awards that were an important part of the primary and young women's programs at church. Receiving these awards in my youth was an important part of learning service, skills, hobbies, and of growing spiritually.

My father was the highest authority as patriarch of our home. When he spoke there was no more discussion and no contrary opinions were voiced. He was highly respected in the community as well as in the church and held many leadership positions, including that of bishop. He was a powerful speaker and leader and, in my mind, I placed him on a par with the *general authorities* of the church. I loved to have religious discussions with him, and he was always well-equipped to answer any of my questions. Often he answered verbally, but sometimes he referred me to books out of his vast library so I could research the answer for myself. One room in the house was set aside for dad's books, which filled shelves on all four walls. As a young woman I believed every book published by the Church in Salt Lake City was in dad's library.

As a teenager, I looked to my parents as such perfect models that I grew up with an unrealistic view of marriage. I can honestly say that in their fifty years of marriage I never heard them quarrel or say an unkind word to each other. That is not to say that they didn't have their problems, but they never showed them openly. This may sound ideal, but in truth it created within me an unrealistic, Cinderella-like dream of marriage, one that made life somewhat difficult for me when dealing with normal problems later as an adult.

Prior to my eighth birthday, we moved from Layton, Utah to Lake Stephens, Washington, where our home was surrounded by five acres of woods. I loved to spend hours playing in the trees and developed a keen sense of closeness and reverence for God as I wandered through His beautiful creation. We lived within five minutes' walking distance of the lake, and we enjoyed picking and eating wild berries on the way home from our summer swims.

Shortly after moving to Lake Stephens, I was baptized. In the LDS Church it is customary that all children be baptized by immersion at the age of eight. My father impressed upon me the importance of this occasion and I would remember it always. I was taught that through baptism my sins were remitted and I was given a clean slate. The next day at church I was confirmed a member of the Church of Jesus Christ of Latter-day Saints when men who held the priesthood laid hands on my head to confer the *gift* of the Holy Ghost upon me. I fully expected to *feel* very differently after receiving the Holy Ghost and was surprised when I felt no different at all.

I looked forward to going to church regularly and especially enjoyed learning all the Bible stories at Sunday school. I was taught that to say no when asked to give a talk or to do any kind of service at church was to say no to the Lord. So, in spite of my shy nature, I tried to do what I was

3

asked to do, although doing anything in front of people frightened me. This inability to say no to the church carried over into my adult life and I responded to any call to serve with a yes even though, at times, I felt very overwhelmed and tired.

I often contemplated how fortunate I was to have been born in the great and free land of America, instead of some third-world country. In addition to this, I rejoiced in that I was born healthy and born into an affluent society and, most importantly of all, into Heavenly Father's true church. I was taught that this was a privilege earned only by *the worthy* in the pre-existence. (Pre-existence is a Mormon belief in a spirit world where all humans existed before this earthly life).

Once, my father had seen a vision in which he saw hundreds of Heavenly Father's spirit-children in this pre-existent spirit world. They were the spirits reserved to come forth in this, the last dispensation of time, and they were divided into two groups—one large and one small. His spirit-guide told my father that the large group was amongst the most rebellious and wicked of God's spirit-children. In the smaller group were some of God's most valiant spirit-children, those who would come forth on earth with the wicked spirits in order to be tested. The youth of the church today were these *valiant spirits* and they would be faced with tremendous trials and temptations.

Because of my father's words, I believed I was one of those valiant spirits and that, because of my worthiness in the pre-existence, God had blessed me exceedingly. This not only made me feel important to God, but it also placed a great responsibility upon me. I was often reminded, "Where much is given, much is expected." I wanted to prove faithful to God while on this earth, as I assumed I had been in the spirit realm before this life, and someday to return to Him again. This was more important to me than anything!

When I turned eleven years old I began playing the piano for Junior Sunday School and the weekly primary children's meeting. This, and many other growing experiences such as teaching and speaking, helped me overcome shyness and develop self-confidence. I loved the piano. It was pure self-expression, my best friend, and something that provided an emotional release for me as a teenager. Mother started teaching me to play at the age of five. The highlight of my day was when my sisters would come home from school and play duets with me. I dreamed of someday becoming a concert pianist but was too afraid and embarrassed to express my fantasy to anyone. In high school when they asked for a pianist to volunteer at school, I was too inhibited to step forward, but I envied the students that accompanied the choirs. I played the viola and, one time when performing Tchaikovsky's Piano Concerto with the college orchestra, I longed to be playing the piano solo instead of the viola. However, I never considered myself good enough to perform publicly and wondered why I had such dreams.

At the age of eighteen, a good piano teacher encouraged me to learn Chopin's great compositions that I had thought were far too difficult for me, although I loved them dearly. Two or three hours at the piano were like minutes to me as I lost myself in the works of the great composers. My teacher was astounded at how fast I learned and made a comment that partially fulfilled the secret longing of my heart.

"I wish I'd found you when you were five," he said. "I would have made a concert pianist out of you."

My twelfth birthday was very memorable because we drove from Washington to attend the General Conference Session on Temple Square in Salt Lake City. I actually got to shake hands with the living Prophet of God, President David O. McKay. I felt very special shaking hands with the man who talked with Heavenly Father and received messages for us.

After five years in Washington we moved back to Ogden, Utah. I missed the green, lush, forest-covered mountains of the Northwest and was amazed to hear the local Utahans frequently express thankfulness for their "beautiful" Wasatch Mountains. I thought their idea of beauty was strange because, by comparison to the forests I was used to, the land seemed dry and barren. The lack of foliage on the mountains made them appear naked to me. In time, however, I learned to appreciate the beauty of the Rocky Mountains and could sing along with all the Saints the beloved Mormon hymn, "Utah, We Love Thee."

Coming back to Utah was like coming home. This was the land of my heritage, a heritage of which I was proud. Utah was the land my Mormon ancestors had settled and developed. My maternal great, great grandfather, William Stimpson, had crossed those rugged Rocky Mountains with the ill-fated Martin Handcart Company in 1856. That

5

was a tragic year for many Mormon pioneers and constituted a sad page in LDS Church history. William Stimpson was among the fortunate who survived this trek of more than a thousand miles on foot. Many others died of hunger, fatigue, or illness, while still others froze to death in the terrible winter storms they encountered.

Some Mormon pioneers that survived this journey were so severely frostbitten they were crippled for life. William Stimpson lost his wife and two sons, ages four and two, in those mountains. [For a startling and more extensive account of the Martin Handcart Company, see A. Appendix to Chapter One.]

As a teenager living at the foot of the rugged Wasatch Mountain range, I was often reminded that many faithful people (my own ancestors included) had risked or even given their lives so that the Church could be established. Because of their faith, perseverance, and extreme sufferings, I now had the privilege of enjoying the cultural and spiritual benefits of a Mormon society—a society and lifestyle that I dearly loved.

Growing, Going, and Knowing

It was great to be in Zion (as we called Utah), where my friends were all Mormons and I could take *seminary* as one of my regular, high school classes. But at school and in the social world I was still shy. It was at church and in Seminary class that I seemed to find my identity as a worthwhile person. My self-esteem and identity as a teenager was closely tied in with my activities at church and in religious settings.

In my early teens I fell in love with The New Testament, especially the four Gospels. One day while reading somewhere in the gospels, I remember a unique experience of feeling an unusual outpouring of God's love that filled my soul with a special warmth and glow. I remember being filled with the desire to obey and follow my Savior, Jesus Christ, and always be true to Him.

At last the time came for me to receive my patriarchal blessing! For Mormons, a *patriarchal blessing* is given by a man set apart and ordained as a patriarch. It is believed that this man is called of God to give you specific blessings and promises for your life that will be received upon one's attainment of worthiness and personal righteousness.

At this time I believed in the church, but I was experiencing some teenage doubts about Joseph Smith. I also wondered if the patriarch was really inspired or if he just had some rhetorical sayings he used in all blessings, changing each one a little. Well, I was quite amazed how my blessing seemed to fit me as an individual. He mentioned my love for nature and music. Receiving my blessing strengthened my faith in the church, but still I could not say that I knew the church was true. I loved the church deeply and was entirely devoted to it. I could not comprehend how the church could be anything but true. Still, the words "I know" were too strong for me, and I wondered how so many people could testify using them.

Didn't God expect us to exercise faith? I wondered. *Once someone knew something, he didn't need faith anymore, did he?* I reasoned.

A Mormon testimony consists of being able to say, unequivocally, "I know the LDS Church is true and that Joseph Smith is a true prophet of God." This testimony is very important to members of the church and is believed to proclaim knowledge received from the Holy Ghost. But I was no longer satisfied with merely *believing*. I wanted to *know*, I wanted a spiritual manifestation from God that would leave me with no doubts. As I listened to others bear testimony that they knew the church was true and that Joseph Smith was a true prophet, I felt that they had experienced a magnificent and powerful spiritual manifestation that left them no doubts or question that they were right. My father had experienced several such evidences, many of which he could not share with us, but many of which he did. By his report, he had heard the voice of the Lord and had personally been in the presence of the Holy Ghost. He believed the LDS teaching that the Holy Ghost was a spirit and did not have a body of flesh & bones; yet, he said that the Holy Ghost appeared to him as a beautiful, glorified man who taught him spiritual truths.

My father was an extremely honest and respected man, and I never questioned or doubted that these experiences were real. I *believed* the church had to be true because of these manifestations he had experienced and his powerful, extensive knowledge of the gospel.

However, I had not experienced any strong spiritual enlightenment myself, so I was hanging somewhat onto the strength of his testimony,

7

exercising faith. I did not have a pure knowledge that enabled me to say, "I know," as others did. I could say I believed it with all my heart, but I was expecting and waiting for the day when I, too, could say, "*I know* this is the *only true church* on the face of the earth," as I'd often heard others say.

I studied other religions and visited a few churches but was extremely thankful to be part of what seemed to me to be a far superior faith. As my dad put it, "Comparing the Mormon Church with any other church was like comparing a Cadillac to a wheelbarrow." I was convinced that my church had the best lifestyle, the best programs, the best doctrines, and the best promises. In no other church could partners marry for eternity. All other marriages were for *time only*. How shallow that seemed. I dreamed of the day when I would find my eternal partner—the one that I had chosen in the pre-existence—and be married to him for all eternity in the House of the Lord, the Holy Temple.

My Mission

At the age of twenty-one, while working as a legal secretary in Salt Lake City, I received a call from my bishop to go on a mission. I had recently turned down a marriage proposal and had another admirer convinced that I was the only one for him. I fasted and prayed for God to reveal His will to me. I wasn't getting any answer, so after three days of not eating or drinking anything, I concluded that God would not want me to turn down a mission call. As I drank some water to end my fast, my entire body was filled with a tingling sensation that I interpreted to be the Holy Ghost confirming my decision to accept the mission call. I had been seeking God's direction and was convinced that this experience was His answer to my question and that I was to go on a mission.

Mission preparations began and it was soon the day to go to the temple, the House of the Lord, to receive my endowments. It was a day I had anticipated with excitement all my life. My parents had gone to the temple regularly, but because the temple is of such a sacred nature, they could never discuss what they did in the temple with anyone. Consequently, like others, I knew very little about the temple ceremony I was to participate in before going. I did know I would be making sacred covenants that were very serious, but I didn't know what those covenants were.

Since the unknown made me anxious, I was very nervous. In addition to this, I had a friend who had been a Mason, as well as an active temple Mormon. He had tried to warn me that the temple might seem different than I expected. He said there were similarities between the Masonic temple and the Mormon temple and that at first it had bothered him. However, after continuing to go regularly he was no longer troubled. He seemed to want to protect me from being disillusioned. All of this added to my nervousness. However, I was mostly very excited that I was actually going to enter the sacred temple—the most holy spot on earth. My parents went through the temple with me. The experience was different from anything I had experienced in my life. It seemed foreign to my church experience. I really had expected to feel the presence of the Lord in the temple and was surprised that I didn't. It was uncomfortably strange. I was told that by being faithful to my covenants and returning to the temple often I would understand the sacred ordinance as I became more spiritual. I concluded that I didn't feel the presence of the Lord in the temple because I wasn't worthy (even though I was morally chaste, lived the Word of Wisdom, paid tithing, and was faithful in attending and serving in callings at church). I was sworn to secrecy to never speak of the things I learned in the temple.

Several months later I was on the other side of the world—in the beautiful and fascinating country of New Zealand. Rather than feeling elated, however, I was struggling. I had anticipated my mission to be very spirit-filled and joyful. Why did I feel such empty, lonely, and dark feelings? I would have loved to trade places with the missionaries who were leaving to go home. However, I knew such thoughts were wrong and I quickly buried them.

The first month in New Zealand seemed like an eternity. I was homesick, surrounded by strangers, living in a poverty-stricken area of Wellington, and desperately wanting God to give me a spiritual witness. The day had arrived when *believing in faith* was no longer sufficient. As a young missionary I was fully expecting God to give me some divine manifestation that would place me beyond faith and enable me to bear testimony, as all the other missionaries did, that *I knew beyond a shadow of a doubt* that the church was true, that Joseph Smith was a true Prophet, and that the Book of Mormon was true.

Gaining My Testimony

At zone meetings (missionary testimonial meetings), giving one's testimony was not voluntary, but compulsory. Row by row, in seating order, each missionary was to rise to his feet, go to the front of the group, and bear (give) his testimony. This was not just a testimony of sharing God's love or sharing some blessing you had received, but it was also stating that you knew the church was true and that Joseph Smith was a true prophet. When my turn came I was the only one to say, "I believe," rather than, "I know." This was almost embarrassing for me.

I assumed that all the other missionaries had experienced a magnificent and powerful manifestation of the spirit that had left no doubt or question in their minds. I was becoming very impatient and desirous for God to give me some kind of spiritual experience that would change my belief in the Book of Mormon and Joseph Smith to *absolute knowledge*. I wanted a testimony—a strong testimony—an unwavering testimony! I not only wanted it, I *needed* it! It was expected and imperative.

After three weeks in the mission field I was asked to speak in church. Speaking in church meetings was not new to me since the church provides opportunities for youth to speak. However, I had never overcome my fear of public speaking. Any kind of performing or speaking before an audience of any size was extremely frightening to me, particularly giving speeches that I had to write myself. My anxieties were intensified for two reasons: first, being a missionary I felt the pressure of the high expectations I had placed upon myself, and, secondly, I had not been able to prepare a talk. My senior companion was a very dedicated, hard-working missionary who had kept us very busy. Besides having no time, I was dealing with homesickness and culture shock, and I didn't feel very spiritual. In addition there had been so much emphasis in the Missionary Training Center on "getting the spirit," which I didn't feel had happened to me yet. This caused me to wonder what was wrong with me. I had hoped to prepare a talk an hour or so before church but my companion, who was choir director, felt it much more important that I accompany her on the piano for choir rehearsal. I was frustrated! How could I give an uplifting, spiritual message in church in thirty minutes when I didn't even have a good feeling inside myself? I was discouraged and wondered if I was cut out to be a missionary. It was one of those moments when I wanted to run from the responsibility in front of me, but I had no place to run. The temptation to give it all up and go home was great, but I didn't want to bring such disgrace and humiliation upon myself or my parents. Such a thought was unthinkable and was simply *not* an option.

In desperation I found a quiet, secluded spot in the women's restroom. I knew my only hope was for Father in Heaven to take over. I could do nothing without Him. My faith in Him was all I had to hold onto. I thought of one of the favorite Bible verses I had memorized at the age of twelve: "Trust in the LORD with all thine heart; and lean not unto thine own understanding. In all thy ways acknowledge him, and he shall direct thy paths" (Proverbs 3:5–6).

He did not let me down. The next few moments alone with Him surprised me. My troubled soul was calmed as a supernatural strength flowed into me. My head became warm, as if a hand rested upon it. My panicky fears melted away, my tense nerves relaxed, and my mind was calmed. Comfort, solace, and peace flowed through me from my head to my feet.

Priesthood-holders had placed their hands on my head at the age of eight to impart to me the Holy Ghost and I felt nothing. *A general authority* of the church had laid his hands on my head and set me apart as a missionary. I felt no change or spiritual feeling within me, as I'd expected. I had often wondered why I never felt any spiritual impact at these times. Even when I went to the temple and received the sacred endowment, I had not felt any spiritual presence. But what had just happened to me now was not from man. It came when I was alone with Father in Heaven, trusting only Him.

My confidence was no longer in myself as I spoke in church on faith. I received many compliments. An elder told me my talk was powerful. I knew it was the Lord, not me. This spiritual experience increased my

11

faith that God was very aware of me and of my needs. I also concluded that the church just had to be true in light of what I had just experienced. However, I was still waiting for the Holy Ghost to give me that special witness to the truthfulness of the Book of Mormon, as promised in the book itself. I had never experienced the "burning in the bosom" that was mentioned in the Doctrine & Covenants. I was very desirous for the Lord to give me some special confirmation from the Holy Ghost concerning the truthfulness of the Book of Mormon. Each morning I read the Book of Mormon on my knees by my bedside, praying for such an experience. Finally, after several weeks, while reading the words of King Benjamin in the Book of Mormon about service and humility, I realized how much I loved what I was reading. I remembered being taught that a testimony was a feeling of love, similar to the warm feelings we have towards our family.

A strong emotion of warmth, goodness, and love filled me as I thought of my family back home, combined with the beautiful words from the Book of Mormon. I concluded that this love I felt was the Holy Ghost confirming to me the truthfulness of the Book of Mormon. It's hard to put into words the feeling that came over me. Unlike the calming spirit that flowed through me and strengthened me when I had previously felt the hand on my head, this was a happy sensation that tingled through me and left me feeling somewhat weak and dizzy. Because of this experience I knew the Book of Mormon was true, and I could testify accordingly. I had received the spiritual witness I had been seeking and anxiously anticipating.

Because of these two experiences, I could finally say, "I know the Book of Mormon is true." Therefore, Joseph Smith had to be a true prophet and the Mormon Church was the only true church on the earth. It was a package deal. One could not be true without the others. I had gained my testimony—a testimony I had earnestly sought and desired, and one I would not question or doubt. It was precious to me, and I resolved I would never let anything or anybody take it from me. For years to come, whenever problems or questions arose concerning Joseph Smith or the Book of Mormon, I remembered these experiences and blocked out anything that would contradict them.

Powers of Darkness

I enjoyed being in New Zealand and had many special experiences there. I also experienced the spiritual powers of darkness in that land. One night my companion and I had been visiting with a Buddhist lady in her home. As we were walking home, suddenly I felt an evil presence and instantly heard a sound that was different from anything I had ever heard. It sounded like a raspy, scratchy voice, but not a human voice. As fear gripped me, I felt this entity grow closer. It was as if it were right next to me. My companion and I said nothing, but I knew she also was experiencing something as she grabbed my arm and looked around with fear in her eyes. There was no one anywhere in sight. Without speaking a word to each other, we both silently prayed. When we arrived at our apartment, we both fell to our knees. She rebuked the evil presence in the name of Jesus and it left. Then we shared with each other what we had felt. We both had heard and felt the same thing.

The second time we visited the Buddhist home we again went through a similar experience. We never returned to that Buddhist home and our zone leader found us another place to live in a much better part of town. We both wondered why this had happened to us. I didn't understand the experience very well, but it had convinced me of the reality of evil spirits in our modern world. I also now believed that these evil spirits were against us, which further strengthened my testimony of the church.

Mission Successful

I soon got over being homesick and became close with the people that we taught. Several families became our families away from home. I made many wonderful friends and fell in love with both the Maori people and the beautiful landscapes of New Zealand.

My mission was a great experience and a time of personal growth. I learned to love people in a new way and gained confidence in myself. There were times of deep discouragement and struggle, as well as many happy times. Yet in all that happened across that year-and-a-half, (LDS missions are two years for young men, but one-and-a-half years for young women) the most important events were the experiences that gave me a testimony of the church and became an anchor of faith that would allow me to serve my mission faithfully and the commitment and determination to serve the Lord all my life.

I finished my mission as the first *supervising sister* in the New Zealand South Mission, a calling I considered to be a great honor.

A. APPENDIX TO CHAPTER ONE:

A Brief Sketch of the Martin Handcart Company

From the time of the church's origin its leaders were very devoted to missionary work. As a result they gained hundreds of proselytes from England. These early converts were counseled to "gather to Zion."

Zion was first designated at Kirtland, Ohio, the city where the LDS Church was located after leaving New York. Because of troubles in Kirtland, the Saints had gathered to Independence, Missouri, where Joseph Smith dedicated a spot for the building of the temple and the establishment of a New Zion. The Saints were driven by the populace from Independence and were given land in Caldwell County. Here, once again, Joseph designated Far West to be the location of Zion and dedicated a plot of land for the building of the temple in the last days.

At Joseph's request, the Saints gathered to Far West, believing they were establishing Zion. The two pieces of property (in Independence and Far West) can be visited as historic Mormon sites, but a temple has never been built on either piece of land, nor was Zion established at either place. From Missouri, the Saints were driven to Illinois. Lastly, following the death of the Prophet Joseph Smith, the Mormons who followed Brigham Young as the succeeding prophet made their famous trek across Iowa, Nebraska, Wyoming and the Rocky Mountains into the Salt Lake Basin in Utah.

The first group arrived in 1847. Utah then became Zion—the new gathering place for these Saints. Several splinter groups started at this time and went in different directions geographically and theologically. The largest splinter group followed Joseph Smith's son as the new prophet and remained in Illinois. Some remained in Missouri and still believe that the temple will be built on the land known as the Temple Lot, which Joseph Smith had prophesied would be the place to which Jesus would return. Members of this splinter group, known as "Church of Christ (Temple Lot)," are today still waiting to build a temple there; they presently do not have the funds to do so.

In a letter addressed, "To the saints scattered throughout the earth," dated September 22, 1851, all LDS saints were admonished by Brigham Young to come to Utah, even if they did not have the necessary equipment to get there:

> O ye saints in the United States, will you listen to the voice of "the Good Shepherd"? Will you gather? Will you be obedient to the heavenly commandments? Many of you have been looking for and expecting too much; you have been expecting the time would come when you could journey across the mountains in your fine carriages, your good wagons, and have all the comforts of life that heart could wish; but your expectations are vain, and if you wait for those things you will never come . . . and your faith and hope will depart from you.

> . . . Some of the children of the world have crossed the mountains and plains from Missouri to California with a pack on their back to worship their god— gold! Some have performed the same journey with a wheelbarrow, some have accomplished the same with a pack on a cow . . . and can you not do the same? Yes, if you have the same desire, the same faith! (A Comprehensive History of the Church, B. H. Roberts, Volume 4, pages 83 and 84.)

B. H. Roberts tells us that another general epistle from the first presidency was sent out in October, 1855, giving definite instructions on the suggested method of immigrating: the wooden handcart. The Perpetual Emigration Fund Company was to help in providing the means for poor saints abroad who could not raise sufficient funds on their own to "gather to Zion." Eight ships were made available to English Mormons for coming to America. From Boston, New York, or Philadelphia, the emigrants were to travel by rail to Iowa City, then the terminus of the railroad.

The saints were to receive their handcarts in Iowa City, along with a few cows for milk and beef cattle, as needed for food. They were then to walk the distance from Iowa City to the Great Salt Lake Basin. This was intended to save expenses and reduce problems that earlier pioneers had encountered. The following is a quote from the Epistle of the First Presidency:

Let the saints, therefore, who intend to immigrate the ensuing year, understand that they are expected to walk and draw their luggage across the plains, and that they will be assisted by the fund in no other way. (ibid, page 85)

The saints in Europe responded, and the following year, 1856, the immigration was unusually large, amounting in all to 4,326 souls. Among these immigrants was William Stimpson, my great-great-grandfather, who had joined the church in 1849. He left Liverpool, England, on May 25, 1856, with his wife and two young sons, ages four and two. On arriving at Iowa City they had to wait for the handcarts to be made. They were organized into a company of 576 persons, 146 handcarts, 6 wagons for supplies, 6 mules and horses, 50 cows and beef cattle. Edward Martin was their leader.

Imagine 576 people, from infants to the aged, weak, as well as strong, starting a trek of more than a thousand miles by foot, with rivers to cross and mountains to traverse! They didn't even have wagons to sleep in at night!

The Martin Handcart Company was the fifth company to cross the plains with handcarts that year. The first three companies of saints arrived in the Salt Lake Valley with great rejoicings in late September and early October, suffering the fatigue and toils that would be expected on such a hard journey. The last two companies, the Willie Company and the Martin Company, met with many more disasters and sorrows.

Because of the delay in waiting for the handcarts to be made (which should have been completed upon their arrival from England), they got off to a late start, leaving Iowa City on the twenty-eighth of July, 1856. Also, the construction of the handcarts was faulty because they had rushed in building them and had sacrificed durability for lightness, replacing iron axles and wheels with wooden ones. As a result the trek was delayed even more by broken handcarts along the way.

They arrived at Florence, Nebraska, on August 22. Here a debate ensued as to whether to venture on so late in the season to Salt Lake or to camp for the winter at some available location in Nebraska. One leader, who was acquainted with the country, was convinced, "that a mixed company of aged people, women and little children . . . could not cross the mountains so late in the season without much suffering, sickness, and death." (ibid, p. 89) He was overruled, however, by the other leaders, and submitted to their decision—with the promise to go and even die with them if necessary. One narrative says, "No man worked harder than he to alleviate the suffering which he had foreseen, when he had to endure it." (ibid, p. 90)

Unaware of the hazards and dangers that were before them, the emigrants trusted the judgment of their leaders. The influence the leaders had in this decision is clearly stated in B. H. Roberts' history:

> But it had been represented to these saints in the handcart companies, and, indeed, to all the saints in Europe, that a special providence would attend this method of migration, and hence they would be apt to discredit any warning that might be given concerning dangers that might overwhelm them. "Know ye not," wrote Elder John Jacques, assistant editor of the Millennial Star, "Know ye not that it is the holy ordinance of the Lord revealed through his prophet, Brigham Young, for the redemption of the humble, faithful poor, and that it will be blessed and sanctified of him to the Salvation of thousands who are not too proud to be saved in his appointed way, while many who will despise that way will be left to perish in Babylon. The Lord has promised through his servant Brigham Young that the handcart companies shall be blessed with health and strength, and be met part way with teams and provisions from the valley. And I am not afraid to prophesy, that those who go by the handcarts, and continue faithful and obedient, will be blessed more than they have ever dreamed of." Religious enthusiasts imbued with these ideas of blessing and favor, would, of course, vote to continue the journey "to Zion" (A Comprehensive History of the Church, B. H. Roberts, Volume 4, p. 90 and 91, quote from the Millennial Star, Volume xviii, p. 370)

They left Florence, Nebraska, on their treacherous journey at the end of the summer, August 25, and arrived at Fort Laramie on the eighth of October, still five hundred miles from the Salt Lake Valley. This part of the journey was extremely hazardous, crossing icy waters and rough mountain terrain ranging between 6,000 to 8,000 feet.

Severe snow storms and biting winds created an overwhelmingly helpless condition. Many of the already weak, starving, and fatigued emigrants did not survive. In order to lighten the loads of the flimsy handcarts on rugged mountain trails, they sacrificed bedding that was desperately needed in the freezing snowstorms. Nevertheless, for the months of October and November they struggled on. To summarize their struggles, I quote from a brief family history about William Stimpson, my great-great-grandfather, written by one of his descendants, Joseph H.Stimpson:

> As seen from this narrative, the early snows made the roads almost impassable and their journey most difficult. Their son, William B., died about the time they crossed the Platte River (October 19, 1856). Their food was getting low and the record says that their rations dropped to four ounces of flour per day per person. When they reached the Independence Peak on the Sweetwater River in Wyoming, his wife and a prematurely born child died and were buried near Fort Bridger. Relief trains were sent out from Salt Lake City to meet them. They found them undergoing extreme suffering. Half a slice of bread, or possibly a cup of flour mixed with water, was all the food they had to sustain him and his son for a day at a time. Finally they reached Salt Lake City on November 30, 1856. The experiences of this trip were of such a nature that William Stimpson refused to talk very much about them. The ground was frozen so that it was almost impossible to dig graves in the ground to bury those who died and they feared that they would be eaten by coyotes even before they could proceed further on the journey. (Sketch of the Life of William Stimpson, by Joseph H. Stimpson, September 22, 1945)

CHAPTER 2

UNREALISTIC EXPECTATIONS

*"Come unto me, all ye that labor and are heavy laden,
and I will give you rest. Take my yoke upon you, and
learn of me; for I am meek and lowly in heart: and ye
shall find rest unto your souls. For my yoke is easy, and
my burden is light."*

—Matthew 11:29–30

Within a month of returning home from my mission in 1965 I achieved my goal of enrolling at Brigham Young University, where I would meet Charles Naylor. We were married in the Salt Lake Temple six months later! This dramatically fulfilled a prophecy made by a Maori friend in New Zealand, who had stated that I would be married within six months of returning home. At the time he said it I laughed at him, but much to my amazement it would soon come to pass.

Our wedding was the realization of a dream and goal I'd looked forward to all my life: being married to a returned missionary in the House of the Lord (the LDS temple) for time and all eternity! After all, being sealed in holy matrimony forever by a Priesthood-holder was one of the requirements for entering the Celestial Kingdom and becoming gods and goddesses (attaining exaltation).

Charles and I started our lives together in a small town in Southern

Utah. I loved being a homemaker—baking bread, canning fruit, sewing, and all the things my Mormon culture had taught me how to do. Charles was the "music man" for the school district—teaching all grade levels, both vocal music and band. I taught piano in our home and we both had several church callings. We had planned to wait a year and adjust to married life before starting our family, but after listening to a talk at General Conference given by Joseph Fielding Smith, then President of the Twelve Apostles, in which he said that young couples using birth control were living in sin, we changed our minds about waiting to have children.

Three days before our first wedding anniversary I gave birth to a baby girl, and nine months later to a two-and-a-half month's premature baby boy. So, on our second wedding anniversary we had a one-year-old daughter, a two-month-old son, and a fifteen-year-old, Indian foster daughter. The church had, at that time, an Indian placement program in which we were encouraged to take in a Native American student from the reservation and provide the opportunity for him or her to attend school and to live in our home. We felt it was an opportunity to help someone and also to serve the Lord. Thus, within two years of our marriage we were a family of five!

My life had started in the *fast lane* and stayed there. The years began to fly by, with several moves, job changes, and (of course) more babies. We moved from Circleville, Utah, to Ogden, then to Salt Lake City, where Charles taught high school choir. At one time it had been his dream, but somehow he was not happy. He accepted a job selling textbooks to school districts, which meant a lengthier move for us— to Phoenix, Arizona. The job ended up being temporary and we were moved to Southern California as Charles continued to sell textbooks. That job turned out to be temporary, also.

During the weeks of unemployment, the church welfare program adequately took care of our needs. Through the church unemployment service, Charles got an excellent job as a representative for an established pharmaceutical company. The moves were fun and refreshing. Since we always had the church wherever we went, and because we were musical, we were always welcomed with open arms into our new ward (church congregation). Moving always came with mixed emotions, but usually turned out to be a "stepping stone" of change and growth. State to state, we experienced cultures that were different than the Utah Mormon culture we had both lived in most of our lives.

Early Family Years

We had been married less than eight years, had moved six times, and I had given birth to our fifth child. My church was my anchor, my support—the one place I felt that others saw me as a success. Yet deep down inside I did not feel successful. I felt very insecure. And because my husband struggled with depression, I often felt that he didn't love me. He was gone a lot on his job, and when he was home he was busy with church callings (usually, Elder's Quorum President). Times of playing and having fun together as a family became fewer and fewer. These were being replaced with stress, tension, and sibling rivalry. Though surrounded by church friends, I felt lonely and smothered—smothered with demands—yet not understanding why.

At the time I was very performance-oriented. Because of my cultural upbringing, which taught the goal of seeking "excellence in all things" and seemed to measure one's very worth by one's level of performance and accomplishment, I placed unrealistic expectations on myself, and often on my family, as well. My desire for excellence seemed pure, righteous, and worthy, but again and again unrealistic expectations robbed me of joy and fulfillment. Instead of being happy to be myself and satisfied with the gifts that God had given me, I experienced a strong sense of inadequacy and guilt because I frequently fell short of the high goals my LDS culture demanded.

For example, I sincerely wanted to support my husband in his priesthood responsibilities, but often felt guilty because I needed or wanted him home with me and the children. At the ward, I longed to sit together as a family and have Charles' help with all the children during sacrament meeting, but because he was the organist he was always sitting on the stand by the organ. I wanted to be an example to our neighbors and never yell at my children but was always falling short. I wanted to keep my house and yard as clean and beautiful as the temple, as I was told I should, but somehow I just couldn't keep up.

Day after day I sought God's acceptance and approval through my performance but always came up short. I frequently felt overwhelmed with responsibility. For every good thing I accomplished, it seemed, I was reminded of several things undone. I wanted to be the perfect example I was supposed to be, but I couldn't quite achieve it. Church meetings were a continual reminder to do more and to lengthen our stride.

In truth, I loved my church callings, which included playing the piano or the organ for church meetings, as well as teaching and leadership assignments. My favorite calling was "Spiritual Living Leader" in the LDS Relief Society (the women's auxiliary of the Church). I wondered how people could be happy without the church because it provided for so many of my needs, yet likewise I often felt overwhelmed with responsibilities and demands.

Maintaining a high level of performance expectation for myself often led me into depression. Because, to my way of thinking, I belonged to the true church, the one that was supposed to make my life happy and fulfilled, I simply didn't understand this depression. Because I was supposed to be an example, I didn't want to let others know of my problems, like increasing periods of sadness and fatigue. I lived in denial of these feelings rather than seek help to resolve them.

At church I always appeared to have it all together. Others would look at us and think we were the ideal family. This did wonders for my self-esteem, but down deep I knew of the unspoken problems that we covered up so beautifully. The praise I received at church would sometimes make me feel like a hypocrite, even though it was a great boost to my ego. I wondered why we were not the "ideal family" who we were supposed to be. Worse yet, I compared myself and my family to the other families at church, thinking they were "ideal families" and wondered what was wrong with my family and me. This only increased my feelings of inadequacy and depression.

Prayer and Scripture study were important priorities in my life, but sometimes I was confused by what I would read. I often wondered what Jesus was referring to when He spoke of His "yoke that was easy" and His "burden that was light."

If Jesus' yoke is easy, why do I feel so burdened? I longed to find rest for my soul and sought it desperately. Where was Christ's easy yoke? *If Christ's burden is light* (I asked myself again and again), *why do I feel such deep, dark depression at times?*

There was another Scripture that bothered me. It was the parable Jesus told of the ten virgins (Matthew 25:1–13). All ten went to meet the bridegroom and planned to go to the wedding banquet. Half of them were wise and half were foolish. Only the five wise virgins who were ready went to the banquet. The other five were shut out.

I knew this parable symbolized Christ's return and spoke of the characteristics of those who would enter the Kingdom of Heaven with Him. From earliest childhood it had been my desire to be ready when Jesus returned for His sheep. I was striving with all my heart, soul, and energy to be worthy to walk with Him. Why did I feel that I was one of the *foolish* virgins waiting for Jesus, one who was not ready? Too often, I felt like I was falling short.

My worst fear was of falling short of exaltation. I did not want to be one of the foolish virgins who did not have sufficient oil. Yet I lived with a constant desire to know what that extra oil was, and I wanted to be sure I had it! I did not want the door to God's Kingdom shut in my face.

What was lacking? I was doing all I could do. I had devoted myself to my family and church service. *Why did I feel unready for Christ's return? What was the extra oil I needed?* These five foolish virgins obviously expected to get into the banquet because they had been eagerly waiting for the bridegroom. They didn't doubt but believed the banquet was going to happen as evidenced by their response to the midnight call. However, later when they returned and knocked on the door, saying, "Lord, Lord, open to us," it was too late. The door was shut. They had missed the wedding banquet! They were told, "I don't know you."

This parable symbolized the Kingdom of Heaven; verse one makes that clear. What a scary thought! Many who think they are going to enter God's Kingdom will be shut out. I did not want to have the doors of heaven shut with me left outside. Why did I have this gnawing fear that I could end up like one of the five foolish virgins when I was trying so hard to make myself worthy of the Kingdom of God? I wanted to make sure I had extra "oil," but I wasn't exactly sure what that was.

I always kept my *temple recommend* current and Charles and I attended the temple as often as time would permit. I was trying to be faithful in my various church callings. Still, I knew that something was missing. What more did I need to do to make myself worthy? The worst thing I could imagine ever happening to me would be to have Jesus say to me, "I know you not." I pondered Jesus' warning:

> Many will say to me in that day, Lord, Lord, have we not prophesied in thy name? And in thy name have cast out devils? and in thy name done many wonderful works? And then will I profess unto them, I never knew you: depart from me, ye that work iniquity.
> —Matthew 7:22–23

I never wanted Jesus to say those words to me. I could think of nothing worse!

CHAPTER 3

MY QUEST

"The unfolding of your words gives light; it gives understanding to the simple."

—Psalm 119:130

One day my twenty-two-month-old daughter tugged at me while chattering something I couldn't understand until I followed her out of the house and down the street. She had discovered a beautiful Labrador Retriever that she was very excited to show me. That's how I met Tobie. She was the owner of the dog and one of the few women in our neighborhood besides myself who stayed home as a full-time mother. Tobie had a one-year-old daughter and was eager to see my new baby— and was very surprised to learn he was my fifth child!

That was the beginning of a unique friendship. This gal was very organized and consequently had her house in order early in the day, so she entertained herself by coming to my home, which was always very active. She became like a sister to me, a friend who loved me no matter what—not for what I could do, but for who I was. I never did feel judged by her, nor did I feel I had to meet certain expectations. We laughed together, cried together, and became very close.

Tobie was Jewish and her strict Jewish parents had taught her to plug her ears at Christmas time, so she wouldn't listen to the name of Jesus when the Christmas carols were sung. Of course, she had nothing to do with Christmas, but she always observed Hanukkah and knew when all the other Jewish celebrations occurred. We both agreed that religion should not interfere with our friendship and it didn't. However, right from the moment I met her, I felt the Lord wanted me to share the truth with her. I invited her to go to church functions with me but she declined. She was Jewish and was not interested in Christianity.

An Amazing Conversion

After being friends with Tobie for four years I felt impressed by the Lord to take her a New Testament. One Sunday evening, I literally felt pushed to her house with my oldest daughter's New Testament.

"Please read the book of Matthew," I said as I handed her the book. The very next morning she was knocking on my door.

With tears in her eyes she said, "After reading the book of Matthew, I know Jesus is the Son of God."

I was amazed. For lack of something better to say, I asked, "You read the whole Gospel of Matthew last night?"

"Yes," she said, "and now I realize that I have been wrong. I have always believed that Jesus was an impostor. I was also taught that the Romans killed Jesus, not the Jews. My parents even taught me that his disciples had stolen Jesus' body from the tomb while the Roman guards slept—the very lie that the chief priests and elders devised and paid the Roman soldiers to say so people wouldn't believe He had been resurrected. As Matthew said, 'And this story has been widely circulated among the Jews to this very day.' I was actually taught that story. However, after reading all about Jesus from the record of Matthew, I know Jesus really is the one He claimed to be. He is the Messiah!"

Wow! I had never experienced anything like this. The spirit had really spoken to her. All she had done was read the gospel of Matthew. Of course, she wasn't going to stop there. She was eager to read the rest of the New Testament. I could see I needed to replace my daughter's New Testament. I did not tell Tobie the Bible I had given her was a loan. It was now her permanent possession. The change in her was permanent—and so was Jesus' permanency in her life.

I was confident that Tobie would finally become a Mormon. She and her husband took the missionary lessons and started attending the LDS

Church. However, they were not the ordinary investigators of Mormonism and were not ready to be baptized at the end of the three-week period in which they were given the six missionary discussions. Tobie was very thorough in her thinking and still had many questions. Since neither she nor her husband were ready to get baptized, the missionaries only called on them occasionally. However, it was the beginning of many hours, days, and weeks of interesting discussions between Tobie and me. I loved our conversations. She believed the LDS Church was true and wanted to be baptized, but still had some questions, concerns, and habits that kept her from being ready for baptism into the Mormon Church.

A year had passed since Tobie had started attending the Mormon Church and my family was now moving from Corona to Cherry Valley, California, about an hour away. I was comfortable that she was grounded in the church and would get baptized soon. Even though we would no longer be having our in-depth conversations, she was attending church regularly and there were plenty of others to encourage her. Besides, she was in God's hands, and I left it at that.

By 1982 five years had passed since we'd moved to Cherry Valley, but close friends remain friends even with miles between them. So it was with Tobie and me. We stayed in touch, but because Tobie now had a job and I now had eight children, we didn't get to visit or see each other very often.

How Could This Be?

One day I received a phone call from Tobie that left me rather stunned. She informed me that she had been studying with the Jehovah's Witnesses for some time. It was evident that she was being heavily influenced by them and no longer believed in certain Mormon doctrines. I couldn't believe it. As I hung up the phone I turned to God with a burdened heart.

If there was anybody who frustrated me as a Mormon, it was a Jehovah's Witness! I was convinced that Satan was the source of their inspiration. Having engaged in numerous conversations with them before, it seemed to me that it was next to impossible to reason with a

Jehovah's Witness. How could it be that my "Golden Contact" (a nickname Mormons give to someone we know is destined to become a member of the church) and my best friend, Tobie, was believing their deceptions! This just couldn't be. She was meant to be a Mormon; I knew it in my heart.

Persistent Problem

Since my teenage years, and especially because of my experiences in the mission field, I had been troubled by the fact that so many sincere people whom I loved rejected Mormonism. It had always seemed to me that honest, sincere people would accept the Church since we were promised that the Holy Ghost would manifest the truth to the honest seeker. The Book of Mormon states:

> And when ye shall receive these things, I would exhort you that ye would ask God, the Eternal Father, in the name of Christ, if these things are not true; and if ye shall ask with a sincere heart, with real intent, having faith in Christ, he will manifest the truth of it unto you, by the power of the Holy Ghost. And by the power of the Holy Ghost ye may know the truth of all things.
> —Moroni 10:4–5

Since the Mormon Church was God's only true church on the face of the planet and in light of the above promise, why did so many people who seemed to believe in God and to honestly seek Him reject the LDS Church? This was an old problem in my life and one that had troubled me as a missionary. While abroad, I had met many people who were devoted to Christ but never got that "witness of the Holy Ghost" that the Book of Mormon was true and that the Mormon Church was true.

Of course, I knew that not everyone was going to accept the truth and that only God knows a person's inner heart. However, Tobie did have faith in Christ and a sincere, honest desire to know the truth. Her conversion to Christ was real. Besides, I believed that the Holy Ghost had given me many evidences that He wanted her to know the truth. Tobie's rejection of the "truth of Mormonism" for what I believed to be the deception of the Jehovah's Witness theology was extremely troubling to me. I got to my knees and prayed:

"Dear Father in Heaven,

I want to understand why good people I love so much turn from Your true church. You said the ordinances and baptism by the correct authority, found only in the Mormon Church, are necessary. Why, then, don't all sincere people get that witness of the Holy Ghost, as You promised in the Book of Mormon that they would—and especially Tobie, since You have already taught her so much? If it is Your will, dear God, please, please help me understand this.
In Jesus' Name,
Amen."

As noted, this old question of my heart ran deep. Now it was renewed with great intensity. If the promise in the Book of Mormon was true, then it seemed that all sincere believers in Christ would accept the Book of Mormon. *Why didn't they?*

Time to Teach

I was committed to defend my religion to my friend. Certainly the Lord did not want her to be deceived. I was convinced that God would help me to support the truth. Although I wasn't eager to debate the Bible with the Witnesses, I was confident that I could defend my Mormon beliefs from the Bible. Besides, I had no doubt at all that the LDS Church was the true church; therefore, I trusted that God would help me to reveal this to Tobie. I was on His side—the side of truth!

As I prepared myself for my first meeting with Tobie and two of her Witness friends, I prayed intently that God's truth would be made manifest at that meeting. I left that meeting with an insatiable hunger to study and understand the Bible more fully. In the days following, a series of intense conversations ensued. These discussions caused me to seize every opportunity to study the Scriptures and to pray often for help. I loved the Bible and believed that both Joseph Smith and the Bible were inspired by God. Therefore, they would be in agreement and I could show my friend the truth from the Bible.

Tobie wasn't interested in Scripture given to Joseph Smith, but she did believe the Bible. I felt the Bible was sufficient to propound the errors of the Jehovah's Witnesses and confirm to her the truth of

31

Mormonism. I believed the Bible contained many truths taught only in the LDS Church. I felt a deep responsibility and commitment to show Tobie that the Jehovah's Witnesses were wrong and that Mormonism was the only true church of Jesus Christ. After all, the Holy Ghost had already opened her eyes to the truth about Jesus. I was confident He would lead her back to the true church. I was merely an instrument in God's hands and I was desirous to be faithful in this calling. The "unfolding of God's Word" had certainly given light to my friend, Tobie, as Psalm 119:130 promises. Now it became my fervent quest to use God's Word to save Tobie from the lies and deceptions of the Jehovah's Witnesses.

CHAPTER 4

DEFENDING MY FAITH

"And the serpent said unto the woman, Ye shall not surely die:
For God doth know that in the day ye eat thereof, then your eyes shall be opened, and ye shall be as gods, knowing good and evil."

—*Genesis 3:4–5*

One of the pillars of Mormon doctrine is the "Law of Eternal Progression." As Mormons we were excited that we knew where we came from, why we were here on earth, and where we were going in an eternal perspective. We had so much more than the Christian world. Joseph Smith had revealed to us that every human who ever lived or will live on this planet began as an intelligence in past eternity. Then, we were all born as *spirit-children* to Heavenly Father by a union with his celestial wives. This was the spiritual creation in heaven before the earth was created and is referred to as the *pre-existence*. It is also called our *first estate.*

As Heavenly Father's spirit-children, we needed to take on physical bodies as part of our progression to godhood. This earth-life is our second estate. Here, we receive various levels of blessing or condemnation according to our faithfulness in our first estate, or pre-existence. According to Mormon doctrine, we also will receive various levels of existence in the next world, according to our worthy efforts in this life. Progression continues in the resurrection throughout eternity and those who are deemed worthy will progress to godhood. As gods, they will create their own spirit-children and worlds for them to live on. So the cycle continues throughout eternity.

This is the "Law of Eternal Progression." It is summarized in the statement, "As man is, God once was; as God is, man may become." Thus, to the Mormon way of thinking, there are in existence many gods, but we only worship the God of this world, who is our Heavenly Father. In addition, just as these gods continue to progress, so is our God still progressing. (*Journal of Discourses*, vol. 6, p. 120 and vol. 11, p. 286.)

My friend Tobie had learned all this from previous discussions with me, but she no longer believed this doctrine. The Jehovah's Witnesses she had been talking with had somehow convinced her that all this wasn't biblical. I realized, of course, that she just needed to see the scriptural evidence for these doctrines, so that now became my focus.

One God, or Many Gods?

Tobie kept insisting that there was only *one* God and she was determined to show me that this was true from Bible passages. Here are some she offered:

> Ye are my witnesses, saith the LORD, and my servant whom I have chosen: that ye may know and believe me, and understand that I am he: before me there was no God formed, neither shall there be after me.
>
> —Isaiah 43:10

> Thus saith the LORD the King of Israel, and his redeemer the LORD of hosts; I am the first, and I am the last; and beside me there is no God.
>
> —Isaiah 44:6

> Is there a God beside me? Yea, there is no God; I know not any.
>
> —Isaiah 44:8

I explained to her that for us, the people on this planet, earth, there was but one God, our Father in Heaven. Paul, the apostle, also explains this in 1 Corinthians 8:6. He said there were gods many and lords many, but to us (the inhabitants of this planet) there is only one God, the one that created us as *His* Spirit-children. I continued to show her that that didn't negate the fact that there were many other planets created by other gods that were inhabited with *their* spirit-children. Besides, I was fully prepared to show her the numerous passages in the Bible that spoke of "gods," revealing that there is a plurality of gods. The Old Testament was full of them!

Tobie wasn't convinced.

"Those Scriptures that mention 'gods' are referring to idol gods of the pagan religions or demon gods," she stated.

I had never heard of "demon gods." Tobie suggested we read the passage in Corinthians that I referred to and insisted that we read the verses before and after the passage of Scripture we were discussing.

We began by reading 1 Corinthians 8:4–6:

> As concerning therefore the eating of those things that are offered in sacrifice unto idols, we know that an idol is nothing in the world, and that there is none other God but one. For though there be that are called gods, whether in heaven or in earth, (as there be gods many, and lords many,) But to us there is but one God, the Father, of whom are all things, and we in him; and one Lord Jesus Christ, by whom are all things, and we by him.

After reading the complete passage, I acknowledged, defensively, "All right. Paul was mentioning idols in this passage, but he still said there were 'gods many and lords many.' "

"Yes," Tobie replied, "but notice Paul says they are 'called gods.' Just because people in false religions worshiped many idol gods and called them 'god' doesn't mean that they are true gods." She read some other verses to explain further:

> Howbeit then, when ye knew not God, ye did service unto them which by nature are no gods?
>
> —Galatians 4:8

> Hath a nation changed their gods, which are yet no gods? But my people have changed their glory for that which doth not profit.
>
> —Jeremiah 2:11

Determined, I said, "Well, Jesus spoke of gods and even said we are gods." We turned to John 10:34:

> Jesus answered them, "Is it not written in your law, I said, Ye are gods?"

Tobie said she needed to get help from her Jehovah's Witness teachers but soon called me with a very clever explanation. Something about small g's and capital G's and that "gods" was translated from the Hebrew word *Elohim*, which had different meanings and could refer to men who were judges over Israel. I was beginning to see just how cleverly Satan had blinded her eyes. However, it was much later in my research that I learned that the Mormon Apostle, James E. Talmage, confirmed her interpretation to be correct in his book, Jesus, the Christ.[1] Then Tobie asked, "If Jesus is teaching here that we are gods in embryo as you interpret this passage, why would He be telling the Pharisees who were picking up stones to stone Him that they were gods?

Was He telling them that they were going to be gods someday when they were rejecting Him and even wanted to kill Him?"

I could see we were getting nowhere with this topic of becoming gods so I decided to show her the Scriptures that teach of our pre-existent state. This doctrine was stated clearly in modern-day revelation given to the Prophet Joseph Smith, but was, I thought, also supported by the Bible.

Pre-existence

The first Scripture Tobie and I read together was Jeremiah 1:5:

> Before I formed thee in the belly I knew thee; and before thou camest forth out of the womb I sanctified thee, and I ordained thee a prophet unto the nations.

That verse definitely shows that Jeremiah existed before his physical birth. How could anything be clearer than that? I thought.

She had another interpretation. According to her this merely meant that God knows everything before He does it. He planned to make

Jeremiah a prophet and knew in his mind what Jeremiah would be and to what purpose he would be created. Rather than saying that Jeremiah had lived as a *spirit child* with God before the creation of the earth, it merely confirms God's foreknowledge of everything.

"OK, let's look at Job 38:4, 7," I said:

> Where wast thou when I laid the foundations of the earth? . . . when the morning stars sang together, and all the sons of God shouted for joy?

I explained that we, as spirit-children of our Father in Heaven in the pre-earth life, were these sons of God and we were present when God laid the foundations of the earth, as was Job.

Again, her understanding of these verses was different. She patiently explained that the sons of God were angels. Angels were of the spirit creation, and we are of the earthly creation. There is a spirit realm, which includes the angels, and then there is the physical realm. We are of the physical realm. Tobie did not believe that the Bible taught we evolved from one type of creation to another—from intelligences, to spirit children, then to humans. She insisted that man began when Adam and Eve were created and used Genesis 2:7 to make her point:

> And the LORD God formed man of the dust of the ground, and breathed into his nostrils the breath of life; and man became a living soul.

Tobie continued to explain, "Besides, Job wasn't present at all when God laid the foundations of the earth. If we put the verses from Job in context we see that God is showing Job how insignificant he really is." As we read chapters 38–40 of Job together, I could see that God was asking Job many rhetorical questions in which He was bringing this man to the realization that he could not comprehend God's abilities. For example, God asked Job:

> Hast thou perceived the breadth of the earth? Declare if thou knowest it all. Where is the way where light dwelleth? And as for darkness, where is the place thereof?
> —Job 38:18–19

Using irony, God continues to speak to Job in order to reinforce the absurdity of the notion that man, God's creation, should think that he can question his Creator:

> Knowest thou it, because thou wast then born? Or because the number of thy days is great?
>
> —Job 38:21

God's humbling interrogation of Job continues:

> Canst thou lift up thy voice to the clouds, that abundance of waters may cover thee? Canst thou send lightnings, that they may go, and say unto thee, Here we are? Who hath put wisdom in the inward parts? Or who hath given understanding to the heart?
>
> —Job 38:34–36

And Job 38:4:

> Where wast thou when I laid the foundations of the earth? declare, if thou hast understanding.

These questions humbled Job and brought him to an awareness of his unworthiness and inability to answer, question, or criticize God.

> Moreover the LORD answered Job, and said, Shall he that contendeth with the Almighty instruct him? He that reproveth God, let him answer it. Then Job answered the LORD, and said, Behold, I am vile: what shall I answer thee? I will lay mine hand upon my mouth.
>
> —Chapter 40:1–4

Job's humiliation brought him to repentance:

> Wherefore I abhor myself, and repent in dust and ashes.
>
> —Job 42:6

I didn't want to admit that her interpretation of Job seemed to be more accurate than mine. Her answers were making me feel foolish, especially since I couldn't deny that her interpretations of these Scriptures fit the context of the surrounding verses better than my interpretations. These chapters were not stating that we existed with God in a pre-existent state at all. Instead of stating that Job was present when the foundations of the earth were laid, these verses were stating the very opposite. God was putting Job in his place and showing him that his perspective was very limited. In other words, Job was pretty small and in no position to question God's actions. Job's response confirmed this:

> I spoke once, but I have no answer—twice, but I will say no more.
> —Job 40:5 NIV

Job was humbled, and so was I. Nevertheless, I was not willing to let her know that I thought her interpretations were sensible. I was still determined that there were many more Scriptures that taught of the pre-existence. I looked up every verse in my *Missionary Pal* reference book under "pre-mortal existence" looking for foolproof, biblical evidence.

I was surprised to find that most of the Scriptures listed referred to Christ's pre-existence, but not ours. However, I finally found a Scripture in the Bible that clearly said that we existed before creation:

> The LORD possessed me in the beginning of his ways, before his works of old. I was set up from everlasting, from the beginning, or ever the earth was. When there were no depths, I was brought forth; when there were no fountains abounding with water. Before the mountains were settled, before the hills was I brought forth . . . When he prepared the heavens I was there.
> —Proverbs 8:22–27

This sounded like good proof of the pre-existence to me . . . until I started reading at the beginning of the chapter:

> Doth not wisdom cry out? And understanding put forth her voice?
> —Proverbs 8:1

When I read the entire proverb it was apparent that wisdom was present during the creation, not humans. "I" referred to wisdom!

I was frustrated that my *Missionary Pal* had apparently misused a few Scriptures, but this only confirmed my belief that the Bible was not sufficient proof to establish truth. The doctrine of pre-existence is taught in the temple and in Mormon Scriptures that were revealed through Joseph Smith. The *Doctrine & Covenants* (93:29) states: "Man was also in the beginning with God."

Our discussion, to my way of thinking, had been a good example of why we need a prophet to give us the correct interpretation of the Bible. I used this opportunity to point out to her why modern-day revelation and a modern-day prophet were so important today. Several doctrines, such as the Law of Eternal Progression, are vague in the Bible, I told her, but God revealed them plainly through the Prophet Joseph Smith.

Tobie didn't seem impressed. She was convinced that the Bible taught that humans began in the Garden of Eden, when God breathed into Adam the breath of life and, "man became a living soul." To her there was no ambiguity in Scripture about that. She kept insisting that the spiritual creation of angels and spirit beings was real, but was separate from the physical creation of which we are a part. It was not a matter of progressing from one to another. Her problem was clearly that she was limiting herself to what the Bible said, rather than trusting Joseph Smith's revelations.

[It was much later that someone pointed out the following scripture that contradicts Joseph Smith's teaching that all humans were created as spirit beings first. When comparing our physical (natural) bodies to our resurrected bodies Paul said: "Howbeit that was not first which is spiritual, but that which is natural: and afterward that which is spiritual." (1 Corinthians 15:46) However, I was not aware of that scripture verse at this time.]

We ended this session with Tobie's question:

"Doesn't the Mormon doctrine of Eternal Progression resemble the Hindu doctrine of Reincarnation just a little bit in teaching that we earn our status of birth and we evolve from one sphere to another according to our worthiness?"

I thought of a research paper I had done in college on Reincarnation. At the time I *had* seen a few parallels between Reincarnation and the Law of Eternal Progression, even though they had many basic differences. The similarities really didn't present much of a problem for me since Satan always counterfeits the truth with a false doctrine, I reasoned. He is a master at that. I explained to Tobie that the Mormon revelation of Eternal Progression was from God, while the Hindu revelation of progression was the devil's counterfeit.

"That brings me to my last question," she said. "Who wants to exalt himself to become God, and who tempted Eve to disobey God by enticing her with the desire to become *like God*?"

We ended with prayer, and I left not wanting to answer her last question. However, I didn't forget it, especially after reading the following Scriptures:

> How art thou fallen from heaven, O Lucifer, son of the morning! How art thou cut down to the ground, which didst weaken the nations! For thou hast said in thine heart, I will ascend into heaven, I will exalt my throne above the stars of God: I will sit also upon the mount of the congregation, in the sides of the north: I will ascend above the heights of the clouds; I will be like the most High. Yet thou shalt be brought down to hell, to the sides of the pit.
>
> —Isaiah 14:12–15

> Let no man deceive you by any means: for that day shall not come, except there come a falling away first, and that man of sin be revealed, the son of perdition; who opposeth and exalteth himself above all that is called God, or that is worshipped; so that he as God sitteth in the temple of God, shewing himself that he is God.
>
> —2 Thessalonians 2:3–4

I didn't like her insinuation that the Mormon doctrine of men becoming gods was connected with Satan's selfish ambition to be worshiped as God. I had prayed so hard that I would be able to defend God's truth at our meetings, and the meetings had not gone as easily as I had thought they would. However, I knew that I wasn't the deceived one.

I stood humbled. And now my quest to defend my faith from the Bible grew even more determined.

CHAPTER 5

BACK TO THE BASICS: APOSTASY, RESTORATION, AND THE PRIESTHOOD

"And when he had called unto him his twelve disciples, he gave them power against unclean spirits, to cast them out, and to heal all manner of sickness and all manner of disease."

—Matthew 10:1

I realized now that defending the Law of Eternal Progression from the Bible was not accomplishing anything as far as Tobie was concerned. She was not mature enough spiritually to grasp this doctrine. She needed to be fed "milk" first. I had been trying to feed her "meat." The doctrine of *plurality of gods and progression to godhood* was a spiritual doctrine that was only for the spiritually mature. In the New Testament, Paul teaches that only those who have the Spirit of God understand the spiritual truths of God. They are foolishness to unbelievers, "because they are spiritually discerned" (1 Corinthians 2:6–3:3).

It was a mistake to discuss these doctrines with Tobie first. I needed to go back to the basics—the Apostasy, the Restoration, and the Priesthood. I needed to help Tobie understand that Christ's church, the one that He established when He was on the earth, had been taken from the earth after the death of the apostles. This was the Great Apostasy. As I had been taught when a child, the church that Christ established, the one with the proper organization and priesthood of God, was not on the earth shortly after His life was over. Then, in the early 1830s, this True Gospel had been restored through the prophet Joseph Smith. When Christ was on the earth, He had established His church with twelve apostles as the foundation, with Jesus being the Head (Ephesians 2:20). The Mormon Church claimed to be the only church today that is built on that same foundation of twelve apostles and prophets.

Tobie had learned these truths when she had been taught the LDS missionary lessons a few years previously, but it was evident that the Jehovah's Witnesses had confused her and that she had forgotten them. I needed to help Tobie understand the foundational need for priesthood authority and that the Church of Jesus Christ of Latter-day Saints was the only church with that authority. Other churches did not have this priesthood authority, nor did they even claim to have it, except the Catholics and a few others. Therefore, God did not honor baptisms or other ordinances performed in other churches.

Christ had given priesthood authority to his twelve apostles when He called and ordained them (Mark 3:14). With this authority, the power to act for God, they could heal the sick, cast out demons, and preach the gospel (Luke 9:1, Matthew 10:1). However, after the death of the twelve apostles, this priesthood authority was taken from the earth. The authority for men to, once again, act for God was restored to the earth when John the Baptist appeared as a resurrected being to Joseph Smith in 1829 and conferred the Aaronic Priesthood upon him, giving him the authority to baptize. Later, Peter, James, and John—three of Christ's apostles—appeared to Joseph Smith as resurrected beings and by the laying on of hands conferred the Melchizedek Priesthood upon him.

Now, Joseph Smith held the same authority, power, and keys to God's Kingdom that Christ had given to Peter. The authority that had been lost from the earth for almost 1800 years was once again restored and given to men. Joseph Smith called twelve apostles and ordained them. He then established the same organizational church upon the earth that Christ had established. The Aaronic and Melchizedek Priesthoods, now resident in the restored Church of Jesus Christ of Latter-day Saints, could only be given to other men by the laying on of hands by one possessing these priesthoods.

Priesthood in the New Testament

For instance, I had several Scriptures that sufficiently said that Jesus had called twelve apostles and ordained them to the priesthood (Matthew 10:1, Mark 3:14, Luke 9:1, and John 15:16). These Scriptures state that Christ gave them power to drive out demons and to heal every disease and sickness. Tobie was unimpressed, insisting there was no mention of priesthood in any Scripture I showed her. That was true, but these Scriptures did say Jesus gave the twelve power and authority, which to me meant the same thing as priesthood. Besides, Mark 3:14 and John 15:16 specifically stated that Jesus ordained the twelve. I explained to Tobie that "ordain" means to receive the priesthood by the laying on of hands by one that has this priesthood authority. She insisted that the Greek word from which "ordained" was translated means "to appoint."

Here we go again! She always had another interpretation. *I suppose her Jehovah's Witness friends think they know Greek*, I sarcastically thought to myself. All we needed was the gift of the Holy Ghost (which they didn't have) to understand the Bible, not an education in the Greek language. I couldn't understand why Tobie wasn't seeing the obvious. It was clear to me, but she just wasn't getting it. The Jehovah's Witnesses she had been talking with had really blinded her to the truth.

The topic of priesthood was very foundational to the true church, because Christ's church today would need to have twelve apostles and the priesthood, the same as the church that Christ established. I knew this priesthood authority was the strong point of Mormonism and that we, alone, had this authority; so I was determined to show my friend no other church could be true because they did not have any authority to act for God. Catholicism was the only other denomination I was aware of that traced their priesthood authority back to Peter. Jesus had given this priesthood authority to Peter when he gave him the keys to the Kingdom. The true church had to be either Catholic or Mormon because we were the only ones claiming this authority. None of the other churches had priesthood authority; therefore, God did not recognize them.

It was all so clear to me. I was frustrated that Tobie refused to acknowledge the obvious. Tobie kept encouraging me to read the Book of Hebrews—especially chapters seven through nine. She believed this passage taught that the Old Testament priesthood had ended with Jesus' death as "the Perfect Sacrifice" for sin and was replaced by a new way of faith in Jesus that was without the need for a priesthood. I read Hebrews but really had a hard time understanding it. It was evident that it spoke of priesthood and of Christ's priesthood, or the *Melchizedek Priesthood*. It was rather confusing because, on the one hand, the restored church— The Church of Jesus Christ of Latter-day Saints—was the only church with the Aaronic and Melchizedek Priesthoods. And yet, on the other hand, Hebrews seemed to indicate that the Melchizedek Priesthood had replaced the old order of priests, the Aaronic Priesthood. So why did we have both in the church today?

Even though I couldn't find New Testament Scriptures that specifically mentioned the necessity of the priesthood in Christ's church, I knew it was true because it worked. I could think of several instances where people had received priesthood blessings and were healed. My mind also thought of several instances where the priesthood didn't work. Of course I didn't want to remember those occurrences, but I couldn't ignore them. For instance, before I met Charles, his father, Joy Naylor, had suffered for several years with heart problems. The decision was made to do open-heart surgery. This was in 1964, when open-heart surgery was a very new medical procedure, so the outcome was extremely uncertain. Before the surgery, the Stake Patriarch gave Joy a blessing by the power and authority of the Melchizedek Priesthood. Joy was told in that blessing that he would live and that the surgery would be successful. He died in the hospital within hours after the operation.

Another troubling instance was the story of our brother-in-law. When suffering with bone cancer, a General Authority gave him a priesthood blessing. In this blessing he was promised that he would walk again. His wife trusted in this blessing so much that she refused the opportunity to take out insurance that would have paid off the house if he should die. She felt that doing so would have shown a lack of faith in the power of the priesthood, but he died of cancer, never walking again.

My husband had experienced giving a priesthood blessing to a sick man in which he felt impressed to promise him that he would live. The man died. This had bothered Charles, but as Mormons we didn't focus on these negative experiences that would weaken our faith. We tried to focus on the positive experiences that were faith-promoting. As I thought of these various priesthood blessings, both positive and negative, I realized that in order to keep my faith strong I now needed to focus on the positive, not the negative. I continued to search for Scriptures to support the necessity of the Melchizedek Priesthood in Christ's church today.

While looking up Scriptures to share with Tobie, I noticed that the religious leaders who rejected Jesus were also very concerned about authority. They asked Jesus: "By what authority doest thou these things? And who gave thee this authority?" (Matthew 21:23, Mark 11:28, Luke 20:2) They thought they could trap Him because He was not of the tribe of Levi, the priestly tribe and the only tribe that had the priesthood. Rather, Jesus was of the tribe of Judah, among whose members there is no mention of priesthood (Hebrews 7:14).

These religious leaders never got an answer to their question because they didn't want to answer the question Jesus asked them: "Was John's baptism from heaven or from men?" That question was rather thought-provoking. Was Jesus insinuating that priesthood authority was given to men from heaven rather than from men? I tried to suppress another bothersome question that popped into my mind: *Were we Mormons thinking like the religious leaders of Jesus day? Did we have exclusive, religious blinders on like they did? How could that be?*

I had to admit that Tobie was right in stating that Jesus never mentioned specifically that "priesthood" was necessary. I discovered another specific passage of Scripture that made me stop and think: "And John answered and said, 'Master, we saw one casting out devils in thy name; and we forbad him, because he followeth not with us.' And Jesus said unto him, 'Forbid him not: for he that is not against us is for us'." (Luke 9:49–50)

This did not fit the LDS view of an exclusive priesthood received by the laying on of hands. Since the man casting out devils in Christ's name did not follow with the other disciples or apostles, he apparently had not been ordained and given the priesthood. Yet Jesus saw no problem with this man using His name to exercise power over demons... without the priesthood. *Considering how important the priesthood is,* I thought, *it's strange there was such a silence about it in the gospels.*

Power in the Priesthood or Power in the Name of Jesus?

I also couldn't help but notice the various ways that Jesus healed others. He did not do it by laying hands on their heads, as it is always done in the church. Sometimes He wasn't even in the presence of the one He healed (Matthew 8:5–13, Mark 7:24–30). One time He healed a blind man by spitting on the ground and putting the mud He formed from it on the man's eyes and told him to wash in the Pool of Siloam. (John 9:6, 7). Though priesthood was never mentioned, something else was mentioned: faith in Jesus and the acknowledgment of who He was—God's Son.

I found the same thing to be true when I looked into the miracles performed by the apostles after Christ's Ascension to heaven. They never acknowledged any priesthood power that they held. Instead, they insisted that the miracles they performed were done through the name of Jesus and by faith in His name. A specific example of this is given in Acts, chapter four, when the reigning religious leaders questioned Peter about his authority. After healing a lame man, the rulers, elders, teachers, and the High Priest asked Peter and John, "By what power, or by what name, have ye done this?" It was the perfect opportunity for Peter to tell them about his priesthood authority, but he didn't. Instead, he said:

> Be it known unto you all, and to all the people of Israel, that by the name of Jesus Christ of Nazareth, whom ye crucified, whom God raised from the dead, even by him doth this man stand here before you whole.
>
> —Acts 4:10

If priesthood was so important, and he had healed the crippled man by the power of the priesthood that he held, why hadn't he said so? Instead he gave all the credit to Jesus and to the name of Jesus.

Tobie was trying to show me that Christ "abideth a priest continually," and that therefore we don't need other priests and especially High Priests. She challenged me to find where the New Testament church had High Priests or where Jesus ordained priests or High Priests. I could not find any mention of the position of priests or High Priests in Christ's original church anywhere in the New Testament.

The Need for a Prophet

All these uncomfortable questions brought me back to my learned belief in the importance of a modern-day prophet. As much as I loved the Bible, I had to admit it was insufficient. I had been wrong. I didn't like admitting it, but I could not confirm or substantiate unique Mormon doctrines from the Bible. We needed modern-day revelation from God and modern-day prophets. That was all there was to it. *That is why Joseph Smith is so important*, I thought. Father in Heaven had restored the truth and the priesthood through him. The problem I faced trying to teach Tobie from the Bible was clear: she trusted the Bible; I trusted the LDS prophets and LDS Scripture. This was a major difference.

It was more than an interpretation problem. It was a matter of trust! I needed to convince her why we needed a prophet today in addition to the Bible. Since she had been so intent on referring to the Book of Hebrews in our discussions about the priesthood, I had her turn to a verse that talked about the Melchizedek Priesthood:

> For this Melchisedec, king of Salem, priest of the most high God, who met Abraham returning from the slaughter of the kings, and blessed him; To whom also Abraham gave a tenth part of all; first being by interpretation King of righteousness, and after that also King of Salem, which is, King of peace; Without father, without mother, without descent, having neither beginning of days, nor end of life; but made like unto the Son of God; abideth a priest continually. Now consider how great this man was, unto whom even the patriarch Abraham gave the tenth of the spoils.
>
> —Hebrews 7:1–4

I was very intent about showing her the significance of the above passage of Scripture because it demonstrated a very important point I had been trying to get her to understand from the beginning of our talks: the need for a prophet today. The above verse didn't make sense if speaking of Melchizedek as a man, "without father, without mother . . . having neither beginning of days nor end of life." I had been telling her that, "We believe the Bible to be the Word of God, as far as it is translated correctly," (*Articles of Faith*, No. Eight) and that this was a good example of a translation error. Joseph Smith had retranslated it correctly to mean the order of the priesthood was without father or mother, not having a beginning or end.

KING JAMES TRANSLATION	JOSEPH SMITH TRANSLATION
Hebrews 7:3 (KJV) "Without father, without mother, without descent, having neither beginning of days, nor end of life; but made like unto the Son of God, abideth a priest continually."	Hebrews 7:3 (JST) "For this Melchizedek was ordained a priest after the order of the Son of God, which order was without father, without mother, without descent, having neither beginning of days, nor end of life. And all those who are ordained unto this priesthood are made like unto the Son of God, abiding a priest continually."

Joseph Smith's correction of the Bible made more sense than the King James translation, which stated that the man Melchizedek did not have parents or a beginning. (Much later, I learned that the statement in the King James Version "Without father, without mother, without descent, having neither beginning of days, nor end of life;" indicates in Hebrew tradition "no recorded genealogy." I did not know it at this time.)

The above correction was only one of the many changes Joseph Smith made to the Bible. Sometimes it was necessary for him to add complete verses to clarify the meaning and correct the text of the Bible since, according to him, it had many "translation errors." Now was the perfect opportunity to convince my friend that the Bible, in itself, was not sufficient. We needed a prophet to help us interpret and understand the Bible. That was the big difference between the true church and all other Christian denominations. The others didn't have a living prophet to receive modern-day revelation. They only had the Bible. The obvious fact that there were so many denominations disagreeing with each other while claiming to believe in the Bible was evidence enough that the Bible was too incomplete and ambiguous for teaching all gospel truths. This was all the more evidence why Joseph Smith was so important and explained how he, "has done more, save Jesus only, for the Salvation of men in this world, than any other man that ever lived in it" (Doctrine and Covenants, Section 135:3). He restored the truth through modern-day revelation to alleviate all of this confusion among the different denominations.

In addition, I reminded Tobie, we needed the Holy Ghost to properly interpret the Bible. It was obvious that others did not have the gift of the Holy Ghost in understanding the correct interpretation because they did not have the Melchizedek Priesthood to confirm the gift of the Holy Ghost.

I affirmed my testimony of Joseph Smith to Tobie and told her that just because many of the unique doctrines of the LDS Church—such as the pre-existence, eternal progression to godhood, plurality of gods, celestial marriage, the temple endowment, and many other doctrines—were not clear in the Bible, didn't mean that they were untrue. They had been revealed to Joseph Smith and were found in the other Scriptures of the church: the Book of Mormon, the Doctrine & Covenants, and the Pearl of Great Price. Along with the Bible, these books are known as the Standard Works of the church. All the doctrines of the church were found in Scripture somewhere. If it wasn't in the Bible, it was found in one of the other authoritative books of Scripture like the Doctrine & Covenants. What difference did it make which book of Scripture it was in? They all came from God. Although many Mormon doctrines were obscure in the Bible, they were still true. After all, that was Joseph Smith's divine mission—to restore lost truths.

I stuffed all the uncomfortable questions that had surfaced from our discussions. I had been given a testimony of Joseph Smith and I had to protect my testimony. All this confusion over Bible interpretation just confirmed how much we needed a prophet to clarify the Bible. *That is why I must follow the Prophet!* I concluded.

CHAPTER 6

A REAL DILEMMA

"Therefore if any man be in Christ, he is a new creature: old things are passed away; behold, all things are become new."

—*2 Corinthians 5:17*

The religious talks between my friend Tobie and her Jehovah's Witness acquaintances continued for several months. They were very intense and I was putting considerable study, prayer, and preparation into these discussions. We had covered many topics— from tithing to temples, from Adam to the afterlife, and everything in-between (at least it seemed that way).

Following one of our visits Tobie handed me a paper with two Scriptures written on it and asked me to read them.

"What are they about?" I asked. "Communicating with the dead," she answered.

I was surprised and didn't think they were relevant to our discussions.

I certainly hope she doesn't think we communicate with the dead, I thought to myself. After all, I knew that was of Satan. I thought of a headline I had just read on the cover of the *National Enquirer* at the grocery store: "Elvis Is Back from the Dead." How ridiculous that she would think I approved of such deceptions. Surely she knew that members of the church recognized séances and other ways of trying to communicate with the dead as deceptions from the devil.

I didn't bother to look up the Scriptures.

Worldwide Deception

Tobie was convinced that I was deceived, and I was convinced that she was deceived. We reminded each other of the many biblical warnings against deception:

> And the great dragon was cast out, that old serpent, called the Devil, and Satan, which deceiveth the whole world . . . .
>
> —Revelation 12:9a

> And the devil that deceived them was cast into the Lake of Fire and Brimstone, where the Beast and the false prophet are, and shall be tormented day and night forever and ever.
>
> —Revelation 20:10

A Testimony Comes from the Spirit

Even though I had some definite questions and genuine concerns that I didn't have when I started these discussions, I was convinced that I couldn't be the one who was deceived. I had received a spiritual witness from the Holy Ghost, which had convinced me that the church was true. Even though I couldn't always prove my testimony intellectually, I wasn't going to let doubts enter my mind; that was a sign of weakness. I would be strong. One gained a testimony of the church by the Spirit, not by facts. Members of the LDS Church could write books about these spiritual experiences. Indeed many books have been written, and I had my own experiences to tell of, as well as my father's convincing experiences. Tobie, however, wasn't impressed by any of those stories.

"Do you want to discuss the thousands of other people not in the Mormon Church who claim such experiences?" was her response.

I felt much discredited and gave her no answer. She really was annoying sometimes. However, her question stuck in my head. Just what and who was she referring to? I continued to bear my testimony to her that I had the truth based on a witness of the Holy Ghost.

My Silent Quandary

Nonetheless, I was bothered by an observation I couldn't deny or easily explain. I was facing a real dilemma—Tobie! It was very evident that my Jewish friend who had rejected Jesus all her life, now had a great love for Him. That wasn't a problem because I knew many people that were not members of my church who believed in the Savior and loved Him, but this was different. Tobie had understood and embraced Mormonism, and now she was rejecting it! Yet, she had feelings and experiences similar to what Mormons consider being a *witness of the Holy Ghost* upon which their testimony of the LDS Church is based.

Her baptism at the Kingdom Hall was one example. I was hoping that she would not go through with it, but she informed me she was going to be baptized and invited me to attend. Of course, I didn't want to go because I believed she was supposed to be baptized into the Mormon Church, not by the Jehovah's Witnesses. Following her baptism, she was eager to tell me all about it. Tobie shared about an inward warm feeling and peace that she had felt. She had been baptized by immersion, but was very emphatic that baptism did not wash away her sins. She explained to me that it was the blood of Jesus Christ that had cleansed her of her sins and confirmed her new belief with Scripture.

Are Sins Washed Away by Baptism or by Blood?

A Scripture-study attempting to answer this question in my debates with Tobie led me to the following:

> In whom we have redemption through his blood, the forgiveness of sins, according to the riches of his grace . . .
>
> —Ephesians 1:7

> But if we walk in the light, as he is in the light, we have fellowship one with another, and the blood of Jesus Christ his Son cleanseth us from all sin.
>
> —1 John 1:7

And almost all things are by the law purged with blood; and without shedding of blood is no remission.

—Hebrews 9:22

Wherefore Jesus also, that he might sanctify the people with his own blood, suffered without the gate.

—Hebrews 13:12

(See also Ephesians 2:13; Hebrews 9:12–14; 1 Peter 1:18–19; Matthew 26:28; Colossians 1:14, 20; Revelation 1:5, 5:9, 7:14.)

Of course I believed in Jesus' sacrifice on the Cross for the sins of the world, and I knew that Tobie recognized that I did. However, I had never thought of his blood washing away my sins, as the above Scriptures stated. Just what did the verse mean, "And almost all things are by the law purged with blood; and without shedding of blood is no remission." (Hebrews 9:22)

Why was *blood* necessary to cleanse us? I thought of the animal sacrifices I had read about in the Old Testament while studying about Aaron's ordination to the priesthood. I also thought about some particular words from the *sacrament prayer* I listened to every Sunday in church before partaking of the sacrament: "That they may do this in remembrance of the blood of thy son . . . ." Every Sunday at church, when I partook of the broken bread that represented Jesus' body and the water that represented His blood shed for me, I meditated on Christ's sacrifice on the cross for me.

This had always been a special time for me to feel close to the Savior. However, I had often wondered why He had to suffer and die on the Cross for us. The missionary lessons that I had taught made it clear that Jesus had to die and be resurrected so that we all could overcome death through Him. But why did He have to suffer for my sins if I was required to repent and earn my Salvation through obeying the laws and ordinances of the gospel? If I was able to return to God's presence because of my own worthiness through obedience and living the best life that I could, and through baptism into the church and the temple endowment, then why did Jesus suffer on the cross? For the past few years, this question had come to my mind regularly during my meditation on Christ's death during the sacrament. Now, I wanted to understand more than ever why it was necessary for Jesus to shed His blood for me and just what it meant to be cleansed by His blood.

I certainly wasn't denying the Scriptures Tobie was showing me, but I didn't understand them. However, I wasn't going to let her know I was perplexed, so I showed her a Scripture that I believed taught that baptism washed away our sins:

> Then Peter said unto them, "Repent, and be baptized every one of you in the name of Jesus Christ for the remission of sins, and ye shall receive the gift of the Holy Ghost."
>
> —Acts 2:38

That certainly said that baptism was for the remission of sins. Didn't that mean washing away our sins? I thought I finally had her.

She didn't have an immediate answer, but still insisted that baptism didn't cleanse us of our sins—the blood of Jesus did. [Much later I learned that the word "for" in this verse means *because of*; in other words, baptism was important because it gave evidence that one had repented and received the remission of sins through Jesus' blood. Baptism is an outward sign of an inward change through faith in Jesus. The same Greek word that is translated "for" in this passage is also used in Matthew, chapter three, verse eleven. The context clearly fits the definition *because of* here also. However, I didn't know this at this time and I was frustrated because Tobie seemed to always have some other Bible interpretation.]

A few years before this she hadn't even read the New Testament, now she had answers for everything! Just how did she get so smart? Feeling irritated, I ignored her and asked, "If your sins are washed away by the blood of Jesus, then why get baptized?"

"Baptism is a sign of our faith that we are cleansed by the blood of Jesus. He paid for our sins on the 'torture stake' (the Jehovah's Witnesses term for the cross.) The immersion in water is symbolic of our old lives of sin being dead and buried, since we have new spiritual lives because of Jesus," she answered. Then she found a couple of Scriptures in Romans:

> Know ye not, that so many of us as were baptized into Jesus Christ were baptized into his death? Therefore we are buried with him by baptism into death: that like as Christ was raised up from the dead by the glory of the Father, even so we also should walk in newness of life.
>
> —Romans 6:3–4

> Likewise reckon ye also yourselves to be dead indeed unto sin, but alive unto God through Jesus Christ our Lord.
>
> —Romans 6:11

Then she continued, "My baptism symbolizes that I am a new person because of what Jesus did for me. He paid for all my sins when He suffered and died."

I was surprised and at the same time perplexed. Why hadn't my Church taught me that deeper meaning of baptism? I couldn't disagree with Tobie's reasoning, nor with the Scriptures she'd showed me. I didn't want her to know it, but I was secretly impressed. I liked her explanation of baptism better than what I had been taught all my life— that baptism was for the remission of my sins and membership into the Mormon Church.

A Living Demonstration

What she had said was not just words. I could see the change in her life also. Tobie was undeniably a new person. Her devotion and love for Christ was evident and powerful. She was more interested in going out and witnessing for God than anything else in her life. She had separated herself from worldly desires. This was an obvious and dramatic change in her.

It wasn't the only obvious change I observed in her. She had really experienced a cleansing of her sins and had found freedom from guilt. She loved the story of the woman who washed Christ's feet with her tears, kissed them, and wiped them with her hair (Luke 7:44–47).

"That's me," Tobie would tell me in a choking voice with tears in her eyes. "He who has been forgiven much, loves much. You know where the Bible talks about being a new person—the old gone, the new has come? Well, that is what has happened to me."

At the time I didn't know where the Bible talked about being a new person, but later I read about it in the following verses: 2 Corinthians 5:17, 1 Peter 2:24, Galatians 6:14, Romans 6:1, 6:5–11, 7:4.

It was evident that Tobie had undergone some kind of supernatural change. Before this, she had seemed rather worldly and been involved in sins I had never done. I had tried so hard all my life to be good. Yet, she seemed to have found what I had been striving for—a solid assurance of acceptance in His eyes and freedom from guilt. This didn't seem fair! Honestly, observing Tobie was a dilemma for me. She had rejected what I believed to be the one and only true church, yet seemed to have Christ in her life in a more alive and meaningful way than I did.

This was my Jewish friend who had never seen a New Testament until a few years ago when I took one to her, and now she couldn't stop talking about it or about Jesus. I found myself almost envying her because she was learning to skillfully teach and defend what she believed from the Bible. I wanted to be able to do that and was finding myself frustrated when being told by my leaders that it was a waste of time to do so. They called such Bible discussions "Bible-bashing."

Help From a BYU Professor

The Dean of Religion at Brigham Young University was speaking at a Southern California church lecture series ("Know Your Religion"). I eagerly anticipated receiving encouragement and answers to some of my questions from him. However, I was completely disappointed by his advice to me:

"You are wasting your time talking with your friend," he said. "You will get nowhere by 'Bible-bashing.' If a person is pure in heart and has the right spirit, he will accept the gospel when he hears the Joseph Smith story. If a person doesn't believe in the Book of Mormon and Joseph Smith when taught, then don't bother with him."

Was the Dean of Religion right? Should I give up my intense drive to teach my friend the truth from the Bible? I knew that God did not want me to do that. I believe the Holy Ghost had whispered to me several years before that Tobie needed the truth. She certainly had found Jesus. To simply give up on her now was not only a lack of faith in God but would be disobedient to Him as well.

Is righteous living a prerequisite for gaining a testimony? I wondered. The Dean of Religion had made it sound like we had to be worthy to understand truth. It wasn't that way when Jesus taught the truth. It was the sinners that accepted Him and the law-abiding, religious Pharisees that rejected Him. Hadn't Jesus said?

> But go and learn what this means: 'I desire mercy, not sacrifice.' For I have not come to call the righteous, but sinners.
> —Matthew 9:13

Besides, I knew Tobie's heart. She was as sincere in following Jesus as anybody I knew.

"Don't Rock the Boat"

My stake president also told me to stop teaching my friend and to discontinue Bible discussions with anyone outside of the church. He went so far as to say, "I would never talk with anyone or read anything that might cause me to have doubts about the church. If I am deceived, I don't want to find out I'm wrong. I'll just stay deceived. I don't ever want to put myself in a position of doubting the church."

Was I "Bible-bashing" or seeking to defend the truth? I felt extremely let down. These two leaders' lack of concern for deception was startling. I didn't want to doubt my testimony either, and since I was seeking reinforcement to strengthen my testimony and more knowledge to defend it, these statements from educated priesthood leaders were disappointing, and yet very revealing. These were men who insisted they knew they were right, yet they had just indicated to me that the way to keep a testimony of the church was to not question it!

I believe we learn by asking questions and that truth will come out on top. *Was seeking answers to scriptural questions wrong?* Besides, was I just supposed to forget my friend, Tobie, because she believed in the Bible and let her be deceived by the Jehovah's Witnesses?

Tobie felt that if people wanted the truth they should be able to study and discuss the Bible in order to help them in their search. She quoted 1 Thessalonians 5:21 to me: "Prove all things: hold fast that which is good." I couldn't help but agree with her. Even if the Mormon Church's position was right—that the Bible didn't contain all the truth, and we still needed a Prophet today—shouldn't we still be able to use the Bible to teach and support the truth? That is what I was doing and was being told to stop. According to the Bible itself, we should be able to do that, for it said:

> All Scripture is given by inspiration of God, and is profitable for doctrine, for reproof, for correction, for instruction in righteousness.
> —2 Timothy 3:16

Did we as members of the true church believe that or didn't we? It was as if we had a double standard about the Bible. We believed it and used it in our missionary work and church meetings. My dad had always taught me that the Bible was the yardstick for measuring truth. Yet when there were problems, were we supposed to blindly trust Joseph Smith and disregard the Bible? We were certainly putting a great deal of trust in the Prophet. I acknowledged the need for our living prophet and felt the importance of following him. Yet, should believing in the Prophet negate the desire and ability to seek scriptural support from the Bible in order to defend the truth, as well as strengthen my testimony?

My testimony of the church was very strong and I considered myself a knowledgeable Mormon. I was well-trained and versed in my religion, but I had received my testimony mainly on the basis of a spiritual confirmation and subjective experiences. Now I needed intellectual evidence to support my testimony. I wasn't disregarding the spiritual evidences, but others also claimed similar spiritual evidences for their beliefs. Could mine also be proven by biblical evidence?

A Bigger Problem

Listening to Tobie tell of the warmth, love, and joy she felt, and seeing her eyes fill with tears as she shared with me her deep emotional and spiritual experience at her baptism posed an even deeper dilemma for me. *Was God pleased with her baptism? How could He be?* I had been taught that the only baptisms He honored were those performed by the correct authority—by the priesthood found only in the Church of Jesus Christ of Latter-day Saints. Yet I couldn't deny that she had experienced a spiritual witness that was real, and one that convinced her that she had made the right decision and was truly following Jesus.

In the past I would have simply shrugged off such a story as a counterfeit spirit of Satan, deceiving others. Now, it wasn't so easy for me to simply classify this as a satanic deception since it was so similar to the feelings Mormons have, and more particularly to feelings upon which I had based my testimony of the Mormon Church. Also, I could not explain the tremendous goodness, zeal for God, and love for Christ that Tobie radiated in her changed, new life.

Previous to this time, I had always quickly and confidently judged the Jehovah's Witnesses to be influenced by Satan. I was becoming less confident and not so hasty to judge others. A reassessment of my predetermined ideas was necessary. What was different between what she experienced and what I experienced? How could I say her experience was of Satan and mine was of the Holy Ghost?

I concluded one of three explanations: a) Either God accepts our acts of faith, overlooks our ignorance, and blesses our obedience to true principles, even when we are deceived and in a false religion (as I believed she was), or, b) Satan has a counterfeit spirit that resembles the Holy Ghost so much that it is extremely difficult to discern which is from God and which is from Satan, or, c) some of these good feelings we interpret to be from God are only our own emotions, human wills, and personal mindsets.

I had always trusted the prompting of the Holy Ghost in my life. The witness of the Holy Ghost was the strength of my testimony, as is the case with most devoted Mormons. The conversion by the Spirit is the basis for belief in the Book of Mormon and the church and this spiritual experience is much more powerful than intellectual facts. If others outside of the church also experience a witness of the Holy Ghost, then this type of experience is not exclusive to Mormons. Then how can we claim that the LDS Church is the one and only true church on the basis of spiritual experiences that are common to others outside the Mormon Church?

CHAPTER 7

EXPANDING MY WORLDVIEW

"Knowing this first, that no prophecy of the Scripture is of any private interpretation. For the prophecy came not in old time by the will of man: but holy men of God spake as they were moved by the Holy Ghost".

—*2 Peter 1:20–21*

Tobie had certain subjects that she would not leave alone. One of these was the question, "Who is Adam?" For some reason this subject seemed very important to her. She was acquainted with Mormon doctrine enough to know that Adam was highly honored as the father of the human race. Joseph Smith's revelations teach that Adam was the "Ancient of Days" and Michael, the Archangel (*Doctrine & Covenants* 27:1, 128:21, 138:38, 116:1, 107:54). As such, Adam helped create the world. Mormon leaders had taught that Adam was a god and that he had temporarily stepped down from his exalted position as a god to start the human race on planet earth after helping to create it (Journal of Discourses, Vol. 1, p. 50; Conference talk delivered on April 9, 1852).

I soon learned why this subject was so important to Tobie. The Jehovah's Witnesses were trying to convince her that Jesus is Michael, the Archangel. She had no convincing biblical support that Jesus was Michael, the Archangel (at least not to me), but neither did I have any biblical support to offer as proof that Adam was Michael, the Archangel.

The idea that Adam was elevated to this high position in LDS theology was very offensive to Tobie because she held Adam responsible for all of the evil and sickness in the world. Her theology seemed so simple: Adam caused the sin problem; Jesus was the solution! According to her, Adam was a sinner who willfully disobeyed God's command not to eat the forbidden fruit. This act of disobedience to God was a grievous sin. She believed that through this sin of believing Satan's lies and partaking of the fruit, Adam gave Satan power over the earth, over himself, and over his posterity.

My Mormon Concept of the Fall

That was very different from Mormon doctrine. I had been taught all my life that it was necessary for Adam and Eve to partake of the forbidden fruit in order to become mortal, instead of immortal. Father in Heaven wanted them to eat the fruit so they could obey His command to multiply and replenish the earth, which they couldn't have done in their immortal state. That's why it was necessary for them to eat the fruit in order to have children and to further man's progression (*Book of Mormon*, 2 Nephi 2:23).

In other words, Father in Heaven had given them two contradictory commandments: not to eat the fruit, but to multiply and replenish the earth. Heavenly Father knew they would have to eat the fruit, and therefore intended for them to eat the fruit. So when Adam fell, it was a fall upwards, so to speak. The Book of Mormon says, "Adam fell that men might be" (2 Nephi 2:25).

Actually, that was one of the doctrines of Mormonism that had never made sense to me. *Why would Father in Heaven give two contradictory commandments? Why would He command Adam not to do something that He wanted him to do, and then punish him for it?*

I tried to find Bible references that held Adam in high esteem, but couldn't find any. However, Tobie found Bible verses to show me that Adam was disobedient to God and, therefore, he should not be honored. We turned to Romans 5:19:

> For as by one man's disobedience many were made sinners, so by the
> obedience of one shall many be made righteous.

It was evident from the context of this Scripture that the *one man's disobedience* meant Adam's disobedience. The Scripture did say, then, that by Adam's act of disobedience, "many were made sinners."

It also said, ". . . by the obedience of one shall many be made righteous."

We both agreed that the "One" referred to here was Jesus Christ. I had no problem agreeing that death comes to all because of Adam and that all will be resurrected because of Christ. I had her turn to a Scripture I had memorized that further confirmed it:

> For as in Adam all die, even so in Christ shall all be made alive.
> —1 Corinthians 15:22

This was one point that Tobie and I agreed on.

Will All Receive Eternal Life in Heaven?

Tobie stated, "It is true that all will be resurrected, but not all will be given eternal life in Paradise Earth." (the Jehovah's Witness concept of heaven)

She knew that Mormon doctrine taught that because all people will be resurrected, *all* (except a few *sons of perdition*) will be given everlasting life in one of the *three degrees of glory*. However, she now rejected that doctrine and believed that only few will be given eternal life and the rest will be condemned to hell, which to the Jehovah's Witnesses was complete annihilation.

"You mean to tell me that you believe Heavenly Father is going to resurrect people just to condemn them to death?" I asked. That sounded pretty absurd to me. From my perspective a loving Heavenly Father would never do that. Of course, in a few days she had some Scriptures for me to read:

> And many of those who sleep in the dust of the earth shall awake,
> some to everlasting life, some to shame and everlasting contempt.
> —Daniel 12:2

65

Tobie pointed out that some would be raised to everlasting life, not all. Then she asked, "You believe what Jesus said, don't you?" We read the following:

> Marvel not at this: for the hour is coming, in the which all that are in the graves shall hear his voice, And shall come forth; they that have done good, unto the resurrection of life; and they that have done evil, unto the resurrection of damnation.
>
> —John 5:28–29

I had a quick defense. "None of those Scriptures say that people will be annihilated," I said. "Besides, the condemnation will be that they will spend eternity in the Telestial Kingdom of Glory without Christ rather than being in a *higher* degree of glory, such as the Terrestrial or Celestial Kingdoms. They *will* feel condemned when they see what they could have had!"

Tobie disagreed and pointed out that there were two destinies for mankind—life or death. She quickly turned to one of my favorite verses, Matthew 7:13–14:

> Enter ye in at the strait gate: for wide is the gate, and broad is the way, that leadeth to destruction, and many there be which go in thereat: Because strait is the gate, and narrow is the way, which leadeth unto life, and few there be that find it.

[Much later I learned that "destruction" is translated from the Greek word *apolia*— the same word translated as "perdition." It means "ruin or loss (phys., spiritual or eternal);— damnable, destruction, die, perdition x perish..." #684 *Strong's Exhaustive Concordance*. However, I did not know this at this time.]

"How can you say that everyone will be given eternal life when Jesus said many would go through the gate that leads to destruction and few would find life," she asked. "They don't reap life and destruction both. It is clear to me that those who reap destruction will not be given eternal life!"

She believed that the words "perish, condemnation, and destruction" were synonymous with the Second Death spoken of in the book of Revelation.

She did have a point, but I wasn't about to let her know that. I was silent.

"Do you know," she continued, "the Bible says that not everybody is going to see the truth. Maybe you are one that will not be able to see it."

That made me mad, and the conversation ended.

However, her words penetrated my soul deeply. They reminded me of the haunting feeling I had lived with for years that I was one of the *foolish virgins,* one who was invited to and waiting for the Wedding Supper of the Lamb but one ultimately left out because she didn't have any extra oil. *Was I that one? How could it be?*

In addition, I was bothered even more because I could see that Jesus did say that some would be given life and others would be condemned. Tobie did have a biblical basis for believing that people would be resurrected, some only to be condemned. When alone with my Bible and the Holy Ghost, more Scriptures concerning this subject seemed to jump off the page and get my attention. Many of them were spoken by Jesus, who said the following:

> Verily, verily I say unto you, he that heareth my word and believeth on him that sent me, hath everlasting life, and shall not come into condemnation; but is passed from death unto life.
>
> —John 5:24

Jesus definitely made a contrast between everlasting life or condemnation, and death or life. Jesus also said:

> For God so loved the world, that he gave his only begotten Son, that whosoever believeth in him should not perish, but have everlasting life.
>
> —John 3:16

This was a very familiar Scripture to me, but I had never noticed how Jesus clearly indicates that people will have one of two destinies— everlasting life or to perish.

In my personal study of the Bible, I soon noticed other Scriptures that supported Tobie's belief that you are either *in* or *out* of the Kingdom of God and if you're out of the Kingdom of God, you are thrown into the Lake of Fire and Brimstone, which the Bible calls the *Second Death.* I could at last understand why my friend believed that only those who entered God's Kingdom would have eternal life. (For more on this subject, see Volume Two, Chapter 19, *Would God Send His Children to Hell?*, and Supplemental Material, 1. *"Are All Saved?"* to be found at the end of that book.)

What Is Meant by Heaven?

Just what exactly was the Kingdom of God? As I thought about this, I wondered if Joseph Smith had classified all three degrees of glory as the Kingdom of God. I opened my Doctrine & Covenants to section seventy-six, which details the qualifications of souls that will be assigned to the Celestial, the Terrestrial, and the Telestial Kingdoms of glory, and read the introduction. It says:

> Prefacing his record of this vision the Prophet wrote: "From sundry revelations which had been received, it was apparent that many important points touching the Salvation of man had been taken from the Bible, or lost before it was compiled. It appeared self-evident from what truths were left, that if God rewarded every one according to the deeds done in the body, the term Heaven, as intended for the Saints' eternal home, must include more kingdoms than one." While he and Sidney Rigdon were engaged in studious and doubtless prayerful consideration of this matter, the glorious vision here recorded was given them.

Section seventy-six of the Doctrine & Covenants is the vision of the three degrees of glory, including the Telestial. According to the introduction, even this lowest degree is considered part of heaven. This is confirmed in verses 109–112:

> But behold, and lo, we saw the glory and the inhabitants of the Telestial world, that they were as innumerable as the stars in the firmament of heaven, or as the sand upon the seashore; And heard the voice of the Lord saying: These all shall bow the knee, and every tongue shall confess to him who sits upon the throne forever and ever; For they shall be judged according to their works, and every man shall receive according to his own works, his own dominion, in the mansions which are prepared; And they shall be servants of the Most High; but where God and Christ dwell they cannot come,

worlds without end.

It is clear that those who inherit the Telestial Kingdom will inherit dominions "in the mansions which are prepared." This was another confirmation that the Telestial Kingdom is heaven. *Who are these people?* Verses 103–105 tell us:

> These are they who are liars, and sorcerers, and adulterers, and whoremongers, and whosoever loves and makes a lie. These are they who suffer the vengeance of eternal fire. These are they who are cast down to hell and suffer the wrath of Almighty God, until the fullness of times, when Christ shall have subdued all enemies under his feet, and shall have perfected his work.

Speaking of these people again, verses 84–85 of this same section say:

> These are they who are thrust down to hell. These are they who shall not be redeemed from the devil until the last resurrection, until the Lord, even Christ the Lamb, shall have finished his work.

Yes, that was one of many differences between Mormonism and the Jehovah's Witnesses and evangelical Christianity. We Mormons believed that *God is love* and therefore would not send any of His children to a permanent hell. Hell is temporary, and even those who go there to suffer for their evil deeds will eventually inherit the lowest degree in heaven.

Concerning this Telestial Kingdom, Eldred G. Smith, former Patriarch of the Church, had said, "The Lord has told us of three degrees of glory. There are three 'heavens,' as it is often referred to. We call them the Telestial, the Terrestrial, and the Celestial. I cannot for a minute conceive the Telestial being hell, either, because it is considered a heaven, a glory. The Prophet Joseph Smith told us that if we could get one little glimpse into the Telestial glory even, 'the glory is so great that we would be tempted to commit suicide to get there.'"

This definitely was not in agreement with Tobie's interpretation of the Bible. She insisted that only a few were going to enter the Kingdom of God, which was going to be Paradise Earth, and the rest were doomed to a permanent hell or destruction. She insisted that there was no *second chance*, and that after this life comes the judgment, which is final.

> And as it is appointed unto men once to die, but after this the judgment.
>
> —Hebrews 9:27

"The Bible never speaks of a second chance," Tobie said. She didn't stop there.

"God has given *everybody* evidence that He exists, even from creation, and the Bible is available if we want to read it. But most people don't seek God because they are too busy seeking their own interests. The only people who are going to be in God's Kingdom are those who know Him. The rest are thrown out and destroyed, just like Jesus taught in the parable about the branches that do not remain in the vine and are good for nothing except to be burned (John 15:6)."

Tobie's religious view sounded so harsh to me. It was so different from my Mormon worldview that provided for a temporary punishment in hell but eventually rewarded everyone (except a few "*sons of perdition*") with immortality in some degree of heaven. I made a brief summary of the differences.

Contradictory Beliefs between Mormons and Jehovah's Witnesses

Subject	My LDS Interpretation	Tobie's Interpretation
Adam	Adam is a God. He is respected and loved as the father of the human race. Partaking of the forbidden fruit was a necessary transgression to bring about man's progress and exaltation.	Adam was disobedient to God and a sinner who caused sin and death. He is not admired.

Subject	My LDS Interpretation	Tobie's Interpretation
How Adam's sin affected humanity	Adam's act caused temporary physical death, but the eternal consequence was good.	Adam "sold" himself and his offspring into slavery to sin and death.
Christ's role	Christ overcame physical death for all. The degree of heaven to which we attain depends upon our deeds (good or bad) and personal righteousness.	Jesus paid the price for Adam's sin. Jesus' sacrifice was the ransom needed to deliver mankind from slavery to sin and death. But only those who will avail themselves of such a release will be redeemed.
Salvation	All will receive immortality in heaven (except the sons of perdition) in one of the Three Degrees of Glory.	Not all will be saved; many will experience God's wrath and will never enter into eternal life in His Kingdom.
Michael, the Archangel	Is Adam.	Is Jesus Christ.
Jehovah	Refers to Jesus	Refers to God, the Father.
Christ's Return	Christ will appear in His resurrected body and will reign on the earth personally during the 1,000 year Millennium.	Christ will be ruling from heaven during the 1,000- year Millennium. He will be invisible to those on earth.
Death	Only the body dies. The spirit is fully alive in the spirit world where it feels, thinks, learns, and can communicate with the living in mortality.	Asleep, unconscious in the grave until the Resurrection. Communication with the dead forbidden. Any such claim is a deception by a demon spirit.
The Bible	Has many translation errors and many truths lost from it. We need a prophet to restore truth through modern-day revelation.	God's accurate and complete Word; we do not need any more.

Priesthood	Necessary today to act for God, just as much as in Old Testament times. The priesthood was lost during the Dark Ages and was restored to the earth through Joseph Smith.	Necessary in Old Testament times only.

The thing that really amazed me was that we both believed in the Bible yet got such different interpretations from it. We definitely believed in two different gospels. I asked myself again and again: *How could we get such contrary interpretations from the same Bible?*

Bible Interpretation

This problem of Bible interpretation was another dilemma I faced. As members of the LDS Church we recognized the need to have the Holy Ghost's enlightenment to understand the correct interpretation of the Bible. While we recognized that the Holy Ghost could occasionally affect an individual, the gift of the Holy Ghost was different. Only members of the LDS Church could receive this gift, and that was by the laying on of hands by one holding the Melchizedek Priesthood.

However, after observing my friend, I could not deny that the Holy Ghost was powerfully working in her life and had given her enlightenment from the Bible. Could I continue to cling to the narrow worldview I had always believed—the view that Mormons alone had the gift of the Holy Ghost, and therefore others could not understand the Bible correctly? No, it was not so easy to just discredit Tobie's views as being satanic deceptions for several reasons: a) the Holy Ghost had certainly spoken to her when she first read the Gospel of Matthew and had given her a testimony that Jesus was the Messiah, b) her changed life witnessed that the Holy Ghost was currently working within her, c) she could back up her interpretation with other Scriptures.

She was convinced that her interpretation was given under the influence of the Holy Ghost and I was equally convinced that my interpretation was the correctly inspired one. How could we desire to obey God, be so sincere, feel God's influence in our lives, and yet come up with such opposite doctrines from the evidence in the Bible?

It was especially frustrating to find out that the Scriptures I prepared to convince Tobie and her Jehovah's Witness friends of my theology were not new to them. They simply explained *their* interpretation of the Scripture, which often made some sense when I read the entire passage, much to my surprise and annoyance. I refused to agree with them, but I learned that through their own eyes they had good basis for their doctrines and beliefs, which I previously had considered nonsense. I was beginning to wonder if one *could* find the truth from the Bible, and I was amazed that we both used the Bible to support such opposite doctrines. Was the Bible that incomplete and vague? The idea of other denominations using erroneous interpretations was, of course, not new to me, but the crafty, clever, and convincing way they did it was an eye-opener!

Who's Teaching Error from the Bible?

It wasn't just that we had different interpretations of the Bible, but the serious problem was that someone here blindly believed a lie while emphatically convinced that they were right. This was very troublesome to me. We couldn't both be right, and yet we were each equally convinced we were right. Neither of us was purposefully twisting God's Word; nonetheless, someone was deceived and teaching deceptions from the Bible. I didn't want that someone to be me. I was becoming more aware of how extremely clever and crafty Satan was at using the Bible to confuse the truth and mislead people. Satan was a master of taking Scripture out of context to teach a lie. *How could I discern the truth and be sure I wasn't wrong?*

Becoming Teachable

I couldn't comprehend how I could be the deceived one, yet something had changed within me. I was humbled enough to listen to another's interpretations and I was given the eyes and ears to understand them. This patience and ability to perceive the mind and hearts of others

73

was a dramatic change in me—something God had done. I had asked Father in Heaven to help me understand why sincere people rejected Mormonism, especially my good friend Tobie. God had answered that prayer, and I now understood her thinking and feelings so well it was almost scary. I had been given a changed spirit that enabled me not only to comprehend the strange views of the Jehovah's Witnesses but to also respect them, even though I disagreed with them.

Previous to this time my attitude had been so closed that I really didn't have any reason to understand them, nor did I want to. Since I belonged to the true church, why would I want to be taught by deceived people who were influenced by the devil? The distrust of anything outside of my church caused me to be rather judgmental and narrow-minded. Over the years I had talked to them many times, but always to prove them wrong, and I usually became very frustrated, intolerant, and condemning of them. Even though I thought I had been listening in the past, I had not heard them. I had been so convinced that I had the truth. I had been blinded by my "one and only" rendition of the Scriptures and my made-up mind.

Now it was different. When I first started these discussions with Tobie, I had asked God to help me understand why sincere people I love reject Mormonism, especially since we are told God will reveal the truthfulness of the church to them if they honestly seek the truth. This had bothered me as a missionary and again now with Tobie.

Yes, I had prayed for understanding and I certainly had been given understanding, but I was not prepared for what was happening to me. Since I had always viewed the doctrines of the Jehovah's Witnesses as somewhat ridiculous, this was an extremely broadening experience for me. It was as if a blockage had been removed from my eyes and intellect. I certainly didn't agree with them, but I was amazed to be able to relate to and appreciate the validity of their viewpoints. In their eyes, they were justified in what they believed, just as I thought I was correct in what I believed. I was in awe of how the Lord had truly answered my prayer and given me understanding to such a degree that I no longer wanted to blindly condemn and scoff at their doctrines. Instead, I respected their ability to defend their beliefs from the Bible.

Silently Bothered

Through the process of being humbled enough to learn from others, I was faced with some new questions. Although I believed I could find answers for them, my safe, secure box of Mormonism—in which I had been enclosed all my life—was beginning to show some cracks. I still felt that truth, however, could hold up under pressure, and believed that my "cracks" would be repaired. Still, the deeper I dug to defend my church, the bigger and more numerous became the doctrinal cracks.

I was frustrated. My dad had taught me that the Bible was God's blueprint. I had confidence in the Bible. Others were saying that I was wasting my time trying to show that the church was true from the Bible. Hadn't God spoken to Joseph Smith? Shouldn't he and the Bible agree and support each other, if both were from God? Surely, since the church was true, then I should be able to defend it from the Bible. *Why was I being told it was futile to do so? And why was Tobie not seeing it?*

I had a testimony of the church because of spiritual confirmations, but now I needed intellectual confirmations. *Was that wrong? And why did it appear that Tobie was experiencing the gift of the Holy Ghost in her life? She certainly couldn't be receiving confirmations from God that would cause her to believe in Jehovah's Witnesses—and reject Mormonism, especially if the Lord had told me through the unmistakable whispering of the Holy Ghost that she was to know the truth?* I had some deep questions, but I certainly wasn't going to let anybody know I was bothered. However, I couldn't hide my secret conflict from God.

From Confusion to Commitment

I turned to Him in prayer for help, as I was in the habit of doing:

Dear Father in Heaven,

I need help. I don't understand what is happening. How could so many people who are dedicated to You be so sure they are right, and yet be in such contradiction to each other? They have their feelings and experiences, also. They have evidences for faith. They believe in the Bible. Why does anybody have to be deceived? I sure don't want to be deceived. Is the Bible Your Word? Didn't You inspire holy men of old to write the Bible? I believe You did. You know if the Bible is accurate or not and what it means. I desire to understand what it means through Your eyes. I want to know the correct interpretation of Your words . . .

Dear God, if You will help me to understand the Bible correctly, according to Your truth, not man's interpretation, then I promise to obey You in whatever You teach me.
In Jesus' Name,

Amen.

I meant that prayer with all my heart, and I knew that God had heard it. However, little did I realize the shocking impact the answer to that prayer was going to have on my life. I wonder if I would have had the courage to make that commitment if I would have known what was coming just ahead . . . .

CHAPTER 8

THE BOOK OF MORMON VERSUS THE BIBLE

"I know that everything God does will endure forever; nothing can be added to it and nothing taken from it."
—*Ecclesiastes 3:14*

After encountering firsthand the frustration of trying to establish Mormon doctrine from the Bible, I realized the translation errors in the Bible were much more abundant and serious than I had supposed. The fullness of the gospel that had been restored to the Prophet Joseph Smith was taught clearly in modern-day revelations given to Joseph Smith, but not clearly taught in the Bible. My current problem had been in trying to establish truth from the Bible instead of emphasizing the need to trust in the prophets of the church and the Scriptures Joseph Smith had given us. How could I have been so naive as to think I could defend these doctrines from the Bible when the Book of Mormon states many plain and precious things had been removed from the Bible? How foolish of me! I had trusted the Bible to defend my Mormon beliefs. Yes, of course, the Book of Mormon had the answer.

Book of Mormon Says the Bible Has Been Changed

Consider this key passage from the Book of Nephi in the Book of Mormon:

> Wherefore, thou seest that after the book hath gone forth through the hands of the great and abominable church, that there are many plain and precious things taken away from the book which is the book of the Lamb of God.

—1 Nephi 13:28

It is clear that this passage is referring to the Bible, not just the gospel as taught by men. The use of the word "book" is frequent in this chapter. Verses twenty-three and twenty-four leave no question that "the book" is referring to the Bible, including both Old and New Testaments:

> The book that thou beholdest is a record of the Jews, which contains the covenants of the Lord, which he hath made unto the house of Israel; and it also containeth many of the prophecies of the holy prophets; . . . and when it proceeded forth from the mouth of a Jew it contained the plainness of the gospel of the Lord, of whom the twelve apostles bear record . . .

—1 Nephi 13:23–24; *Book of Mormon*

The Book of Mormon goes on to make it very clear that, "because of these things which are taken away out of the gospel of the Lamb, an exceeding great many do stumble; yea, insomuch that Satan hath great power over them" (1 Nephi 13:29).

Yes, that was my answer! Now I could understand why I had so much difficulty trying to defend Mormon doctrines from the Bible. Many of them weren't there. They had been removed by the "great and abominable church . . . that they might pervert the right ways of the Lord, that they might blind the eyes and harden the hearts of the children of men" (1 Nephi 13:26, 27).

This was a deliberate perversion of God's Word, done by men of the "great and abominable church, which is most abominable above all other churches" to purposely lead the children of men astray. I had always been aware that the Book of Mormon taught that many plain and precious things were removed from the Bible, making it incomplete, but that wasn't all the Book of Mormon said. It states that men were conscious of their attempt to sufficiently change the Bible in order to "pervert the right ways of the Lord."

If the Book of Mormon is correct, then the Bible is a very insufficient guide for confounding error and establishing truth. Why didn't we just admit that instead of repeating the rhetorical statement that the Bible had translation errors? I realized that wasn't even what we believed. Why did we as Mormons say that the Bible is a measuring stick for truth and teach from it—and then say we believe men have corrupted it? Was the Bible still God's Word, or is it a perversion of God's Word, purposely changed by men?

Now I could see my problem. I had trusted the Bible instead of Joseph Smith and the Book of Mormon. Since the Book of Mormon says that the Bible was leading people astray, "insomuch that Satan hath great power over them," I could no longer trust it as the authoritative Word of God if I believed the Book of Mormon. That was a big difference between Mormons and other Christians, I suddenly realized. The Christians I was talking with accepted the Bible as God's Word—authoritative and correct—while Mormons accepted Joseph Smith and their current prophet as their authority and looked upon the Bible as God's Word "as far as it is translated correctly."

According to the Book of Mormon, it certainly wasn't translated correctly by the hands of the "great and abominable church;" therefore, how could it be respected as the inerrant Word of God or as the authority to trust for truth? The Book of Mormon wasn't talking about translators, however; rather, about a willful, deceitful, changing of the Bible's text and meaning.

Keystone of Our Religion

Which was I going to trust as the Word of God—the Book of Mormon or the Bible? The keystone of the Mormon Church is the Book of Mormon, not the Bible. Joseph Smith said: "I told the brethren that the Book of Mormon was the most correct of any book on earth and the keystone of our religion, and a man would get nearer to God by abiding by its precepts than any other book" (History of the Church, 4:461).

The teaching from the Book of Mormon that many plain and precious things had been taken out of the Bible was something I had heard all my life. However, this belief had never penetrated me with the clarity and impact that it did now. The Book of Mormon wasn't referring to innocent translation errors made accidentally by well-meaning scribes and translators. Human error is quite a different thing than purposeful perversion. The idea that the Bible had been copied and translated so many times, consequently robbing it of perfection from human error, had made sense to me. But believing that men had been successful at changing the Bible so as to cause people to be in Satan's power is truly disqualifying the Bible as God's trustworthy Word!

It was as if Mormons were double-minded to say we believed the Bible, and yet also believed it had been corrupted. If men had perverted the words of God with the intention of perverting the right ways of the Lord, then those words of the Bible were no longer God's words, but were the words of wicked men. Which was it? Either God had preserved His Word, the Holy Bible, as a guide for us against false doctrines, or God had allowed it to be changed. Therefore, it would no longer be an accurate guide for truth.

For the first time in my life I realized that if the Book of Mormon was translated by the gift and power of God, as the introduction to the Book of Mormon states (also in Doctrine & Covenants, Section 135:3), then I could not trust the Bible or use it alone to prove all things and to find the truth. However, if the Bible was accurate the way it is today, and God had preserved it for us to be a blueprint and guide for finding truth and exposing false teachers, then the Book of Mormon was wrong. They could not both be the trustworthy, inspired Word of God as they read today.

This was a devastating thought to me! I had always believed that they both came from God and I was strongly committed to both. It was as if I were being split in half.

Deep Conflict

I had always loved the Bible and read it avidly. I believed it to be the yardstick by which truth is measured. It had always been a tremendous influence for good in my life. As a child I loved learning Bible stories from the Old Testament. I had just recently read the entire Bible from Genesis to Revelation. I was highly offended when Tobie first said that Mormons really didn't study the Bible. I couldn't believe she could say such a thing. Mormons take great pride in believing they understand the Bible more completely than any other Christians. However, in comparison to the way Tobie, her Jehovah's Witness friends, and other Christians I had met studied and revered the Bible as the authority of truth, we didn't study the Bible that thoroughly. It was obvious that we Mormons did not have the same respect for the Bible as other Christians did. We loved it and believed there was tremendous truth in it, but the Bible was not "the" authority for truth to members of the LDS Church; Joseph Smith and its current prophets were.

Christians believed that the Bible contained the fullness of the gospel, whereas the Book of Mormon teaches that Satan led others astray because they only had the Bible. Was the Bible that wrong and incomplete? Was I now being led astray by studying the Bible so intensely and therefore under Satan's power? I could not deny that I was being changed by the power of the words I was reading in the Bible and that the Spirit behind those words was working on my mind and heart. Was the Spirit behind the words I was reading in the Bible from God or from Satan—the Father of Lies, the Great Deceiver? If the Book of Mormon were true, then I was making a mistake by trusting the Bible entirely too much.

A thought almost too frightening to think hit me. The Book of Mormon was the first work of Joseph Smith. It was printed even before the church was organized. These statements about the Bible were at the beginning of the Book of Mormon (the thirteenth chapter of 1 Nephi). If Joseph Smith could be successful at invalidating the Bible as God's infallible Word, then he could come forth with new revelations, and they would not always need to agree with the Bible. What a perfect way for Satan to deceive people. I shuddered at myself for thinking such a thought. Yet, it persisted.

A Bible Promise

I was deeply troubled. Would God allow His Word to become corrupted? What about the statements in the Bible that promised that God's Word would endure: "But the word of the Lord stands forever. And this is the word which by the gospel is preached unto you" (1 Peter 1:24–25). Also, Jesus said: "For verily I say unto you, till heaven and earth pass, one jot nor one tittle shall in no wise pass from the law, till all be fulfilled" (Matthew 5:18).

The word "jot" represented the equivalent of the smallest letter in the Greek alphabet. In the King James Version it is combined with "tittle" (Revised Standard Version, "dot") which means a small part of a letter. The phrase, as used by Jesus, emphasizes that nothing will be removed from the law, not a letter, not even part of a letter, until all be fulfilled.[2] Had God failed to keep His Word pure?

Again in Matthew 24:25 we read: "Heaven and earth will pass away, but my word will not pass away."

Was Jesus wrong? Did God let men delete parts of His Word against His promise? If I couldn't trust these words of the Bible, how could I trust any of it?

Jesus also warned against worldwide deceptions. How could we test false prophets and doctrines of demons (1 Timothy 4:1), if God hadn't kept His Word pure for us? And how was I to know which parts of the Bible were changed and which parts were accurate? I was trusting Joseph Smith as to what was true and what wasn't true, including the Bible. Before my recent studies and efforts to defend Mormonism from the Bible, I thought Joseph Smith's teachings were biblical. However, now I was seeing many discrepancies and he was beginning to look very suspicious.

A Bible Warning

I tried not to think about the numerous warnings in the Bible concerning false prophets, but they wouldn't go away.

For there shall arise false Christs, and false prophets, and shall show great signs and wonders; insomuch that, if it were possible, they shall deceive the very elect. Behold, I have told you before. Wherefore if they shall say unto you, Behold, he is in the desert; go not forth: behold, he is in the secret chambers; believe it not.

—Matthew 24:24–26

Dear friends, do not believe every spirit, but test the spirits to see whether they are from God, because many false prophets have gone out into the world.

—1 John 4:1

Let no man deceive you with vain words: for because of these things cometh the wrath of God upon the children of disobedience.

—Ephesians 5:6

I did not want God's wrath upon me. Was it possible that I could be deceived? I resisted that question and reminded myself that I must be strong and hang onto my testimony. I refused to admit even to myself that I doubted Joseph Smith. That was too scary. After all, I had received that good feeling about the Book of Mormon, which I believe had been the Holy Ghost confirming its truthfulness. I might be in danger of committing the unpardonable sin if I didn't stay faithful to my testimony. In addition, I had made sacred covenants in the temple that I dared not turn from or I would be in Satan's power. The temple endowment, the Book of Mormon, and other LDS Scriptures all came from Joseph Smith. I couldn't allow myself to doubt him. There was just too much at risk.

CHAPTER 9

WHO WRESTS
THE SCRIPTURES?

"... as also in all his epistles, speaking in them of these things; in which are some things hard to be understood, which they that are unlearned and unstable wrest, as they do also the other Scriptures, unto their own destruction."

—*2 Peter 3:16*

In the Scripture verse above Peter is referring to Paul's writings and other Scriptures that, "the unlearned and unstable wrest." Words used in place of wrest in other translations are distort, explain falsely, misinterpret to their own ruin, and twist. According to Peter, those who "wrest" God's Scripture will reap destruction. It is a serious thing to teach a false interpretation of the Word of God!

Having my eyes opened to what the Book of Mormon really taught about the Bible was troubling enough, but that wasn't the only thing troubling me. Since I had asked Father in Heaven to help me understand the Bible according to His truths, not man's interpretation, it was as if a veil had been removed from the window of my mind. I was definitely given the ability to see another clear interpretation of Bible passages. This opening up of my mind was a miracle from God.

A simple analogy is the well-known picture called "My Wife and My

Mother-in-Law" by the cartoonist W.E. Hill.

When looking at it, some people see an old woman; some see a beautiful, young woman. Both women are in the one picture. If you see the young one, it is difficult to see the old one, and visa versa. Your mind keeps focusing on what it already sees. The first step in seeing the other woman is wanting to see her. Then it helps a lot to have somebody describe her features and point them out to you.

So it is with seeing another interpretation of Scripture. In the case of the picture, if you can see both the young and the old woman, at first you cannot see them at the same time. You visualize one, then go back to the other, but you do not see both simultaneously. While both images of the women are correct, that is not the case with Bible interpretation. In discerning the meaning of a Scripture, there is only one correct view and that is God's view. Of course, as we continue to study the Bible we get different inspirations from it at different times and we see new insights in Scripture that we didn't see before as God continues to speak to us through His Word, but two opposing doctrinal interpretations cannot both be correct.

In the case of religion it is much more difficult to see the opposite viewpoint because our emotions are deeply involved, sometimes more than our intellect. Also, when one is convinced that he is right because of his feelings, as well as his intellect, then it is easy to become positive and closed-minded. When our minds are made up it is hard for us to learn or comprehend or give credibility to an opposite view-point. It becomes even more difficult when one is bound by a spiritual experience.

Another example of the importance of perspective in interpreting anything we see is found in the arrow in the FedEx® logo. You may never know it is there, but once you see it you are amazed how clear it is. These are trite examples of what was happening to my mind. All my life I had only seen these Scriptures through my LDS interpretations. Now, since I had promised Heavenly Father that I would obey His truth if He would just help me understand what the Bible meant from His perspective, I was seeing these Scriptures in a new light. Sometimes the enlightenment of the new interpretation came to me when I was alone with the Bible and the Lord; not directly influenced by Tobie's interpretation. A religious mind block had definitely been removed. (For more on this subject, see Supplemental Material, I. "Mind Blocks" to be found at the end of this book.)

I was not only understanding the Bible through new eyes, but more and more I could see that certain Bible Scriptures I was using to defend my Mormon beliefs seemed to be taken out of context. In the LDS Church we frequently accused others of "taking statements out of context and twisting them" in order to accuse our prophets of teaching error. This "anti-Mormon" practice was very offensive to us, so it was extremely unsettling and worrisome to think we could be doing this ourselves.

More and more, this was not just a few isolated cases of misused Scripture; it was becoming a frequent problem for me when defending principle doctrines of Mormonism. It was an even bigger problem to have Tobie's interpretation of Bible passages make sense and frequently fit the context of the Scripture better than my interpretation. I wanted to ignore this problem but I couldn't.

Although I suppressed it, I was bothered. A very penetrating and piercing thought persisted: As a Mormon, was I taught incorrect interpretations of Scripture? Had I taken Scripture out of context unconsciously as a missionary, isolating certain verses, reading into them what I had been taught rather than understanding what they really said?

Let's look at a few examples of my problem.

The Stick of Judah and the Stick of Joseph – Ezekiel 37:15–17

> The word of the Lord came again unto me, saying, moreover, thou son of man, take thee one stick, and write upon it, For Judah, and for the children of Israel his companions: then take another stick, and write upon it, For Joseph, the stick of Ephraim, and for all the House of Israel his companions: And join them one to another into one stick; and they shall become one in thine hand.
> —Ezekiel 37:15–17

This passage is used in the church as a prophecy of the coming forth of the Book of Mormon. I was taught that the word stick refers to a book, since anciently they wrote books on scrolls rolled up on sticks. Therefore, Mormons believe that the above Scripture refers to two different books. The first book (or stick) is for Judah and his companions and is interpreted to refer to the Bible. The second book (or stick) is to be written for Joseph and his companions, and is interpreted to refer to the Book of Mormon—allegedly the descendants of Joseph, son of Jacob. Verse 17, above, states that they would be joined together, "and they shall become one in thine hand." This is interpreted by the Mormon

Church to imply that the Bible and the Book of Mormon would be used together as Scripture from God.

When I continued to read the rest of Ezekiel, thirty-seven, I realized that God gave His explanation of the two sticks. They represent the divided nation of Israel, the Northern Kingdom and the Southern Kingdom. The Northern Kingdom (ten tribes) had two names, Israel and Ephraim (Joseph's son). The Southern Kingdom (two tribes) was called Judah. The uniting of the two sticks together symbolized a time when Israel would no longer be divided into two kingdoms or scattered among other nations, but would be gathered into its own land and would become one nation with one king or shepherd ruling them. Ezekiel 37:15–28 is a prophecy of Israel being gathered back to their homeland, and of their ultimate redemption, when Christ will return to be Israel's king and ruler.

The Lord gave this interpretation when He spoke the following to Ezekiel:

> And the sticks whereon thou writest shall be in thine hand before their eyes. And say unto them, Thus saith the Lord God; Behold, I will take the children of Israel from among the heathen, whither they be gone, and will gather them on every side, and bring them into their own land: And I will make them one nation in the land upon the mountains of Israel; and one king shall be king to them all: and they shall be no more two nations, neither shall they be divided into two kingdoms any more at all.
> —Ezekiel 37:20–22

The rest of the chapter confirms this explanation of the sticks.

I decided to look up the Hebrew word for "stick" that Ezekiel used in this passage. This was a second confirmation that Ezekiel was not referring to books or scrolls.

The Hebrew word used in Ezekiel 37:15–20, from which stick is translated, is "ets" and it literally means "stick." Following is the definition from the Hebrew Dictionary:

> Ets, ates, from 6095; a tree (from its firmness); hence wood (plur. sticks):+ carpenter, gallows, helve, + plus pine, plank, staff, stalk, stick stock, timber, tree, wood. (*Strong's Exhaustive Concordance*, #6086, Hebrew and Chaldee Dictionary, p. 90)

I discovered that there was another Hebrew word that means book or scroll. It is "ciphrah."

> **Ciphrah**, writing (the art or a document); by impl. a book; bill, book, evidence, x learn[-ed] (-ing), letter, register, scroll. (*Strong's Exhaustive Concordance*, #5612, Hebrew and Chaldee Dictionary, p. 84)

"Ciphrah" is the word that Ezekiel correctly used in the first part of his book (Ezekiel 2:9) where he refers to "a roll of a book." But he did not use this word in Ezekiel 37. Obviously, Ezekiel knew the correct meaning of these two different words. If he had been referring to the Bible as the "stick of Judah" and the "Book of Mormon" as the "stick of Joseph," I believe he would have used the correct word (ciphrah) for book or scroll as he did in chapter two. But he didn't; he used "ets" for "stick."

This makes even more sense when we understand that the Israelites often used sticks symbolically to represent themselves and their tribes. (See Supplemental Material, II. *"The Stick of Judah and the Stick of Joseph"* the be found at the end of this book.)

When we put Ezekiel 37:15–17 in context with the rest of the chapter, it is easy to see why Ezekiel would hold up two sticks, symbolizing the two kingdoms, and then hold them as one in his hand, symbolizing the one nation of Israel. Today, we see Ezekiel's prophecy being fulfilled. In 1948, Israel was made a nation after not existing since its destruction in 70 AD. Today it is one nation and we have witnessed Jews pouring back into their land that God promised them. When Jesus returns He will be their king and they will never be divided into two nations again.

(For more information on this subject, see Supplemental Material, II. *"The Stick of Judah and the Stick of Joseph"* to be found at the end of this book.)

Celestial, Terrestrial, and Telestial Kingdoms

A second example is 1 Corinthians 15:40–42:

> There are also celestial bodies, and bodies terrestrial: but the glory of

the celestial is one, and the glory of the terrestrial is another. There is one glory of the sun, and another glory of the moon, and another glory of the stars: for one star differeth from another star in glory. So also is the resurrection of the dead. It is sown in corruption; it is raised in incorruption.

I had always believed that these verses referred to the Celestial, Terrestrial, and Telestial Kingdoms of Glory, where almost everyone (says Mormonism) will reside in the resurrection. I had not only believed it but taught it as a missionary, and it had always made sense to me. However, when I put these verses in context with the rest of the chapter, I could see it meant something different. In verse 35 Paul says: "But some man will say, How are the dead raised up? And with what body do they come?"

Then Paul talks about different kinds of bodies, whether it is beasts, fish, birds, grain, or men. Then he goes into celestial and terrestrial bodies. It is easy to get his point when we realize that celestial means heavenly and terrestrial means of this earth. Paul is simply comparing our present earthly (terrestrial) bodies with our future heavenly (celestial), resurrected bodies. This is confirmed in the verses that follow and in the rest of the chapter, where Paul makes more comparisons between our physical bodies and our future, resurrected bodies. Verse forty-four leaves little question about what Paul is talking about when he says:

It is sown a natural body; it is raised a spiritual body. There is a natural body, and there is a spiritual body.

Again, in verse forty-nine Paul says:

And as we have borne the image of the earthy, we shall also bear the image of the heavenly.

(For more information about this subject, see Supplemental Material, III. "*Three Degrees of Glory*" to be found at the end of this book.)

Another Uncomfortable Discovery

One of the topics Tobie and I had been discussing was, "Who is Jehovah?" In Jehovah's Witness theology, Jehovah is the Old Testament Hebrew name for God, the Father. In Mormon theology, Jehovah refers to Jesus Christ only, not the Father. It seemed we both could defend our positions quite well using different passages. One of Tobie's favorite Scriptures, which she used frequently to make a point, was Psalm 83:18:

> That men may know that thou, whose name alone is JEHOVAH, art the most high over all the earth.

Tobie loved quoting that verse to me, and I really missed the point because I was busy looking for Scriptures to confirm my own opinion that Jesus was Jehovah. It was later that I realized the impact of the above verse, when Tobie had me read Luke 1:32–35, where it referred to Jesus as the "Son of the Highest."

"You surely don't believe that Jesus conceived Himself and was His own Son, do you?" she asked.

Of course I didn't believe that, and she knew it! However, the verses in Luke helped me to understand what Psalm 83:18 was saying. It did say that JEHOVAH was the Most High over all the earth. That had gone over my head before. I certainly didn't believe that Jesus was the Most High over all the earth—Heavenly Father was. [I was confused about all of this at the time, but later a Seventh-day Adventist evangelist made sense of it all when he explained that the name "Jehovah" could be applied to God, the Father, and His Son, Jesus Christ, much like a family name would be.]

Before I understood all of this, I was seeking Scriptures to support the Mormon teaching that Jehovah is the Old Testament name referring to Jesus only, and not to God, the Father, as the Witnesses believed. I turned to a much-quoted, authoritative book, Mormon Doctrine, for help. The author, Bruce R. McConkie, was a highly respected Mormon apostle, a member of the "Quorum of Twelve" that presided over the church.

Under the word "Jehovah" in his encyclopedia-style volume, Elder McConkie states: "Christ is Jehovah; they are one and the same Person."[3]

I kept reading, hoping that he would use a Bible passage to support this statement so that I could show it to Tobie. He did, and I was excited!

I quote exactly how Elder McConkie refers to and quotes Isaiah:

> The death and resurrection of Jehovah (and the consequent resurrection of all men) is foretold in Isaiah in these words: 'In the Lord Jehovah is everlasting strength. . . . Thy dead men shall live, together with my dead body shall they arise. Awake and sing, ye that dwell in dust: for thy dew is as the dew of herbs, and the earth shall cast out the dead. . . . The earth also shall disclose her blood and shall no more cover her slain'; Isaiah 26:9, 19, 21.[4] (*Mormon Doctrine*, Bruce R. McConkie, page 359)

Elder McConkie was quoting from Isaiah to show that Jehovah would be resurrected from His dead body, which of course would have to refer to Jesus, not God the Father.

I at last had a clear Bible passage to support Mormon doctrine that Jehovah was Jesus' name and not God the Father's name. However, I had learned to go to the Bible and put quotes in context to make sure I was understanding them correctly.

My excitement over McConkie's quote turned to disappointment when I did this. McConkie had mistakenly applied this passage to Jesus' resurrection, but that was not what Isaiah said. Let me explain.

I discovered that in Isaiah, Chapter twenty-six, Jehovah is not the one speaking; rather, it is a prayer to Jehovah the LORD.[5] Throughout this chapter, Isaiah is speaking, using first person pronouns, such as; I, me, we, our, etc. In verse nineteen, Isaiah says: "Thy dead men shall live, together with *my* dead body shall they arise."[6] (emphasis mine) When put in context, it is clear that Isaiah is speaking of his own resurrection (as well as other men's), not the resurrection of Jesus.

Isaiah starts this chapter with a song. It appeared that verse four was part of this song of praise: "Trust ye in the LORD for ever: for in the LORD JEHOVAH is everlasting strength:"

McConkie had quoted the last half of this verse (accidentally typed as nine in the reference in his book) and combined it with verse nineteen to say:

> In the Lord JEHOVAH is everlasting strength. . . . Thy dead men

shall live, *together with my dead body shall they arise.* (emphasis McConkie's)

McConkie had combined part of verse four, which used the name "Jehovah," with part of verse nineteen, "together with my dead body." When read this way, it sounds like Jehovah is referring to his dead body that shall rise. Thus, McConkie makes his point that "Jehovah" refers to Jesus. However, McConkie doesn't notice that Isaiah is talking here, not Jesus. Therefore, how could "my dead body" refer to Jehovah's dead body? It does not! It refers to Isaiah's dead body.

McConkie emphasizes his incorrect point that "my dead body" refers to the body of Jesus by prefacing the two partial Scriptures with this statement: "The death and resurrection of Jehovah (and the consequent resurrection of all men) is foretold in Isaiah in these words: . . ." He then quotes the two combined verses above. This is the only Bible Scripture he gave to support his conclusion that JEHOVAH referred to Jesus.

While there is nothing wrong with putting Bible verses together to emphasize a point, I had already learned the serious consequence of twisting or distorting the Word of God—destruction. I was especially offended because we Mormons were always accusing the "anti-Mormons" of taking statements of our leaders out of context and putting them together to misrepresent them. I had a natural abhorrence for such a deceptive practice. I was surprised and devastated to discover that the respected and trusted Apostle McConkie was guilty of such a practice with a Bible passage. Whether knowingly or innocently, he was guilty! Before this time, I could have easily shrugged this off as an innocent mistake. However, now it had an impact because I saw it as a glaring example of reading into Scripture what we want it to say, rather than simply accepting what it said.

My stomach was suddenly feeling sick. I had asked Father in Heaven to show me who was misinterpreting or twisting His Word. Were we, the Latter-day Saints, "wresting the Scriptures to our own destruction?" I now wondered.

I did not want to accept the reality of the answer to that question. Trying hard not to be bothered, I excused away the examples of misused Scripture that I was seeing as the error of men. I would not let these kinds of mistakes affect my testimony of the church. I reminded myself that these errors certainly didn't reflect in any way upon the truthfulness of the church. There were far too many evidences of its divine truthfulness to let these human errors cause me to doubt my testimony. After all, the leaders of the church were human and subject to error just like the rest of us, weren't they?

Human or Inspired?

Nonetheless, a gnawing, uncomfortable thought would not leave me alone. I was bothered because following the leaders of the church implicitly and without question was a fundamental, underlying teaching of the church. The Council of the Twelve (of which Bruce R. McConkie was a member) consisted of a dozen men who were all sustained as prophets, seers, and revelators. They weren't just Bible scholars or learned men. Members of the church look to them as divinely inspired men of God. If God inspired the Bible through ancient prophets, then a modern-day prophet, seer, and revelator wouldn't interpret it incorrectly. If the leaders of the church were true prophets, then they should understand the true meaning of Scripture, shouldn't they? These men should not be teaching erroneous interpretations of the Bible. God's servants would never use His Word deceitfully! Yet I knew Bruce R. McConkie had done so in this case, and in my studies I had discovered many other doctrinal cases of misinterpreting the Scripture.

Paul taught that it is very important that we handle the Word of God correctly, encouraging followers of Christ to be among those who, "have renounced the hidden things of dishonesty, not walking in craftiness, nor handling the word of God deceitfully" (2 Corinthians 4:2).

Deep Significance

There was yet a much deeper significance to all this that I could not ignore, nor excuse. I had sincerely asked Father in Heaven to open my eyes to the correct meaning of Scripture and to give me discernment as to who it was that was twisting Scripture. I had become acutely aware that the leaders of the church were lifting isolated Scriptures out of context in order to teach and validate the doctrines of the church.

This was not just a few isolated cases of insignificant individuals trying to justify their own points of view, but instances of Scriptures being used by the church to support fundamental doctrines of Mormonism—doctrines taught by LDS prophets.

I had been taught these interpretations all my life, using Scriptures I had been trained to use as a missionary, years ago—Scriptures that are still being used by thousands of missionaries all over the world today— Scriptures and doctrines taught in respected, authoritative, oft-quoted books. These doctrines were not found in the Bible, yet they were read into the Bible through the church's interpretation—doctrines that leaders and members of the church fully believed were from God.

Did the leaders of the church know what they were doing, or were they innocently blinded by their own interpretations? Were these men guilty of conforming the Bible to their predetermined beliefs rather than conforming their beliefs to the Bible? I felt confused, fearful, and betrayed.

Follow Blindly, or Think?

At church I became keenly aware of how frequently church leaders were quoted, especially in lesson manuals. It was clear how much members of the church were following their leaders with blind faith and not personally checking out what they were told. It was also apparent to me that it would be easy to be led astray by such a method of learning— a method of trusting men rather than of searching out Scripture for oneself. I could see that I had been following the church leaders more than I had been following the Bible. I now resolved that I would be like the Bereans, who, ". . . examined the Scriptures every day to see if what Paul said was true" (Acts 17:11 NIV).

Rather than blindly trusting what my church leaders said, I realized that their teaching had to be held accountable to what the Scripture said and that I needed to check those things out for myself. However, this new resolve to validate what I was taught at church by the words written in the Bible wasn't church policy. The oft-quoted phrase, "Follow the Brethren" (brethren meaning the General Authorities of the Church) was the direct opposite of checking them out. This expression was even the title of the new priesthood manual.

Within the church these men were the unquestioned authorities. Devoted Mormons did not challenge, question, or disagree with them. All my life I had been taught that criticizing leaders was the road to apostasy. I was becoming intensely aware, however, that there was a big difference between criticizing and having the ability to think for oneself and form one's own opinion.

Was being aware of a fault in a Mormon leader and disagreeing with him considered the same as criticizing? Was it a sin to question? Was it wrong to do my own thinking? Were we to be like sheep and to follow blindly? I wanted to be sure I was following Jesus, not men. If the Mormon leaders did speak God's truth, then there should be no conflict. However, I could see many errors of men here; I felt a conflict.

It was not easy for me to question the church's interpretation of the Bible, or to disagree with its authorities. However, I had promised God I would obey Him. I had asked for His correct meaning and interpretation of Scripture and had prayed specifically to understand the Bible according to His will, not man's interpretation. Was He really trying to show me that my church was guilty of twisting the Scripture? I had to admit that He had, indeed, shown me that the church was undeniably guilty in some cases.

I needed to be honest and to reevaluate my strong, stubborn position. No longer could I be so absolute about my past religious experiences as proof that I was both right and beyond deception. I had asked to know who was falsely interpreting the Bible. Even when done innocently, it was serious and either my friend was guilty or I was. I certainly had not expected to find out that the leaders I trusted were guilty and consequently that I, myself, was as well. I felt even more betrayed, bewildered, and confused.

What Can I Trust?

I had learned a valuable lesson—not to blindly trust men. I had trusted and followed the Mormon prophets and leaders with confidence all my life. Now I didn't know who or what to trust. Could I trust these leaders? Could I trust my feelings? Could I trust an experience? Could I trust Joseph Smith and his Scriptures? Could I trust the Bible?

In spite of my feelings of betrayal I knew that God had heard my prayers and I trusted Him to help me through this tunnel of problems and confusion. I did not want to be deceived. I prayed frequently and intently for God to enlighten me and not let Satan deceive me with his craftiness.

Since I had prayed and asked Father in Heaven to help me understand the Bible according to His truth, not man's interpretation, I was seeing Scripture in a new light. I had also learned that many devout people who believe in the Bible are led to believe erroneous doctrines because they are following incorrect interpretations of the Bible made by other men. Obviously, because of many major doctrinal differences, many who sincerely believe in their church and in their own interpretations of the Bible are thereby deceived. I could not in all honesty exclude myself from the possibility of being among the deceived after my studies brought me to the following three conclusions:

1. The interpretation of the Scriptures I presented to defend Mormon doctrine did not always fit the context of the Bible and were interpreted incorrectly. These were not my interpretations but interpretations taught to me by my church, which was led by prophets. A true prophet would not teach an erroneous interpretation of God's Word.

2. The unique Mormon doctrines that distinctly set the church apart from the rest of Christianity could not be supported by the Bible. They were taught in Joseph Smith's Scriptures, but not in the Bible. The Scriptures in the Bible that the church used to teach these doctrines were often quoted out of context.

3. Once I started understanding the correct interpretation of the Bible, I discovered many contradictions between the teachings of Joseph Smith and the Bible.

These conclusions were not easy for me to accept, but I also could not deny them. As the weeks passed I spent much study and prayer time in God's Word, ". . . which they that are unlearned and unstable, wrest, as they do also the other Scriptures, unto their own destruction" (2 Peter 3:16).

My search was modeled on the mandate of Paul, who directed Timothy to, "Study to show thyself approved unto God, a workman that needeth not to be ashamed, rightly dividing the word of truth" (2 Timothy 2:15).

B. APPENDIX TO CHAPTER NINE

"Out of Context" Chart

The following chart presents a few examples of the many scripture verses I found that have been misinterpreted.

Scripture	Mormon Interpretation	Christian Interpretation
Book of Mormon		
John 10:16 "And other sheep I have, which are not of this fold: them also I must bring, and they shall hear my voice; and there shall be one fold, and one shepherd."	Refers to Christ's visit to ancient America, as described in the Book of Mormon.	Refers to Gentiles. They will be included in God's family, along with the Israelites.
Ezekiel 37:15–17 (Two sticks: 1 for Judah and 1 for Joseph – quoted in this chapter on page 88.)	Prophesied the coming forth of the Book of Mormon. The stick of Judah refers to the Bible; the Stick of Joseph refers to the Book of Mormon.	A prophecy that the divided nation of Israel would become one nation with one Shepherd (see vs. 22). The stick on which Ezekiel wrote "For Judah" symbolizes the Southern Kingdom, called Judah; the stick on which Ezekiel wrote "For Joseph" symbolizes the Northern Kingdom, called Ephraim (Joseph's son), as well as to Israel.
Plurality of Gods		
1 Corinthians 8:15 "For there are gods many and lords many."	There are many gods and we each can also become a god.	The reference to "gods" refers to the idol gods of pagan nations.

The Restoration		
Scripture	Mormon Interpretation	Christian Interpretation
Acts 3:20–21 "And he shall send Jesus Christ, which before was preached unto you: Whom the heaven must receive until the times of restitution of all things, which God hath spoken by the mouth of all his holy prophets since the world began."	The restitution of all things is the restoration of the Church of Jesus Christ of Latter-day Saints that was restored through the Prophet Joseph Smith in the 1820s, and is the only true church on earth.	The restitution of all things will happen when Christ returns (as stated in the passage), evil will be destroyed, Christ will establish his millennial reign of peace on earth, and the earth will be restored to its original state of beauty. The events detailed in the Book of Revelation must happen first, as the prophets in the Old Testament also predicted.
Daniel 2:34, 35 "Thou sawest still that a stone was cut out without hands, which smote the image upon his feet that were of iron and clay, and brake them to pieces. Then was the iron, the clay, the brass, the silver, and the gold, broken to pieces together, and became like the chaff of the summer threshing floors; and the wind carried them away, that no place was found for them; and the stone that smote the image became a great mountain and filled the whole earth."	The stone cut out without hands is another prediction of the restoration of the gospel of Jesus Christ through Joseph Smith in the 1820s and is the Kingdom of God on earth.	The stone that broke the image and became a great mountain that filled the whole earth is symbolic of the end of this present system of things. The nations and governments of men will be destroyed when Jesus Christ returns as King of Kings and Lord of Lords and establishes His Kingdom on earth, as foretold in the Book of Revelation. When this happens, Christ's Kingdom will never be destroyed.

The Apostasy		
Scripture	**Mormon Interpretation**	**Christian Interpretation**
Acts 20:29–30 "For I know this, that after my departing shall grievous wolves enter in among you, not sparing the flock. Also of your own selves shall men arise, speaking perverse things, to draw away disciples after them."	Paul is predicting the Apostasy—a complete apostasy, meaning that Christ's Church and the priesthood power that He gave to His apostles would be taken from the earth.	Many will arise teaching false doctrines, but this does not say Christ's Church would be taken from the earth. While the New Testament predicts in many places that heresies would be taught by false teachers and false prophets who professed to be Christians, the true gospel of Jesus Christ is still taught in the New Testament today as the apostles taught it and wrote it. Jesus said the *gates of hell would not prevail against His church* (Matthew 16:18).
Authority		
Hebrews 5:4 "And no man taketh this honour unto himself, but he that is called of God, as was Aaron."	Men must be called and ordained by one possessing the priesthood or they have no authority to act for God. The Mormon Church claims this priesthood exclusively. It is passed from man to man by the laying on of hands.	Jesus, as our High Priest, was called of God, not ordained by men. Hebrews 7:16, 18, 23–25. Later I learned that Christ's priesthood (the Melchizedek Priesthood) is non-transferable.
Three Degrees of Glory		
1 Corinthians 15:40–41 (Quoted in this chapter)	After the Resurrection, everyone will dwell in one of three kingdoms or *degrees* of glory: the Celestial King-dom (highest degree), Terrestrial Kingdom (middle degree), and Telestial King-dom (lowest degree).	Paul is teaching that in the Resurrection we will have heavenly (celestial) resurrected bodies, as compared to our present earthly (terrestrial) bodies.

Men Can Become Gods		
Scripture	Mormon Interpretation	Christian Interpretation
John 10:34 " Jesus answered them, 'Is it not written in your law, I said, Ye are gods?' "	We are all gods in embryo.	Surely Jesus wasn't calling the Pharisees who hated Him and wanted to kill Him gods in embryo. What then, did He mean? Jesus is quoting Psalm 82:6. Eloheim (the Hebrew word from which God is translated) also means human magistrates and rulers. In Psalm 82:6, Eloheim (translated *gods*) refers to Israel's judges. Notice Psalm 82:7 says, "You will die like mere men." (The Mormon apostle, James E. Talmage, confirms this in his book, *Jesus, the Christ, on pages 489 and*
Pre-Existence		
Jeremiah 1:5 "Before I formed thee in the belly I knew thee; and before thou camest forth out of the womb I sanctified thee, and I ordained thee a prophet unto the nations."	Man existed as spirit beings with God before the creation of the world.	God knew He was going to form Jeremiah to be a prophet. God knows everything before it happens.
Job 38:4 and 7 "Where wast thou... When the morning stars sang together, and all the sons of God shouted for joy?"	Morning stars and sons of God refer to the entire human race, who existed as *spirit children* in the pre-existence before the creation of the earth.	Morning stars and sons of God refer to angels. They are created spiritually; humans are created physically and we don't "progress" from one state to the other.

Baptism for the Dead		
Scripture	**Mormon Interpretation**	**Christian Interpretation**
1 Corinthians 15:29 "Else what shall they do which are baptized for the dead, if the dead rise not at all? Why are they then baptized for the dead?"	The Bible teaches that the living should do baptisms by proxy for the dead. These spirits of the dead are in the spirit realm, waiting for this important ordinance so that they can progress.	Paul and the Christians were not the ones performing these baptisms. Notice Paul changes from the first person "we," to the third person "they."

CAN I TRUST THE BIBLE?

"The grass withers, the flower fades, but the word of our God stands forever."

—Isaiah 40:8

Just how trustworthy was the Bible? Was it a sufficient guide for truth, or not? I had been insisting to Tobie that the Bible had many translation errors. This oft-repeated statement within the Church that, "We believe the Bible to be the word of God as far as it is translated correctly" (LDS Article of Faith, No. 8) was, however, not an accurate representation of what the Book of Mormon taught. It said that men of the "abominable church" willfully changed the text of the Bible. Also, Joseph Smith had said, "I believe the Bible as it read when it came from the pen of the original writers. Ignorant translators, careless transcribers, or designing and corrupt priests have committed many errors" (*Teachings of the Prophet Joseph Smith*, p. 327).

Translation errors was an understatement! Joseph Smith taught, as does also the Book of Mormon, that men had willfully changed God's Word for their own evil purposes. There was a big difference between *accidental* translation errors having been made innocently and corrupt priests committing many errors. However, I had trusted what I had been taught, and I repeated the rhetorical statement I'd heard so often that the Bible had "many *translation errors*." Tobie challenged that claim.

"Use any translation you want," she confidently stated. "It doesn't matter that much. The message is the same in all of them. The wording is a little different, but they all contain the truth. Just what do you mean by translation errors, and can you produce evidence to back up your statement?"

I started to explain that there were missing books that had been written during Bible times. She quickly pointed out that that was another subject. Whether or not there existed other writings that we do not have in our Bible didn't determine whether our current Bible had been translated correctly. I had challenged the accuracy of what we do have. She insisted there was conclusive manuscript evidence to support the current Bible as being extremely accurate. (Note: Jehovah's Witnesses, however, are strong in using their own "New World" translation, in which they have made a few changes.) In the end, this was the issue: Could I accept and trust what I read in the Bible as God's inerrant Word, or had men changed it?

In all honesty, I knew next to *nothing* about Bible manuscripts and translations. I had trusted my church leaders and been boldly stating a fact I had no evidence to back up. I knew nothing about the history of the Bible. *Who'd translated it? Who had decided it was Scripture? How accurate or inaccurate was it?* It was time to do some serious personal research on the subject.

I discovered a series of articles in our church magazine, The Ensign, entitled, "How the Bible Came to Be." It was perfect. Just what I wanted to know—and published by the church! If there was any evidence of translation errors, I would probably find it in these articles. I was also eager to see if these articles showed evidence to support the Book of Mormon claim that the "great and abominable church" had taken "many plain and precious things" from the Bible.

I had been taught from my youth that the "great and abominable church" was the Catholic Church. The Mormon Apostle, Bruce R. McConkie, makes this clear in the 1958 edition of *Mormon Doctrine*. On page 129, under the headline, "Church of the Devil," we read:

> There are two scriptural senses in which the titles "church of the devil" and "great and abominable church" are used: 1) All churches or organizations . . . which are designed to take men on a course that

leads away from God . . . 2) The *Roman Catholic Church* specifically— singled out, set apart, described, and designated as being "most abominable above all other churches." (McConkie references 1 Nephi 13:5.)

Continuing on page 130 of the same book, we read:

It is also to the Book of Mormon to which we turn for the plainest description of the Catholic Church as the great and abominable church. Nephi saw this 'church which is most abominable above all other churches' in vision. He 'saw the devil that he was the foundation of it;' and also the murders, wealth, harlotry, persecutions, and evil desires that historically have been part of this satanic organization.
(McConkie references 1 Nephi 13:1–10.)

The above statements about the Catholic Church were deleted in the 1966 edition of *Mormon Doctrine* and have remained deleted.

A Parenthetical Insert about Changes in LDS theology

It is important to me as the author to make a statement regarding the changes that have occurred over the years in the LDS religion. My reader may even encounter things in reading this book that they would question because they have never heard them taught in the LDS Church today. If this is the case, trust me. I was taught true Mormon doctrine in my generation.

While we can be fair and acknowledge that men's understanding of things certainly does change, we need to be objective and acknowledge that not all changes within Mormonism can be swept under the carpet so easily because of the error of men. The church attributes these changes to *continuing revelation*. However, when it is a reversal or a negating of a former revelation, I don't think it is fair to call it "continuing revelation."

The Quorum of Twelve Apostles of the LDS Church, of which Bruce R. McConkie was a member, has been sustained by the world-wide membership as "prophets, seers, and revelators." Therefore, one should not be afraid to put them to the test as to whether they are true prophets of God or false prophets. Obviously they can err in their own opinions, but when their teachings go back to the first prophets of the church and have been taught as Mormon doctrine and believed by the membership of the church for over one hundred years, I think it creates some problems.

For example, the teaching that the Catholic Church was the "great and abominable church" was not given as a revelation, but I had been taught this all my life by the leaders of the Church. The problem of changing doctrines within the LDS Church becomes magnified when a particular teaching was allegedly given as a revelation of the Lord and later changed because of "people pressure." Some of these changes would include the "sacred" temple endowment, the revelation on the worthiness of African Americans to go to the temple and be ordained to the Priesthood, polygamy, living the United Order (communal living), changes in the Book of Mormon, and changes in the *Book of Commandments* (now the Doctrine & Covenants). Of course, there are the old teachings that most Mormons today wouldn't even know about, such as the Adam/God Doctrine and Blood Atonement, preached and practiced by Brigham Young.

Changes happening today are more gradual, as the church seems to be moving towards biblical Christian teaching and promoting fewer of the original, unique Mormon teachings. These gradual changes include the teaching that "God was once a man and man may become a god." Even though their Scripture still contains the teaching that men can become gods and many Mormons still believe this, the LDS missionaries seem to be downplaying this LDS doctrine by promoting the idea that they believe men can become "godlike." Another change is that the current leaders occasionally even speak of the cleansing power of the blood of Christ. This, as well as the doctrine of grace, was not taught from LDS pulpits for the forty years that I was a strong, active Mormon.

I think that abandoning error and accepting truth is very commendable. Yes, it would be wonderful if the LDS leaders would renounce their past errors, embrace the truth, and join the Body of Christ as the Worldwide Church of God has done. However, this would require

an honest confession that they were wrong instead of denying the former teachings of their prophets. Is it honorable to quietly change and reverse what their prophets have taught and still tell the world they are true prophets of God? Is it honest to proclaim to the world that they alone are the only true church and claim that the rest of Christianity is apostate while they gradually incorporate biblical Christian doctrines to which they once were opposed and now claim as their own beliefs? Wouldn't it be better to embrace   the truth   and honestly admit their errors? However, to do so
would be an admission that those who taught the falsehoods were false teachers and false prophets who deceived millions and the foundation of Mormonism would collapse.

Now having said all that, let's get back to the claim made in the Book of Mormon that changes were made in the Bible by the "great and abominable church." Whether it was the Catholic Church or another group of men who supposedly made these changes in the text of the Bible, the LDS belief is that they were made after the time of Christ. According to the Book of Mormon, both the Old and New Testaments had been altered from their original state. The chapter in the Book of Mormon that says "there are many plain and precious things taken away from the book, which is the book of the Lamb of God;" mentions both the "record of the Jews, which contains the covenants of the Lord, which he hath made unto the house of Israel . . ." and "the fullness of the gospel of the Lord, of whom the twelve apostles bear record;" (1 Nephi 13:23–28).

A careful reading of 1 Nephi 13 makes it clear that these deletions from the Bible could not have happened before the time of Christ because the book went "forth from the Jews in purity" (vs. 25) by the hand of the twelve apostles:

> And after they go forth by the hand of the twelve apostles of the Lamb, from the Jews unto the Gentiles, thou seest the formation of that great and abominable church... Wherefore, thou seest that after the book hath gone forth through the hands of the great and abominable church, that there are many plain and precious things

taken away from the book, which is the book of the Lamb of God.

—1 Nephi 13:26, 28

Tobie was claiming that there were manuscripts of the Old Testament that predated Christ and showed that it had been transmitted to us with amazing accuracy. She said that there was more manuscript evidence for the Bible than for any other work of antiquity. (For more detailed information on manuscript evidence, see Supplemental Material, IV. *"The Holy Bible: God's Double-Edged Sword"* to be found at the end of this book.)

If the claim my church made was true, (contrary to what Tobie said) the articles in the Ensign should have some specific knowledge to shed on when and how the "changes in the Bible" were made.

I was surprised that these articles did not give evidence to support changes made by "a great and abominable church." On the contrary, I had more confidence in the Bible after reading them. A few years later, the author of these articles published the same information in a book entitled "How We Got Our Bible." The following quotes are taken from the book although I first read them in the Church magazines.

Reliability of Old Testament Copies

The first thing I learned was that the Old Testament was originally written in Hebrew and then hand-copied by Jewish scribes. Their task was taken on with great seriousness, and often, in war time, at the peril of their lives.

> The preservation of records was of great concern to the Hebrews . . . The official scrolls were the holiest objects in the synagogue and were treated in every way like treasures. New scribes were carefully instructed about the sacredness of their task: "My son, be careful in thy work, for it is heavenly work, lest thou err in omitting or in adding one jot [the smallest letter in the Hebrew alphabet] and so cause the destruction of the whole world."[7]

From other sources I learned that the Jews were so faithful at keeping the text of the Old Testament accurate that they were referred to as "God's librarians." The reason we don't have the original manuscripts of the Bible is that, out of reverence for God's Word, the Jewish scribes would burn the worn and aged copies so that clarity would not be a problem in copying them.

The painstaking process of transcribing the text of the Old Testament was handed down from the time of Ezra. The Jewish scribes, whose job it was to copy it, were known as the *Sopherim* (counters). They later came to be known as the *Masorites*. The way they would keep the copies accurate was by counting. Since every Hebrew character has a numerical equivalent, the Masorite scribes would add up each line they copied, and if it did not equal the line in the original text, they would burn the entire scroll they were working on. They were just as careful and meticulous in other areas. For example, they noted that the Hebrew letter *aleph* occurred 42,377 times in the Old Testament.

The New Testament was written in Greek. One of the first translations of the Old and New Testaments was done by Jerome and was finished in about 405 A.D. It was translated into Latin and became known as the *Latin Vulgate* (Vulgate meaning *common text*). This became the Bible used by the Christian Church for about a thousand years.

During this period of time, different men who loved the Scriptures and memorized them also put them into song in the Anglo-Saxon language. They would sing these songs to the common people with a desire to bring the Scriptures to them. Many people would memorize the Bible by hearing it since they didn't have copies to read.

Because copying the Bible was an extremely tedious task, few Bibles were available in this era.

> Those made were elaborate, with covers and cover pages beautifully ornamented and gilded, and with painstaking embellishments in the copy. The effect of such labor was to make the Scriptures 'treasures of art,' but not of knowledge. In a sense, then, the Bible became a holy relic. It was not meant to be read or studied, for even monks came to regard its contents as 'sacrosanct but ill-understood lore, a venerable mystery.' Its contents were no longer penetrated by eager minds, nor memorized, nor treasured by softened hearts. In general, it became an unopened enigma, only to be kissed and superstitiously revered.[8]

Translators— Guilty or Godly?

Learning about the men who first translated the Bible was fascinating to me. In the early 1300s, a godly man by the name of John Wycliffe studied the Bible with great reverence as the Word of God. He was dismayed by the pomp and power within the church at that time, as opposed to the humility of Christ and how He had related to the poor and common people. The following quote paints these contrasting pictures:

> Because of his study of the Bible, Wycliffe felt confident that his religious convictions were consistent with the principles taught by the prophets and apostles. He understood that the true standard for the church must be meekness, not worldliness; and when he saw two opposing popes fighting for status and power, he could not withhold his dismay.[9]

> Disillusioned with the contemporary church and feeling that its actions were inconsistent with the teachings of the Bible, Wycliffe came to the conclusion that the only just guide that the people still had was The Bible. It was "God's Law," and he felt that under present conditions men should be held accountable to it alone. The people, however, could not be held accountable for a law they did not know. The goal of his life, then, became taking "Goddis Lawe" to the people in the language they understood, which was English.[10]

Wycliffe and those who assisted him in translating the Bible were severely persecuted. They were hunted, excommunicated, imprisoned, tortured, and burned. Not only the translators were persecuted, but also anyone possessing a Bible, even hearing a few pages of it, was risking their liberties, properties, and even their lives.

In 1414, a law was established that would cause those who read any part of Scripture in English to "forfeit land, catel, lif[e], and goods from their heyers [heirs] forever." The church was in earnest about this law, and there were many prosecutions. One woman was accused of heresy simply for listening in the secret of the night to her husband read the words of Christ. Others suffered for memorizing the Bible's passages, regardless of the content. Another woman was tried for teaching someone else "the Epistle of James, the first chapter of Luke, and the Sermon on the Mount." She was strictly instructed to teach the Bible no more, especially to her children. Many men and women who were convicted were burned at the stake, often with their Bibles hung around their necks.

> The church [Catholic Church] claimed the right to interpret the Scriptures to the masses. But, having generally abandoned the Scriptures as a basis of the faith, the church did not fulfill that duty. All church services were in ceremonial Latin, which few of the parish priests themselves understood. Nor did they understand any better their Latin Bibles. Consequently, the clergy could not feed the sheep, for they had no knowledge with which to feed them.[11]

It was obvious that the church had kept the Bible a secret. The Catholic Church had not changed the Bible; rather, they had treated it with such adoration that they were afraid to have it taken out of the original language so it could be read by common people.

I felt a deep gratitude for the men who had long ago given their lives so that we could read the Bible today. I had never been taught about Jerome, John Wycliffe, or any of the others who had made such sacrifices so that we could know God's truth.

Another such man I learned about through my personal studies was William Tyndale. He was born about the time that Columbus discovered America and was a contemporary of Martin Luther, who was then translating the Holy Bible into German. The Dark Ages were being replaced with the Renaissance, the Reformation, and many new inventions and discoveries—including Johann Gutenberg's moveable-type printing press. Tyndale was highly educated and deeply committed to studying the Scriptures. He was eventually reprimanded for staying true to what the Scriptures taught, even though it meant standing alone against the clergy.

> At one point, during an encounter with a learned gentleman, Tyndale was provoked to exclaim that if God would spare his life, before many years the boy who guided the plough would know more Scriptures than those who were supposedly learned.[12]

By 1525, Tyndale had completed his first goal of translating the New Testament into English. The Catholic Church was still adamantly opposed to any translations of the sacred Scripture. They made claims that the translations were full of thousands of errors and anyone found with these translations would have to give them up for burning or be excommunicated. The church built a huge bonfire and publicly burned any Bibles they found.

> Tyndale later commented that "in burning the New Testament, they did none other thing than I looked for; no more shall they do if they burn me also, if it be God's will it shall so be."[13]

As God often uses irony, it is interesting to note that Tunstal, one of the strongest opponents to the Bible being translated and someone who was largely responsible for the burning of thousands of Bibles, unknowingly financed the printing of more Bibles by buying them for burning. Little did he know that the money was being returned to Tyndale, who was continually having more Bibles printed!

Tyndale worked constantly at improving his translation of The New Testament. Tyndale himself complained that if there were even so much as an "I" undotted, someone would call it heresy. He also insisted, "I never altered one syllable of God's words against my conscience; nor would do so this day, if all that is in the earth, whether it be honour, pleasure, or riches, might be given me."[14]

He also desired to translate the Old Testament. The manuscript of his first translation of the Pentateuch was destroyed in a shipwreck. After retranslating it, it was also sought for burnings. Tyndale had literally spent his life fleeing to safe places and often living like a fugitive in order to preserve his life so that he might accomplish his dream of giving the people God's Word—the Bible.

> Tyndale revealed much of what he had suffered for the cause, including 'poverty, exile out of my natural country, and bitter absence from my friends . . . my hunger, my thirst, my cold, the great danger wherewith I am everywhere encompassed . . . and hard and sharp fightings which I endure.' He insisted that death would be more pleasant than life if it were really true that men could not endure truth and that knowledge of the Scriptures would bring more harm than good. Appeals were made to the German emperor to surrender him, and instructions were given to kidnap him. Living like a fugitive, he

managed to elude his pursuers.[15]

In 1535 Tyndale was betrayed by someone he thought was his friend and was imprisoned.

> He would never be freed from the dungeon there, suffering its isolated darkness and dampness for over sixteen months . . . Just two events brought Tyndale out of his dark dungeon. One was a bitter trial; another was an attempt to disgrace him by publicly stripping him of his ecclesiastical authority. Throughout his imprisonment, he endured intense pressures to recant. Finally, on October 6, 1536, twelve years after he'd left England, he was led from prison to the stake. There he was strangled, and then his body burned. He had time to utter one last cry: 'Lord, open the King of England's eyes!' It is one of the ironies of history that Tyndale died not knowing that the battle was nearly won. [16]

A Lack of Evidence that the Bible Had Been Changed

After learning about the Bible translators, my love of, appreciation for, and faith in the Bible was much greater. I was surprised that I had not found any detailed, conclusive evidence to support the common statement in the Mormon Church that the Bible had many translation errors. This early teaching had instilled in me a natural distrust for the translators, but now I had great respect for them. The translators I had read about had been God-fearing men with a tremendous reverence and love for Scripture. They were very mindful of their holy responsibility in translating. They believed that:

> . . . a translator hath great need to study well the sense both before and after, and then also he hath need to live a clean life and be full devout in prayers, and have not his wit occupied about worldly things, that the Holy Spirit, author of all wisdom and knowledge and truth, dress him for his work and suffer him not to err. By this manner, with good living and great travail, men can come to true and clear translating, and true understanding of holy writ, seem it ever so hard at the beginning.[17]

There was no evidence that wicked men from the Catholic Church, or any other church, had changed the Bible. On the contrary, the Catholic Church excommunicated, hunted down, and killed godly translators because they translated the Bible into everyday languages that the common people could understand.

These men gave their lives so that everyone could read the Bible. From what I had learned, the corruption was not in the Bible, but rather in men straying from the Bible because the Catholic Church had treated it as "too sacred to be read." The problem was not the Bible, but a *lack of reading* the Bible. It seemed to me that this was the same problem we have today!

I realized that the accusation I had been taught all my life that "Bible translations have many errors," had originated with the Catholic Church. *How ironic!* All my life I had believed they were guilty of corrupting the Bible. Rather, the papacy had believed that translating the Bible and making it available to the common and ordinary people was corrupting it. It appeared that Satan had not been able to corrupt God's Word, but he had tried to prevent it from being read.

My respect and trust for the Bible and the translators had grown tremendously. However, the lack of evidence to support the Book of Mormon's claim that, "many plain and precious things" had been removed from the Bible was not conclusive enough to satisfy my need to be fully confident that no one had tampered with the text of the Bible over the past nineteen hundred years. Was there any concrete evidence to establish accurate transmission of God's Word from the original writings to us today? I needed to know.

The Dead Sea Scrolls

Tobie and her Jehovah's Witness acquaintances kept insisting there was conclusive evidence from hundreds of ancient manuscripts to support the Bible's accuracy. Some of these manuscripts had been discovered in our lifetime—among them, the Dead Sea Scrolls.

I really didn't know too much about this subject, except that I had heard some talks by LDS scholars showing similarities between the Dead Sea Scrolls and Mormonism, which was evidence, to them, that the LDS Church was the true church. I really had not been informed how the Dead

Sea Scrolls validated accurate translation of the Bible.

I looked in the Bible Dictionary in the back of my LDS Bible and read the following about the Dead Sea Scrolls:

> In 1947 in an area known as Qumram, near the northwest corner of the Dead Sea, some significant rolls of leather and a few copper manuscripts were found preserved in earthen jars in some dark caves. They were found quite by accident by goat herders. As a result of further searches in the area, many documents have been discovered and translated. The language is Hebrew. Some were dated as early as 200 B.C., others a century or so A.D. Complete copies and/or fragments of every book of the Old Testament have been found, except the book of Esther. Deuteronomy, Isaiah, and Psalms are the most numerous. Books of regulations and 'manuals of discipline' produced by the people who made the scrolls have also been located.
>
> The contents of the scrolls are interesting to historians, textual critics, and readers of the Bible. It is to be expected that such discoveries will support and supplement many principles and ideas that are already known to us through latter-day revelation.[18]

That was interesting! If these scrolls contained a large part of the Old Testament and they dated back to two hundred years before Christ, then it would be relatively easy for Hebrew scholars to compare them to our present King James Bible translation to see how different they were. This would be pretty good evidence since these scrolls have been buried in the ground for almost two thousand years—untouched and unchanged.

Although the Bible dictionary in the back of my LDS Bible mentioned that textual critics were interested in the scrolls, it did not mention the results of any comparative studies. Yet Tobie and the Jehovah's Witnesses insisted that they showed our present-day Bible to be very accurate. I didn't want to trust them; I didn't even know who to trust at all. Too bad I didn't know Hebrew myself. Still, there must be some reliable information on this subject since it was so important.

After doing more research, I learned it was believed by most scholars that a Jewish sect called the Essenes had established a community located on the northwest shore of the Dead Sea. They had buried hundreds of scrolls in caves. These Essenes occupied this area from the second century B.C. to around 68 A.D. when they fled the advancing

Roman armies. Before they abandoned their community they carefully hid their library in the nearby caves of Wadi Qumran. The Essenes buried their own religious books including the "Manual of Discipline" along with multiple copies of the Hebrew Bible.[19]

I soon realized some similarities that Mormons had talked about between the beliefs and practices of the Essenes and the Mormons came from the Essenes own books and writings. A few similarities were: they followed a strong religious leader, believed in a communal lifestyle (the United Order was practiced in Joseph Smith's day), and they lived by strict rules.

In spite of LDS scholars' desires to find support for Joseph Smith's "latter-day revelations" from the Dead Sea Scrolls, the differences far outweigh the similarities. The Essenes lifestyle resembled a monastic type of living more than a Mormon lifestyle. They were dedicated to asceticism, voluntary poverty, and abstinence from worldly pleasures, including marriage.

I found it very interesting that the talks I had heard at the Mormon Church about the Dead Sea Scrolls had excluded the most important part of this exciting and significant discovery—the scrolls confirm that our Old Testament has been preserved and transmitted to us with amazing accuracy, contrary to "latter-day revelation" from Joseph Smith.

Insight from a Mormon Scholar

Charles and I attended a Book of Mormon symposium at which a BYU professor, Robert J. Matthews, expounded on the statement in the Book of Mormon that men of the abominable church had deleted plain and precious things from the Bible in order to pervert the right ways of the Lord. Afterwards, I asked him if he knew what the Hebrew scholars had discovered when comparing the Dead Sea Scrolls to our current Bible. His answer dumbfounded me.

"Strangely enough, the Dead Sea Scrolls have the same deficiencies as does our Bible. Therefore, the changes in the Bible were made before the Dead Sea Scrolls were copied," he said.

Wait a minute. Scholars dated the scrolls as early as 200 B.C. or earlier. This BYU professor was saying the changes had to occur before that time since the scrolls agree with our current Bible. That was a direct contradiction to the Book of Mormon. It says the changes happened after the book went forth by the twelve apostles of the Lamb. That was definitely after the New Testament was written—not prior to 200 B.C.

The more I thought about it the more I realized how incredible Robert J. Matthews' statement was. The Dead Sea Scrolls were in existence at least two centuries before Christ and during his life. This point is very important when we realize that Jesus validated the Old Testament of his time. I found this especially significant for a Mormon because the Book of Mormon states that when Jesus appeared to the inhabitants of the American Continent, he pointed out errors in their scriptures and made sure they were correct. Surely he would have done the same for the Jewish Scriptures. But he didn't. Instead, he validated them. Remember, these unaltered Dead Sea Scrolls agree with our current Old Testament.

Jesus Endorsed the Old Testament

When tempted by the powers of Satan, Jesus used Old Testament Scripture to overcome the enemy; thus demonstrating the Scripture's power over the clever and powerful attacks of the destroyer.

Jesus confirmed the authority and accuracy of the Old Testament after His resurrection when He said, in Luke 24:44, "And he said unto them, These are the words which I spake unto you, while I was yet with you, that all things must be fulfilled, which were written in the law of Moses, and in the prophets, and in the psalms, concerning me."

Here Jesus mentions the three categories of writings that are contained in the Old Testament; one, the writings of Moses—the first five books of the Bible, known as The *Pentateuch*; two, the writings of the prophets; and three, the Psalms.

Luke 24:25 states, "Then he said unto them, O fools, and slow of heart to believe all that the prophets have spoken . . . ." Notice that He said, "all that the prophets have spoken," confirming the Jewish books of the prophets. Jesus also promised that "not one jot or tittle" would pass from the law (Matthew 5:18) and that heaven and earth would pass away, but that His Word would never pass away (Matthew 24:35).

Jesus validated the Old Testament in many different Scriptures. (See Supplemental Material, IV. *"The Holy Bible: God's Double-Edged Sword"* to be found at the end of this book.) The fact that Jesus endorsed the Old Testament gives us confidence that it was accurate in His time. Think about it. The Essenes buried their Hebrew copies of the Old Testament shortly after Jesus validated the Old Testament. There they lay undisturbed and untouched until their discovery in 1947, and they affirm our current translations. What a powerful witness God provided to erase any doubts as to the trustworthiness of our current translation.

An Abundance of Manuscript Evidence

Furthermore, the Dead Sea Scrolls are only one of thousands of ancient manuscripts that are available today for comparison of not only the Old, but also the New Testament. However, since the work of men is not perfect, there are variances in the manuscripts, but according to textual critics these variances do not change the message of the text and are rather insignificant. They involve different spellings of words or arrangements of phrases. Scholars have spent years studying these manuscripts and their efforts show our Bible to be complete and trustworthy today. (For more detailed information see Supplemental Material, IV. *"The Holy Bible: God's Double-Edged Sword"* to be found at the end of this book.)

More than two hundred known manuscripts in existence date back to the fourth and eighth century. Three of the most well-known ancient manuscripts are: 1) the Vatican Codex, dating back to the fourth century, which contains almost the whole New Testament; 2) the Alexandrian Codex, dating back to the fifth century, which contains almost all of both the Old and New Testaments; and 3) Sinaiticus manuscripts in London. These manuscripts have been buried for centuries and therefore provide good comparisons to see what errors, if any, appear in our Bible today. A comparison of these manuscripts gives us overwhelming evidence that the entire Bible has been meticulously, or should we say *miraculously*, preserved. God has not only kept His Word pure, but He has brought forth overwhelming evidence to disprove any false claims that would discredit its accuracy!

Mormon scholars defend the claim that the original manuscripts were changed by saying that the change had to occur before the third century, or shortly after they were written. However, fragments of the New Testament have been found that date back as early as 125 A.D. These ancient copies validate our Bible today! Another strong evidence to show the accuracy of our New Testament text comes from the writings of the early church fathers. They quoted so much from the New Testament that we can reconstruct almost the entire New Testament from their writings, which date back to the second and third centuries. These early church fathers' writings and Bible quotations agree with our New Testament of today.

Personal Reflection

I stopped for a moment in my studies to reflect on the truth of the statement, "God works in mysterious ways." God had worked through me to get Tobie to read the Bible. Now He had worked through Tobie to get me to trust the Bible!

> The grass withereth, the flower fadeth: but the word of our God shall stand for ever.
> — Isaiah 40:8

> For ever, O Lord, thy word is settled in heaven.
> — Psalm 119:89

> Heaven and earth shall pass away, but my words shall not pass away.
> — Matthew 24:35

> For verily I say unto you, Till heaven and earth pass, one jot or one tittle shall in no wise pass from the law, till all be fulfilled.
> — Matthew 5:18

For more recommended reading, see list on page 324.

CHAPTER 11

THE TRANSFORMATION

For I testify unto every man that heareth the words of the prophecy of this book, If any man shall add unto these things, God shall add unto him the plagues that are written in this book: And if any man shall take away from the words of the book of this prophecy, God shall take away his part out of the Book of Life, and out of the holy city, and from the things which are written in this book.

—Revelation 22:18–19

As a young Mormon missionary in New Zealand I had confronted opposition to Mormonism many times with the above Scripture. This was frequently thrown at us to show that Joseph Smith was a false prophet because he had brought forth more Scriptures, specifically the Book of Mormon, thus adding to the Bible.

In seminary training, I was equipped with the Mormon answer. The word "book" in that Scripture, I was taught, refers to the Book of Revelation, not the Bible. If the *correct interpretation* of Revelation 22:18–19 meant that God would not reveal more Scripture to us, we would not have some of the other books in the New Testament, since some of them were written after John wrote the book of Revelation. As a matter of fact, the first five books of the Bible that Moses wrote would be all we would have of the Bible since there is a similar Scripture found in Deuteronomy 4:2 and 12:32. Obviously, these passages did not mean that God couldn't continue to give more revelations to mankind if He chose to do so.

The Joseph Smith Translation

This particular day, however, these Scriptures that warned against adding to God's Word had a new impact upon me. I was studying my new LDS–published Bible—the King James Version with new LDS footnotes and references. Among these footnotes were references to *The Joseph Smith Translation*. This is a Bible in which Joseph Smith made changes and additions, which the church accepts as inspired. Originally, this Bible was called *The Inspired Version*. The new title, *The Joseph Smith Translation*, is somewhat misleading since Joseph Smith was not translating the Bible from the original Greek and Hebrew languages, nor any other language. He was simply "fixing" the King James translation. While the King James translation is the official Bible used by the church, when a discrepancy occurs between the King James version and church doctrine, the church accepts *The Joseph Smith Translation* as the authoritative version.

When I was a teenager, I often wondered why we didn't use *The Joseph Smith Translation* if it was the correct one. Some LDS leaders said he hadn't finished it, but some said he had. Some excerpts from *The Joseph Smith Translation* were included in the back of my new LDS Bible. Following is just one example:

King James Translation	Joseph Smith Translation
John 1:1	John 1:1
"In the beginning was the Word, and the Word was with God, and the Word was God."	"In the beginning was the gospel preached through the Son. And the gospel was the word, and the word was with the Son, and the Son was with God, and the Son was of God."

While comparing several passages that Joseph Smith had changed, the verse in Revelation that warned against adding to God's Word kept going through my mind: "If any man shall add unto these things, God shall add unto him the plagues that are written in this book" (Revelation 22:18).

Of course, I believed this verse applied just to John's book of Revelation, the last book in the Bible, not the entire Bible. Had Joseph Smith added words to the book of Revelation? I checked excerpts from *The Joseph Smith Translation* in the back of my Bible and found that he had! I felt as if I had just been pierced with a sword–right through the center of my heart. I was devastated and overwhelmed by the seriousness of what I had just discovered and immediately thought of a similar warning that Moses had given about adding to the first five books of the Bible, the Jewish Torah.

I noticed that Joseph Smith had made many additions to it, as well. One change was approximately fifteen verses added to the last chapter of Genesis which included a prophecy that alluded to himself. Searching further, I saw that Joseph Smith had made various significant changes throughout the Bible. That was a problem. (For a few examples, please see Supplemental Material, IV. *"The Holy Bible: God's Double-Edged Sword"* to be found at the end of this book.)

According to my recent research, the Bible didn't need fixing. If the Bible has been transmitted to us accurately, these changes were indeed convicting evidence against Joseph Smith. I had just received an answer to my question, "Who changed the Bible?" It wasn't the Bible translators, nor was it the Catholic Church. It was Joseph Smith! What a devastating thought! My heart sank within me.

Were the plagues in the book of Revelation going to fall on Joseph Smith because he'd added words to the book of Revelation, as well as the entire Bible? What about his followers? What about me? I certainly did not want to be in that category, nor even have a slight chance of having those plagues upon me.

The Attack

My doubts about Joseph Smith's credibility were becoming so strong that I could no longer ignore or suppress them. I compared some more studies and, at this time, I rose to get a pencil and notebook to record my findings and thoughts, but I couldn't move. I was instantly surrounded by a presence of evil that petrified me and stopped me in my tracks. My head was pounding as voices threatened me loudly within.

"You wouldn't dare write down those negative thoughts about Joseph Smith. How could you even think them? You need to repent of your evil thoughts about Joseph Smith or you will be destroyed. We will destroy you."

I was scared! I wanted to escape but didn't know where to run—or whether I could run at all! The power and influence upon me was so oppressive and frightening I felt paralyzed. The presence of evil spirits all around me was terrifying and horrible.

Since I was alone in my house, my thought was that I needed my husband to rebuke the evil spirits by the power of the priesthood. Then I realized I myself was not helpless against the darkness around me. I had faith in the name of Jesus. I didn't need the priesthood or my husband to speak forth His name. These spirits could be rebuked by the power inherent in the name of Jesus. I could call upon Jesus myself! I fell to my knees and asked God to rebuke the evil spirits in the name of Jesus. They did not leave. I poured out my soul in apologies to God, for at that moment I wondered if my doubting of Joseph Smith had caused God to become angry with me. Had God allowed me to be engulfed in the presence of darkness as a consequence for thinking negative thoughts about Joseph Smith? I didn't know! The only thing I could do was stay on my knees and keep praying. I told God that if He had, in fact, appeared to Joseph Smith in the grove of trees in the spring of 1820, that I certainly was sorry for doubting him. If Joseph Smith were God's true prophet, I wanted to believe in him and continue to be a servant in his church. I pleaded with God to forgive me, but the evil presence persisted. It did not leave.

I didn't want to doubt Joseph Smith, but I couldn't help it. I wanted to ignore and deny my doubts, even to myself, but I knew that God knew my mind. I couldn't lie to Him. After all, I had promised I would obey Him. I would believe whatever He wanted me to believe. Continuing on my knees, I desperately petitioned God in the name of Jesus to remove the terrible presence of evil that was surrounding me.

In these moments of struggle and terror I realized I didn't want to die and get to the other side—only to find out that I had been deceived. If

126

Joseph Smith *were* a false prophet, and I had been deceived, and these evil spirits were there in defense of him, I wanted to know now. I was finally ready to let go of everything I loved and surrender everything I was holding onto so tightly—even my precious testimony of the church, if it were not the truth. I was broken and helpless. I was ready to submit to God's truth, regardless of the consequences. At that moment, I wanted to be right with God more than anything else in the world.

Set Free

It was when I stopped apologizing to God for disbelieving in Joseph Smith and submitted to God's truth and will for me that the evil left. In an instant, terror and smothering bondage were gone. The dark, fearful, evil presence was not only gone, but it was replaced with the most wonderful peace, joy, light, and love that I had ever experienced. This was a miracle that only God could have performed. The freedom that I felt—from dark oppression into light and joy—was dramatic and real. In an instant, I had been set free.

God heard my prayer and He removed the fears that engulfed me. He let me know that I was not guilty of offending Him, but that the presence of evil had tried to scare me so intensely so that I would no longer pursue my quest for truth. The threatening voices of destruction had been replaced with Christ's voice saying, "You belong to me, Carma. I love you. I suffered and died on the cross for you. Is that not enough? Believe and accept my sacrifice for you and stop striving to make yourself acceptable through human effort. You don't need the Mormon activities, laws, ordinances, and temple rituals added to what I already did when I suffered, bled, and died for you. I am the Way, the Truth and the Life. I am sufficient."

What liberation! What peace! God had not only removed the evil spirits and my fear, He had also lifted me up, filled me with His love, and given me a full assurance that I belonged to Him. He had accepted me just as I was!

I felt like a bird that had been in a cage all her life and was suddenly let out to fly and explore a whole new world. My mind and spirit had been set free from a powerful, blinding, spiritual control—a control and power that I had not been aware of until I was set free from it. I could now understand what I read in the Bible so much better. Now I was a person no longer bound by religion. Now I was a person no longer bound by a spirit of fear to question and think for myself, but instead one who was given a spirit of freedom to "prove all things" (I Thessalonians 5:21) and find the truths that would make me free from stress and guilt! (John 8:32).

I had experienced what Paul refers to in his epistles as "freedom in Christ." He well knew what this meant because he, too, had been set free from the blinding power of religion. This did not mean that he had a desire to sin, but a freedom to submit fully to the leading of the Holy Spirit, rather than religious rules. My desire to obey God and live for Him increased rather than diminished as a result of this being set free.

There was so much I didn't understand, but I knew that Jesus had claimed me as His own, and His sacrifice for me was sufficient.

When my children arrived home from school they noticed how unusually vibrant and joyful I was. My husband wondered at my patience, a virtue I was very short of previous to this time. Yes, God had filled me with the fruit of His Spirit and my life would never be the same again.

I experienced freedom from the unrealistic expectations I had lived under my whole life. It was the beginning of experiencing what Jesus meant when he said:

> *Come unto me, all ye that labour and are heavy laden, and I will give you rest. Take my yoke upon you, and learn of me; for I am meek and lowly in heart: and ye shall find rest unto your souls. For my yoke is easy, and my burden is light.*
>
> *—Matthew 11:28–30*

CHAPTER 12

COULDN'T BELIEVE IT, BUT COULDN'T LEAVE IT

Lord, I believe; help thou mine unbelief.

—Mark 9:24

The spiritual encounter I had just experienced, along with all the Bible information I had been learning, dramatically reversed my belief in Joseph Smith and left me with many unresolved questions. Although I had a new confidence to be honest with myself and God, I was not going to make premature decisions. I had to be sure. I did not want to fall into the trap of interpreting an experience, or the Scriptures, according to my limited knowledge—or, worse yet, according to my own emotions and desires. I really wanted to understand God's messages to me correctly. I did not want to be deceived!

My Secret Struggle

This dramatic reversal of my belief in Joseph Smith caused me to be deeply perplexed about many things. *How could the church be false?* It seemed so good! Why had God allowed me to believe in the church if it were not true? I had been so convinced that the Holy Ghost had given me a testimony. All my life I had tried to be a faithful servant in the church—convinced that everything I had done there I had done for the

Lord. Surely He would not have allowed me to be so deceived! Yet when it came to my beliefs about Joseph Smith, either I had been deceived in the past or I was being deceived now. *How could I be getting such contradictory messages?*

I was not ready to verbalize my opinions, especially to Tobie. I certainly did not want to give her any indication that I doubted my religion. Nor did I want to encourage her desire to convert me to the Jehovah's Witnesses organization. Heaven forbid! That's the last thing I would let happen to me. Before that very thought left, however, I was convicted by another: *Didn't you make a promise, Carma, that you would obey God in whatever He taught you? Doesn't that mean that you will be what He wants you to be? What if the Jehovah's Witnesses are God's true organization?*

That was a heavy thought! I was humbled as I realized that I had been put on a new path of learning to surrender my will in exchange for God's will—something I could never do without God's strength.

Even though I was keeping my experience and thoughts a secret, Tobie could see a change in me. I was hungry to learn, instead of resistant to everything she said. It wasn't long before I had visitors at my door—a very nice, elderly couple. I was sure Tobie had sent them. Actually, I enjoyed my discussions with these Jehovah's Witnesses. They were willing and available to feed my insatiable hunger to study and understand the Bible.

My husband, Charles, had been very supportive of my religious talks with Tobie. Surprisingly, he was not opposing my conversations with the Jehovah's Witnesses now, either. He was confident that nothing would shake my Mormon testimony.

I decided to share my recent experience with Charles. We had never kept secrets from each other in our seventeen years of marriage and now was no time to start. I was apprehensive about sharing my deep doubt and disbelief of Joseph Smith, but I believed he would respect my experience. Besides, if Joseph Smith were a false prophet, it was critical that Charles and our children find out. I was hurt by Charles' reaction.

"You just pushed too far with your questions. The devil answered your prayer because you doubted!"

A Confusing Quandary

Was my husband right? After all, I had believed in the church for almost forty years and had borne strong testimony for nineteen years that I knew the church was true and that Joseph Smith was a true prophet. *Had I lost the Spirit because I doubted?*

I was confused because my life had been filled with so many evidences that had convinced me the church was true. I couldn't just forget or ignore them. What about the answered prayers and priesthood blessings I'd received?

For example, many years ago when our first child Nancy was four years old, she would wake up in the night screaming and thrashing out of control. It was behavior that was contrary to her nature, and it seemed very strange. After each incident, it would be extremely difficult to get her calmed down. This happened regularly for several weeks and seemed to be growing in intensity. She didn't have an ear infection and these fits were much more intense than a child waking up from nightmares.

I started wondering if she was being bothered by an evil spirit. My husband did not give much credibility to this idea and thought I was thinking irrationally. However, after several nights of struggle with our daughter and my importuning him to rebuke any evil influence by the power of the priesthood, Charles reluctantly consented to give her a priesthood blessing.

Nancy sat in a chair as my husband laid his hands on her head and began the way every priesthood blessing starts: "By the authority of the Melchizedek Priesthood which I hold, I lay my hands on your head and give you a blessing."

It became very awkward for Charles to continue because as soon as he started the blessing, she started screaming.

"Get your hands off my head! I don't want a blessing."

This behavior was not typical of her. Charles didn't stop but continued with the blessing. Then he ended with strong words.

"I command any evil spirit to leave, in the name of Jesus Christ. Amen."

As soon as Charles said the name, Jesus Christ, the room became silent (except for the "Amen"). Nancy stopped screaming and literally

131

wilted in her chair. No one moved or spoke. I think Charles was speechless. I was silently thanking the Lord for the miracle we had just witnessed. After a few seconds the silence was broken when Nancy very softly and innocently asked, "Mommy, can I have a bath?"

She was free and clean inside and wanted to be washed on the outside, too. Teary eyed, we watched her happily splash and laugh in the tub at 2:00 a.m.! It was a dramatic change and more than coincidental. This was only one of many convincing evidences that the priesthood my husband held was the true priesthood of God.

More Evidences for My Mormon Testimony

Of course, I could not forget receiving my testimony of the Book of Mormon twenty years ago as a missionary in New Zealand. And what about the comforting hand I'd felt on my head? What about the converts in New Zealand who had received a testimony of the church after we had taught them the gospel?

I thought of numerous experiences that had contributed to my strong testimony of the church: the times we had been blessed for paying our tithing, the times of hearing and reading beautiful Scriptures that had formed my life and increased my faith in God, the joy that came to me from the many times of giving and serving in the church, the bonding and sisterhood within the church that had been a major part of my life, and the inspired programs and activities that blessed our family and helped in raising LDS children with standards. All these had formed a testimony in me—a testimony that I loved—and one that went deep into the core of my soul. It was more than a testimony. It was me and my faith.

My testimony was a great feeling of love. It was a love I felt for members of the church and the love they had for one another as they shared their intimate expressions of appreciation and love during a fast and testimony meeting. It was a love I felt for the Savior each Sunday when partaking of the Sacrament (the bread and water in remembrance of Him) as I meditated on His divine sacrifice for me. And it was a love I felt for Heavenly Father and the Savior each Sunday while singing beautiful hymns such as *I Stand All Amazed*:

I stand all amazed at the love Jesus offers me;
Confused by the grace that so fully He proffers me.
I tremble to know that for me He was crucified.
That for me a sinner He suffered, He bled and died.
Oh, it is wonderful that He should care for me enough to die for me.
Oh, it is wonderful, wonderful to me!

I think of His hands pierced and bleeding to pay the debt.
Such mercy, such love and devotion can I forget?
No, no, I will praise and adore at the mercy seat.
Until at the glorified throne I kneel at His feet.
Oh, it is wonderful that He should care for me enough to die for me.
Oh, it is wonderful, wonderful to me!

How could anyone sing such beautiful hymns without experiencing a warm glow within and closeness to God? How could anything that feels so good be wrong?

And what about testimony meetings? You got up to bear your testimony and had your heart beating so fast in your throat you could hardly speak, or you were so choked up that you literally couldn't speak, then tears would flow that you tried to hold back, but they wouldn't stop. They weren't tears of sorrow, but tears of a deep reverence, adoration, and love for all that God has done for you.

This feeling of love was my Mormon testimony. I could not deny it, nor did I want to. To do so would be to deny God and to become a liar. It was real and powerful. It was worth hanging onto and fighting for. *How could anything that generates these wonderful feelings be wrong?*

An Inseparable Connection

These experiences were such a deep part of my life, with so many good memories. I felt as if these memories *were me* and what I had become through all my training and formation. They had molded me and been an expression of my faith and love for Heavenly Father and Jesus Christ. They represented my church, my faith, my connection to God— everything that was good in my life! How could I not believe in my church? It was like denying myself, like denying a deep love within me. It was my culture, my heritage, my identity as a person. My life and my

133

faith in God seemed inseparable from Mormonism. I was a Mormon! I could not separate myself from me, nor could I stop being a Mormon! But how could I be a Mormon and not believe in Joseph Smith?

This extreme paradox of trying to reconcile my past experiences in the Church with my current experiences was too much to deal with. I was in a spiritual and emotional upheaval. There was too much at risk to make a definite decision. According to the temple endowment, if I went against the covenants I had made in the temple for nineteen years, I would be in Satan's power.

Is This a Test?

Maybe God was testing me as He had Abraham. Even though God asked Abraham to offer his son, Isaac, as a sacrifice, in the end he didn't have to do it. Maybe this was a test for me—to see if I would really sacrifice my church and everything dear to me . . . especially since I had promised God that I would obey whatever He taught me. Maybe this was a test to see if I would be willing to be a Jehovah's Witness.

Yes, maybe all this was a test! After all, I had asked to understand why other people who believed in Jesus rejected Mormonism. I certainly hadn't expected to understand to *this* degree. If it were a test to see if I would hang onto my faith, God would eventually lead me back to believing in Joseph Smith with an even stronger testimony!

Proceed With Caution

I was very careful not to jump to hasty and irreversible conclusions. I had done that in the past and did not want to make the same mistake again. I needed to remain teachable rather than positive and closed-minded. I was especially cautious about using the words, "I know." When repeated often—as they were at testimony meetings, these words put a person under a tremendous binding power. I had already seen that one way Satan could deceive people and keep them blinded was to make them so sure that they were right that they were no longer teachable. That's where I had been, and I never wanted to be "locked into" such a positive religious mindset again. Besides, at this point I was still not sure who to trust, but I did trust Jesus and the Bible as God's Word to me.

Avoiding the "Shipwreck of My Faith"

As for my position now, I could admit only to myself and God that I didn't believe in Joseph Smith. I did, however, believe in God. I didn't have answers for what was happening to me, but I could hang onto the faith I did have. To strengthen my current faith, rather than sink in a sea of confusion, I inwardly recounted times when God had specifically answered my prayers.

One experience that came to mind was when I was about eight years old. I was walking home from school and I lost a silver coin that meant a lot to me. I looked and looked in the weeds along the side of the road. It just wasn't there. I decided to pray. As soon as I opened my eyes a bright reflection from the sun was glaring in my eyes. It was my silver coin! I was excited and thankful to have my coin again. However, far more valuable than the coin was the knowledge I gained that day that God did hear my prayers, that I was important to Him, and that He was aware of even my smallest need.

I also remembered a time as a teenager when I was very discouraged and depressed. I knelt down and poured my troubles out to Heavenly Father. He lifted the depression from me and replaced it with a joy and love that I knew came only from Him. I knew that I could not have done that to myself!

These and other answered prayers had given me a faith in God and in the power of prayer. I'd also felt His Spirit and help flood into my life from certain Bible passages that I loved. It was very important to hang onto this faith now, rather than give up and experience a shipwreck of my faith.

"Faith Isn't Faith until It's all You're Holding Onto"

Faith is believing, even if things don't make sense. "By faith Noah, when warned about things not yet seen, built the ark to save his family" (Hebrews 11:7). What a comforting thought! He didn't have absolute

135

knowledge about what was coming, but he obeyed and trusted in God. Faith isn't knowing, nor is it having all the answers. That would not be faith. Hebrews 11:6 says:

"But without faith it is impossible to please him: for he that cometh to God must believe that he is, and that he is a rewarder of them that diligently seek him."

Faith is believing, not *knowing*. The thought that it was impossible to please God without faith was very comforting to me. God didn't expect me to *know*. He just wanted me to exercise faith and trust in Him.

"Be Still"

Psalm 46:10 says, "Be still, and *know* that I am God." I could do that. Now it was time to "be still" and listen. I had been so intent on teaching—on defending my testimony—on saying "I know the Church is true." Now I needed to be taught.

My concern was that I listen to God, not a deceiving spirit. I had to be sure I wasn't trusting the wrong thing. I needed to be patient and wait on the Lord. I would ponder these things in my heart. I decided to keep attending church with my family and give God every opportunity to show me if I were wrong. I would continue to take one step of faith at a time in the light I had been given, without jumping to conclusions. My prayer was, "Lord, I believe; help thou mine unbelief" (Mark 9:24).

CHAPTER 13

EXPERIENCES AND THE PRIESTHOOD

"By stretching forth thine hand to heal; and that signs and wonders may be done by the name of thy holy child Jesus."

—Acts 4:30

As I understood more and more of the opposite meanings others derived from Scripture, I became more humble and teachable.

Now, instead of being so positive, I realized that I really knew practically nothing when it came to understanding God. It was then that God was able to teach me the most. It was when I became humble enough to admit that just possibly I may have misunderstood God's Word, that my tunnel vision opened up and I began to see.

I gained respect for people holding other religious opinions, so that I could allow myself to be taught by them. Before this process changed me, I had been so intent on teaching that I had not been able to learn or accept any viewpoint different from my own. I believed that since I knew I was right, they had to be wrong. Therefore, why would I want to learn from them?

Now I loved to talk to anyone who would discuss the Bible with me. I was intrigued by the different beliefs of others. I had been humbled by God and was starving to learn His truth. I wanted to know what the Bible meant more than anything else in the world. I took my Bible with me everywhere I went, hoping to get a chance to read it in-between my busy schedule of keeping up with the many activities of my Mormon lifestyle and a large family. I realized that I had been in a famine—a famine not of physical food, but of the Word of God.

> Behold, the days come, saith the Lord GOD, that I will send a famine in the land, not a famine of bread, nor a thirst for water, but of hearing the words of the LORD.
>
> —Amos 8:11

I was thirsty and hungry and God was filling me with His Word— the words of the Bible. I was feasting upon them, and I couldn't get enough. Knowing the truth became more important to me than eating and sleeping.

Limiting myself to attending the Mormon Church did not satisfy my quest for truth. Also, my desire not to be deceived was a compelling one. I decided to visit the Kingdom Hall of the Jehovah's Witnesses— just to see what their way of worship entailed. Shaking like a leaf and arguing with myself all the way, I was driven by a power stronger than my resistance.

The Jehovah's Witnesses were very friendly, sincere people, seeking God just like the rest of us. Once again it was confirmed to me that through their limited knowledge and experience they also had validity for their beliefs—at least through the lens of their worldview.

That particular Sunday they were studying an article on AIDS in the current Awake magazine. This was during the era that the knowledge and awareness of the disease was very new. The article pointed out that a person could get AIDS from a blood transfusion which, of course, confirmed their strong position against blood transfusions—one of many confirmations to them that they were in the truth.

I was amazed at how much like Mormons the Jehovah's Witnesses were in focusing on information that would confirm their beliefs but ignoring or rejecting information that would discredit them. I soon recognized this as a common behavior with most people, especially those in churches that claimed to be "the one and only."

About this same time I received a card in the mail announcing a

"Revelation Seminar" at a local Seventh-day Adventist church. The books of Daniel and Revelation were going to be studied in detail. My mind flashed back to a few years previous when I was reading the book of Daniel and I had prayed that God would lead me to people who could help me understand what I was reading. The seminar was three nights a week for several weeks. I would go.

It wasn't easy going to strange churches by myself. Besides, what would everyone think? *Was I crazy? Me, Carma Naylor, who had been so sure of myself, so positive my Church was the only true church, now going to strange, unfamiliar churches!* I had always thought the Seventh-day Adventists were somewhat odd because they kept Saturday as the true Sabbath day. However, I did recognize they had similarities to Latter-day Saints in their clean lifestyle and health code, which included permitting no alcoholic beverages or tobacco.

Christian Churches under Satan's Influence

Going to other churches was emotionally difficult, especially a church with a cross on it. The Cross had been offensive to me in the past since it was a Christian symbol used by Christian churches, which I had been strongly convinced were under Satan's influence.

Of course, they all had some good in them, but Father in Heaven and Jesus had told Joseph Smith, "that all their creeds were an abomination in his sight; that those professors were all corrupt," that, "they draw near to me with their lips, but their hearts are far from me, they teach for doctrines the commandments of men, having a form of godliness, but they deny the power thereof" (Pearl of Great Price; Joseph Smith History 1:19).

Also, the Book of Mormon clearly teaches that there are only two churches: one is the Church of the Lamb of God; the other is the church of the devil (1 Nephi 14:10). Since the Mormon Church was the only true church of Jesus Christ, and the only church with whom God was pleased (Doctrine & Covenants 1:30), the only conclusion was that all others comprised the church of the devil. That belief had been deeply imbedded in my mind by part of the temple ceremony, in which the devil hires a Christian minister to teach the Christian creeds to Adam and his posterity. (This was deleted from the temple ceremony in April, 1990, along with other significant parts of the temple endowment that were exposed in *The Godmakers* movie.) In the past, as a strong Mormon I certainly never had a desire to spend my time being taught by teachers of false religions influenced by the devil. Of course, we (LDS) always recognized that other churches all had good in them and were comprised of many good people, however our church, The Church of Jesus Christ of Latter-day Saints, was the only true church on the earth.

Illumination on My Path

God was certainly dealing with these past prejudices. The closed walls that had been built around my mind and spirit were gone—replaced with a hunger and thirst to learn from those who studied and respected the Bible as their authority of truth. I was experiencing a wide spectrum of emotions, ranging from excitement to nervousness, as I drove to the Seventh-day Adventist Church for the first in the Revelation series talks.

I forgot my loneliness and pride as I walked through a beautiful garden courtyard that led to the sanctuary. All my apprehensions left when a beautiful stained glass picture of Jesus holding a lamb lit up the front of the sanctuary. I was flooded with a love and a peace of Jesus Christ, and I believed He had led me there. In the bottom left-hand corner of the work of art was an oil lamp; in the right-hand corner was an open Bible. I was sure the lamp and Bible were representative of Psalm 119:105, "Thy word is a lamp unto my feet and a light unto my path." I had recently memorized this verse, which spoke to me with power, and it has never left me.

The stained glass art reminded me that God's Word was what I needed to trust. It was the illumination that could guide me along on my pathway of confusion. No wonder I was going to churches where they studied the Bible! I had experienced a great expansion of understanding from studying with the Jehovah's Witnesses and now I believed my thinking was going to be broadened even more by Seventh-day Adventists.

There was so much I needed to learn about Bible interpretation, teachings, and prophecy. I had so many questions and I truly was seeking truth. Even though I was confused and very apprehensive about not trusting man's interpretation, I knew God was using these churches to open my eyes to further accept and understand the Bible. After all, that had been my prayer—to understand the Bible. He was teaching me His way, according to the Bible, instead of a particular denomination's way.

A Significant Story

Learning the Seventh-day Adventist interpretations of Daniel and Revelation was very enlightening and exciting since we had never studied these books at the Mormon Church. However, there was so much more I was learning. It was incredible how the Lord was leading me to just the right person who had information for me at the very time I needed it. I was especially fascinated with the personal experiences with God that I was hearing.

One was of particular interest to me. The evangelist giving the seminar was explaining his belief in the *gift of tongues*. He had experienced firsthand this gift when doing evangelistic work in Mexico. He was from England and did not know Spanish, but he had been given the ability to speak it fluently for a couple of hours when preaching to the people there. Afterwards he had many individuals come up to him and shake his hand in appreciation for his message. However, he could not understand what they were saying to him. The gift was gone and he needed an interpreter after that point.

There was a very good reason why this story had great significance to me. My father had experienced a similar personal incident as a young Mormon missionary in Holland. I had heard him tell this story many times in the various Mormon wards in which he spoke. As a devoted missionary, my father had two disappointments. First, his companion did not share my father's devotion and commitment. Instead, he wanted to "enjoy himself, rather than do missionary work." His second big disappointment was that he thought he would be able to learn the Dutch language but couldn't. He became so discouraged about this that he considered leaving the mission field. The remainder of the story is told in my father's own words, as recorded in his life's story:

> Well, as I knelt down, I prayed to my Heavenly Father and told Him
> that if He wanted me to stay on a mission in Holland, that night as we
> spoke at this street meeting, He would speak through me in the Dutch
> language . . . and if He did this, I promised that for the remainder of
> my life I would do whatever He bid me do. But, if He didn't speak
> through me that night in the Dutch language, then I was all through
> with the mission and I was going on the bum in Europe. I would not
> remain in the mission field.
>
> I was humble, even though this doesn't sound like it! Maybe if I
> wasn't humble, I was at least sincere and very, very honest. I also
> made another request, and why I made it I do not know. But I
> requested that the people in Alkmar would not continue to walk back
> and forth and stop for a minute, but that they would stop dead still
> and stay stopped during the entire time I was talking to them in the
> Dutch language.
>
> That night came and we started our street meeting, sang songs, and
> had our opening prayer. My companion had spoken to the people,
> then he turned to me and said, 'It's your turn to speak,' and he started
> walking out with me to translate, as he always did. I stopped and I
> looked at him and I told him that I didn't want him to walk out to the
> center of this bridge with me, that I was speaking in the Dutch
> language, or I wasn't speaking at all. I said if I do not speak in the
> Dutch language out there, I shall continue walking off the bridge, I
> shall turn and continue to our room, there I shall pack up and I'm
> through.
>
> He was so flabbergasted, and I guess he saw that I was very sincere
> and earnest that he was taken aback, and he did exactly as I said. He
> didn't endeavor to follow me to the center of the bridge at all, but
> stayed on the side.
>
> I stood in the center of the bridge, and for forty-five minutes I spoke
> the Dutch language more fluently than I have ever learned to speak
> English. For forty-five minutes those people in Alkmar that were
> anywhere near the area came into this main street and they stood
> shoulder to shoulder and very compact, and for half-a-block down the
> street—from window pane to window pane—people were standing
> side by side, and beyond this half-block point, where we could see
> the end of the street turn, there was absolutely not a movement in that

street of any kind, not a dog or a cat, not even a bird. There was no wind. It was perfectly still.

After I had spoken, my companion had the meeting closed with prayer and then the people started bustling around and out of the crowd. Many came to me and shook my hand and said something to me in Dutch and, to this day, I don't know what they said, for I did not understand them. By the time I gave my first lecture on my own in the Dutch language, which was approximately four or five months after this, I had forgotten the Dutch words that were spoken to me. My companion, with tears in his eyes, said that he had been reared in the finest schools in Holland, he had been taught by the finest teachers of the Dutch language, and he had never heard the Dutch language spoken so fluently.

—Autobiography of Nicholas Baker, p. 2

I loved hearing this story in my childhood and youth and never tired of listening to my father tell it. Hearing it convinced me that the Church just had to be true. What a surprise! There I was, sitting in a Seventh-day Adventist church listening to the evangelist tell a very similar story. My dad's experience had been a vital, integral part of my testimony. If that had been evidence to me, as it had been, that the Mormon Church was true, then the Seventh-day Adventists had the same evidence that *their* church was true.

Evidences for Faith, but Not Limited to a Particular Denomination

Did the Seventh-day Adventists' experience validate Ellen G. White as a true prophetess? No. It didn't have anything to do with her. Likewise, my dad's experience did not validate Joseph Smith as a true prophet. It didn't have anything to do with Joseph Smith, yet we had used it as evidence to confirm our belief that the Mormon Church was true and that Joseph Smith was a true prophet.

I soon found myself visiting other churches. My eyes were being opened to the reality of God working in Christian lives beyond denominational barriers. A Baptist shared how he had received blessings from paying tithing. I had received blessings as a Mormon for paying tithing, and it had convinced me that my Church was true.

A Christian I worked with told me that he had prayed and laid his hands on his daughter's eye that was badly infected and covered with a film. He saw it was instantly healed.

A Seventh-day Adventist lady told me that she had breast cancer and was scheduled for a mastectomy. The thoughts of this surgery were very traumatic for her. The night before her surgery she was in bed praying that God would heal her if it were His will. She felt the healing take place inside of her and started singing praises to God.

In the morning when she went to her scheduled appointment at the hospital, she told her doctor that she wasn't going to need surgery. He, of course, thought she was going into shock, patted her hand, and assured her that she was going to be all right. However, it was he that went into shock when he took more X rays and looked at them. There was no trace of cancer. The Lord had healed her!

Another Seventh-day Adventist evangelist shared miracle after miracle in his life. He was led by the Spirit to go into the ministry, and God guided him daily in his work as an SDA evangelist. All around me I was hearing of spiritual experiences, miraculous healings, blessings for paying tithing, answered prayers, lives being changed through faith and prayers—all from people outside of the Mormon Church, without the priesthood—from people who were quick to give God the glory and honor. These Christians did not praise their church or a priesthood; they praised Jesus. These experiences came as a result of their faith in Jesus Christ, without the LDS Priesthood.

Power in the Name of Jesus, or in the Priesthood?

As I reflected on the priesthood blessings that had caused me to believe that the Mormon Church was true, I thought of the incident with our daughter, Nancy, (as told in the previous chapter) when she was four years old and Charles gave her a priesthood blessing to rebuke the evil spirit that was bothering her. Yes, it had definitely worked and had been a remarkable experience that we certainly never forgot. However, I was realizing an important truth I had never thought of before. It wasn't until the end of his blessing, when Charles said, "In the name of Jesus Christ . . .," that Nancy stopped screaming and became calm. She'd started screaming when he put his hands on her head and said, "By the authority of the Melchizedek Priesthood that I hold . . ." The priesthood had no affect. The power was in the name of Jesus!

It was the power in the name of Jesus that had released our daughter from spiritual oppression, not the Priesthood that Charles held. We had wrongly interpreted this experience as validation of his priesthood as true, the Mormon Church as true, and thus, Joseph Smith as a true prophet. That was the major problem with gaining a Mormon testimony. Whenever God answered a prayer or did something good in our lives, we interpreted that to be evidence that the Mormon Church was true and that Joseph Smith must therefore be a true prophet.

My Observation

The average Mormon's testimony, based on experiences and good feelings, became weak in comparison to the testimonies I was hearing from many Christians in other denominations. Time and space do not allow me to tell all of them in this book, but it was very evident that my own personal experiences, as well as those of others in the Mormon Church, were not evidence that my church was the one and only true church, anymore than all these other Christians could interpret their denomination to be the only true church because of their experiences.

Interestingly enough, other than the Jehovah's Witnesses, they did not interpret their experience in that way, nor did most of them claim to belong to a "one and only" true church. Experiences and miracles were evidence to them of God's power working in their lives through faith in Jesus. My conclusion was that God is much bigger than any church denomination and cannot be put in a box. He wants us to glorify Him, not a particular church! No longer were such stories evidence to me that I belonged to the "one and only" true church and that Joseph Smith was a true prophet. These and other experiences were evidence that God is powerful and at work and does not limit Himself to certain religious groups in order to bring about His purposes. Nor does he work only

145

through an exclusive priesthood.

Did the Apostles Claim to Hold the Priesthood?

I decided to spend some time studying the priesthood more thoroughly in the New Testament. This proved to be very revealing. The first thing I noticed was that Christ's apostles never gave credit to a priesthood power but frequently gave credit to the name of Jesus as their source of authority. For examples to show that they preached, baptized, and did all that they did in the name of Jesus, see Acts 8:12, 16; 9:27–29; 10:43–48; Ephesians 5:20; Colossians 3:17; 2 Thessalonians 3:6; James 5:14–15.

A great story that demonstrates that the apostles acted in the power of the Name of Jesus rather than in the authority of a priesthood invested in themselves is found in Acts, chapters three and four. Here, Peter and John heal a man who has been crippled from birth. Peter, making eye-to-eye contact, says, "Silver and gold have I none; but such as I have give I thee: In the name of Jesus Christ of Nazareth rise up and walk" (Acts 3:6).

Peter then takes him by the right hand and helps him up. Instantly the man's feet and ankles become strong and he excitedly walks, jumps, and praises God. The people who witness this miracle are filled with wonder and amazement. Peter immediately seizes the opportunity to glorify God and to preach to them about Jesus:

> And when Peter saw it, he answered unto the people, "Ye men of Israel, why marvel ye at this? or why look ye so earnestly on us, as though by our own power or holiness we had made this man to walk? The God of Abraham, and of Isaac, and of Jacob, the God of our fathers, hath glorified his Son Jesus; whom ye delivered up, and denied him in the presence of Pilate, when he was determined to let him go."
>
> —Acts 3:12–13

Notice that Peter did not mention a priesthood power or authority that was invested in himself, but gave all the glory for this healing to

Jesus. The man's healing was the result of his faith in the Name of Jesus. This is verified by Peter in verse sixteen:

> And his name through faith *in his name* hath made this man strong, whom ye see and know; yea, the faith which is by him hath given him this perfect soundness in the presence of you all.
>
> —Acts 3:16

To emphasize even further that the man was healed by faith in the name of Jesus rather than a priesthood given to man, let us finish the story. Peter uses this opportunity to let the people know that they had killed the Prince of Life, the Messiah, whom the prophets had foretold, and that they needed to repent. The Jewish priests, temple guards, and Sadducees were very disturbed by Peter and John's preaching and had them thrown in jail. The next day, Jewish leaders met together to discuss the matter and brought Peter and John before them to question them. A very important question is recorded in verse seven of chapter four:

> By what power, or by what name, have ye done this?

If Peter's power had been through a priesthood received from Jesus, this would have been the perfect opportunity for him to answer by saying, "By the power of the Holy Melchizedek Priesthood that I hold." However, Peter does not say that. Instead he gives glory to Jesus. Peter takes no credit himself, nor does he mention any priesthood power or authority. Once again he affirms that the man was healed through the name of Jesus:

> Then Peter, filled with the Holy Ghost, said unto them, Ye rulers of the people, and elders of Israel, If we this day be examined of the good deed done to the impotent man, by what means he is made whole; Be it known unto you all, and to all the people of Israel, that by the name of Jesus Christ of Nazareth, whom ye crucified, whom God raised from the dead, even by him doth this man stand before you whole.
>
> —Acts 4:8–10

Salvation in the Name of Jesus

Peter concludes his brief speech with this impacting paragraph:

> Neither is there Salvation in any other, for there is none other name under heaven given among men whereby we must be saved.
>
> —Acts 4:12

The above verse is a strong statement regarding the power that resides in the name of Jesus. Only in His name will we receive Salvation.

John puts it this way: "But these are written that ye might believe that Jesus is the Christ, the Son of God; and that believing ye might have life through His name." (John 20:31)

His name is not only the power to preach, to baptize, to heal, to cast out demons and perform other miracles, but it is the power of eternal life!

Jesus Did Give His Apostles Power and Authority

The second thing I observed from studying the priesthood in the New Testament was that Jesus gave the seventy authority (Luke 10:18). He also gave the twelve power and authority over demons and to cure diseases (Luke 9:1; Matthew 10:1; Mark 6:7). I had been taught all my life that this power and authority was the Priesthood of God found only in the LDS Church today. However, I could not find one place in the gospels where Jesus referred to this power as "priesthood authority."

I had learned from my discussions with Tobie not to read something into a Scripture that it didn't say. I wondered what the word for power meant in the Greek. That was something else I had learned—that if I wanted the correct interpretation it helped to know what word was used (and its meaning) in the original language in which it was written. I looked up the word power found in the above passages of Scripture in the Greek dictionary. The word was exousia, #1849:

> power (in the sense of ability); privilege, i.e. (subj.) force, capacity, competency, freedom, or (obj.) mastery (concr. magistrate, superhuman, potentate, token of control), delegated influence;—

authority, jurisdiction, liberty, power, right, strength.

There was no mention of priesthood here, either. This was another instance that I needed to deprogram my mind from a strong mental image—the mental image I had learned from my church that the power Jesus gave to the twelve and the seventy was the priesthood power that was lost after the death of Christ's disciples and apostles, and was restored through Joseph Smith.

I decided to look up the word "authority" since, in the LDS Church, the word "authority" was often linked and equated with "priesthood," as was the word "power."

Interestingly enough, the same Greek word exousia, #1849 was listed.

What Does Ordain Mean?

I decided to look up another important word used in the above passages when Jesus gave power to the twelve. This word was ordain, and it definitely had made a deeply imbedded image in my brain. A common painting used in the church was one of Jesus with His twelve apostles. Jesus is standing, laying His hands on the head of one of the apostles. The other apostles are waiting their turn to likewise be ordained as apostles with the priesthood. This picture and the following two verses went hand in hand:

> And he ordained twelve, that they should be with him, and that he might send them forth to preach, and to have power to heal sicknesses, and to cast out devils.
>
> —Mark 3:14–15

> Ye have not chosen me, but I have chosen you and ordained you, that ye should go and bring forth fruit, and that your fruit should remain: that whatsoever ye should ask of the Father in my name, He may give it you.
>
> —John 15:16

The image of Jesus laying His hands on the apostles heads and giving them the priesthood was what the word 'ordain' had always meant to me. The above verses did say that Jesus ordained the twelve, but what did *ordain* mean in the original language? Did it mean ordaining them to the priesthood by the laying on of hands, like I had always been taught?

I looked up the word for *ordained* as used in the above two Scriptures. This became very interesting since the one word ordained comes from several different Hebrew words in the Old Testament and about fifteen different Greek words in the New Testament, none of which include *priesthood* or *laying on of hands* in their definitions.

Mark 3:14 says, "And he ordained twelve, that they should be with him, and that he might send them forth to preach." In this verse the Greek word for ordained is #4160 poleo (poyl-eh'-o). It means:

> poleo to make or do (in a very wide application, more or less direct): —abide, + agree, appoint, avenge, + band together, be, bear, + bewray, bring (forth), cast out, cause, commit, + content, continue, deal, + without any delay, (would) do execute, exercise, fulfill, gain, give, have, hold, journeying, keep, + lay wait, + lighten the ship, make, mean, + none of these things move me, observe, ordain, perform, provide, + have purged, purpose, put, + raising up, secure, shew, shoot out, spend take, tarry, + transgress the law, work, yield.

Wow! One Greek word could mean all that? I found this very crucial because with all those words there is no mention of priesthood or laying on of hands. I found this to be true in all the fifteen Greek words from which *ordain* had been translated, but all of them included the definition *appoint*.

When I compared Mark 3:14 in seven different translations, I found that the word *ordained* is used only in the King James Translation. Five of the seven chose to use the word *appointed*, and one used the word chose.

I also noticed in Hebrews 9:1-5 (King James Version), that the author is describing the Old Testament tabernacle and its contents, including the candlestick, the table, the shewbread, the Ark of the Covenant including the golden pot of manna and the other contents in the ark. Verse 6 is very significant: "Now when these things were thus ordained..." Obviously, these "things" were not given the priesthood. These items were "appointed" or "set apart" for use only in the tabernacle for God's purpose.

Tobie had been right! When we had discussed priesthood, she'd insisted that *ordain* meant to appoint, choose or set apart.

Once again I needed to deprogram an erroneous image in my mind and replace it with the correct meaning. The idea that Jesus had given the twelve the priesthood by the laying on of hands was a strong, foundational teaching in the Mormon Church, but it was not what the Bible said.

What Did Jesus Say?

I checked in the Strong's Exhaustive Concordance to confirm that nowhere in the four gospels does Jesus mention priesthood. However, He does repeatedly emphasize the use of His name. (See John 14:13, 14, 26; 15:16, 16:23; Luke 24:47; Mark 9:38-41)

> And these signs shall follow them that believe; *In my name* shall they cast out devils; they shall speak with new tongues; They shall take up serpents; and if they drink any deadly thing, it shall not hurt; they shall lay hands on the sick, and they shall recover.
>
> —Mark 16:17–18

Notice in the above verse that the two qualifications are belief and the use of Jesus' name, with no priesthood required. Even baptism was to be done in the name of the Father, the Son, and the Holy Ghost, not by a priesthood power.

> Go ye therefore, and teach all nations, baptizing them *in the name* of the Father, and of the Son, and of the Holy Ghost.
>
> —Matthew 28:19

Even preaching was to be done in the name of Jesus.

> And that repentance and remission of sins should be preached *in his name* among all nations, beginning at Jerusalem.
>
> —Luke 24:47

(Emphasis in above scriptures is mine.)

I could find no reference in the Bible that said the priesthood was

151

necessary to baptize, heal, cast out demons, or to perform any other acts for God.

No Priests or High Priests in Christ's Original Church

The third significant thing I noticed was that Jesus never ordained priests or high priests, nor did the apostles; neither are these offices of the priesthood mentioned in the New Testament Church. It seemed that the references to priests or high priests in the gospels were about those who hated Jesus and wanted Him crucified.

For how important the priesthood was to the LDS Church, there was an obvious silence about it in the gospels and epistles with the exception of 1 Peter and Hebrews. There is a good reason for this. I didn't understand it at this time in my journey, but later it became very clear that the priesthood was all about animal sacrifices—the shedding of blood—in the Old Testament under the old covenant law. Jesus fulfilled the old covenant when He shed His own blood for sins. This is made clear in the Book of Hebrews. Jesus replaced the old covenant with its priesthood (priests and a high priest) with the new covenant in which Jesus fulfilled the role of the high priest and ended the need for animal's blood to be shed. Consequently, this also ended the need for the priests and the high priest whose duty was to shed blood. Jesus is the perfect, sufficient and only High Priest of the new covenant. (See Volume 2, Chapter 22- Jesus, Our High Priest Forever)

A Royal Priesthood

Peter tells all the Christians to whom he is writing (not excluding women) that they are "a royal priesthood" (1 Peter 2:9). Also, Paul speaks to the believers about, "the exceeding greatness of his power to us-ward who believe, according to the working of his mighty power" (Ephesians 1:19). I noticed that the power is "to those who believe," not to those who have been ordained to a special priesthood by the laying on of hands.

Much later I learned that Martin Luther, as a Catholic monk and priest, believed that the priesthood was exclusive to the Catholic Church until he came to understand the above biblical truths. Then he referred to this power as "the priesthood of all believers."

This brings us full circle to a very important point: the power for God to work in the life of a believer is through faith in Jesus and in His name. It is available to all who have put their faith and trust in Jesus. This is validated by Jesus and the writers of the New Testament.

Not Exempt from Deception

It was becoming evident to me that experiences do not determine truth. So how could one be sure he or she is not being deceived? Also, how could I discern which doctrine was true and which one was wrong? Did doctrine even matter? Paul, the writer of a large portion of the New Testament, certainly thought so:

> . . . that thou mightest charge some that they teach no other doctrine,
> Neither give heed to fables and endless genealogies . . .
> —1 Timothy 1:3, 4

Paul gives a clear warning that false doctrines will cause some to depart from the faith:

> Now the Spirit speaketh expressly, that in the latter times some shall depart from the faith, giving heed to seducing spirits, and doctrines of devils.
> —1 Timothy 4:1

Paul wasn't the only one who warned us against being deceived by false teachings. I never wanted to fall under the condemnation that Jesus said would befall some:

> Many will say to me in that day, "Lord, Lord, have we not prophesied in thy name? and in thy name have cast out devils?" and in thy name done many wonderful works? And then will I profess unto them, "I never knew you: depart from me, ye that work iniquity."
> —Matthew 7:22–23

What a thought-provoking and scary verse! Many who do wonderful works in the name of Jesus will not enter into His Kingdom. They even cast out demons using Jesus' name, yet they will be thrown out and even accused of working iniquity. This was a definite confirmation to me that God will honor the name of Jesus when accompanied by faith, but not necessarily honor the person using it. It was also confirmation to me that any answered prayer or *priesthood blessing* done in the name of Jesus did not validate the priesthood, the Mormon Church, or Joseph Smith. Yet my entire life in the LDS Church I had been programmed to believe that such experiences meant that the LDS Church was true. Now I could see that that was a faulty foundation for finding truth. *How disillusioning!*

As Matthew 7:22, 23 makes clear, an experience does not assure us of our salvation. Neither does it mean we are above deception. It does not validate us, nor our doctrines as correct, or the priesthood, our church, or its prophets as true. God will honor the name of Jesus when He chooses to honor it to fulfill his purposes. This is not to be interpreted that He is honoring the individual who is using the name of Jesus.

It was evident to me at last that experiencing miracles did not make one exempt from deception. It was apparent that good people are deceived, sincere people are misled, people devoted to God with great zeal and conviction can be following doctrines of demons, and people who give their lives to their religion can believe lies—people convinced that they are right can be wrong. *How could I, as a Mormon, claim that my experiences meant I was right and others wrong when they had similar experiences?* I could no longer do so!

I never wanted Jesus to tell me He *never knew me* and to depart from Him. Instead, my desire was for Jesus to say to me:

> Well done, thou good and faithful servant: thou hast been faithful over a few things, I will make thee ruler over many things: enter thou into the joy of thy lord.
>
> —Matthew 25:21

God's Word, the Cutting Tool

What was the cutting tool used to separate and discern true doctrine from "doctrines of devils?" (1 Timothy 4:1). *How could one be certain he or she was not "giving heed to seducing spirits?"* Just because something was spiritual, it did not mean it was of God. My mind raced with questions that demanded an answer only God could give me. And He did!

Hebrews 4:12 says: "For the word of God is quick, and powerful, and sharper than any two-edged sword, piercing even to the dividing asunder of soul and spirit, and of the joints and marrow, and is a discerner of the thoughts and intents of the heart."

Certainly God's two-edged sword—His Word—was the cutting tool that divided truth from deception. The Bible declares 3800 times, "God said," or, "Thus saith the LORD." Therefore, the Bible is the Word of God, based on its own claim, or it lies in making this claim and therefore could not be God's Word.

Of course, one could say the same for the Mormon Scriptures produced by Joseph Smith. They are either filled with truth to trust and obey—or they are deceptions to discard. There is no in between.

During this season of my spiritual journey I was still researching the accuracy of the Bible. The more I learned, the more convinced I became that it was accurate and trustworthy, with conclusive evidence to support the Bible's claim to be God's Word. There is no reason to question its trustworthiness. (For more information on this subject, see Supplemental Material, IV. *"The Holy Bible: God's Double-edged Sword"* to be found at the end of this book.)

In Ephesians 6:13–18 Paul tells us to "put on the full armor of God so that we can stand in the evil day." An important part of that armor is, "the sword of the Spirit, which is the word of God" (verse 17).

I was now convinced of three things: 1) Experiences do not determine true doctrine; 2) All experiences, as well as all prophets and prophetesses, need to be tested against God's Word—the Bible—His two-edged sword; and, 3) the power of God was through faith in the Name of Jesus.

> And the seventy returned again with joy, saying, Lord, even the devils are subject unto us through thy name.
>
> —Luke 10:17

CHAPTER 14

TOSSED BY THE STORM

"That we henceforth be no more children, tossed to and fro, and carried about with every wind of doctrine, by the sleight of men, and cunning craftiness, whereby they lie in wait to deceive."

—Ephesians 4:14

Attending my church became increasingly difficult. The emotional trauma of still loving my church and wanting it to be true, and yet seeing more and more problems was extremely difficult for me. I would frequently leave a meeting only to go to the car and sob. The experience was so hard on my emotions that it affected my health as well. I would often experience intense headaches and be physically drained from Sunday until Tuesday of every week. It was like attending the funeral of someone I deeply loved every week, over and over again— remembering how wonderful that person was and how much I loved that person— knowing I had to let go and not quite able to do so.

I loved my church and its people and I couldn't let go; but neither could I believe in Joseph Smith or in some of his teachings. Even more crucial I could not let go of my promise to obey God, so I was dealing with some strong emotional conflicts.

When I had started the discussions with Tobie, I was so confident that I was right. I had not expected to find out I was wrong! I thought of the Apostle Paul and how shocked he must have been when his beliefs were radically reversed. He had hated and persecuted Christians to their death, only to find out later that they were right and to become one of them. So had I been so sure that Joseph Smith was a true prophet but the more I prayed, studied, and attended church, the more convinced I became that Joseph Smith was a false prophet.

Nonetheless, I didn't want to be positive in my current beliefs and thereby become closed-minded, as I had been in the past, so I kept my convictions to myself. Even though I was not speaking forth my opinions and conclusions, I was asking numerous questions and presenting theological problems and contradictions to my husband and friends. The change in me was obvious to all who knew me. They were startled, but concluded I must be in a midlife crisis. None of them knew the depth of my disbelief in Joseph Smith. Rather, they believed I was struggling with my testimony in some kind of temporary confusion.

Several leaders and friends attempted to "straighten me out." Conversations inevitably ended with them becoming frustrated and annoyed with me. They would counsel me to forget my questions and problems, serve more diligently in the church, and focus on the good in the church, not the problems.

Sometimes I was severely condemned and told I must be committing some grievous sin that had caused me to lose "the Spirit." I was told to repent and cleanse my heart and hands of sin. The bottom line was always that it was my fault that I had questions about the church and that I must be guilty of some bad behavior. Otherwise I would not be questioning or doubting, especially since I had been given such a strong testimony by the Spirit. I was even accused of having an affair. My husband was very offended by these false accusations. He knew the one thing I wanted was truth.

A Visit from My Parents

My parents decided it was time to come for a visit from Utah. My husband was relieved. If anybody could straighten me out it would be my father. Mother was great at taking over the kitchen and helping with household chores, which freed up my time so Dad and I could talk for several hours each day. I had great respect for my dad and had been highly influenced by his testimony. Even at the age of forty, I felt very intimidated by his influential, persuasive, and authoritative personality. Tobie and I agreed to temporarily stop our discussions while my parents were visiting. She wisely did not call or come to visit.

My father had always taught me that the Bible was the blueprint for truth, so our discussions centered on the Bible. I shared with Dad that I could not believe in both the Bible and Joseph Smith, because there were too many discrepancies between them. There was no hesitation in Dad's response.

"I know the gospel was restored through the prophet Joseph Smith," he said. "I know that because I've been taught by the Holy Ghost when He appeared to me in the form of a beautiful man. However, I also know there was an apostasy and a restoration because the Bible teaches it. Even if you've found some problems with Joseph Smith, that does not matter. He was human like the rest of us. The important thing is that God used him, in spite of his faults, to restore the true gospel and the priesthood."

A Complete Apostasy?

We turned to the familiar verses that Mormons use to teach that there was a complete apostasy of Christ's church after the death of the apostles:

> For I know this, that after my departing shall grievous wolves enter in among you, not sparing the flock. Also of your own selves shall men arise, speaking perverse things, to draw away disciples after them.
> —Acts 20:29–30

> Let no man deceive you by any means: for that day shall not come, except there come a falling away first, and that man of sin be revealed, the son of perdition.
> —2 Thessalonians 2:3

I pointed out to Dad that these Scriptures, and many others, warned of false teachers that would come and teach untruths and would deceive many, but these Scriptures did not say that there would be a complete apostasy of Christ's church.

161

"Actually," I said, "in Matthew 16:18, Jesus said that the gates of hell would not prevail against His church. If His church and the priesthood (the authority to act for God) were taken from the earth after the death of the apostles, wouldn't that mean that Jesus had made a false prophecy?"

Dad didn't like that at all, but rather than respond to my statement he proceeded to discuss Matthew 16:18:

"Now Carma," he said, "this passage shows the importance of the restoration. Jesus said here that He would build his church upon the rock of revelation. That's why it is so important to have continuing revelation, which we have in the church, and only in the church through modern-day prophets. Now the Catholics believe that the rock is Peter and, therefore, trace their apostolic authority back to him through the lineage of Popes. However, we know that Peter appeared to Joseph Smith and gave him the Melchizedek Priesthood. You know all this!"

"Well, Dad," I responded, "it seems to me that when we put this Scripture in context, the rock Jesus is talking about is for sure not Peter, as you say the Catholics believe. And I don't believe it is referring to modern-day revelation through a prophet of the LDS Church. I think it is quite clear that the rock is the specific revelation that Peter received from Father in Heaven that Jesus was the Christ, the Son of the Living God. That must be the rock on which Jesus said He would build His church. It was *knowing Jesus and acknowledging that He is the Christ*, meaning the *Messiah*. The true knowledge of who Jesus is can only come from Father in Heaven, not from man."

I was quite surprised at myself as I spoke, for I had never seen this so clearly before. Dad didn't seem impressed. As a matter of fact, I wasn't sure he had heard what I'd said at all. He was busy looking up another Scripture.

The Restitution of All Things

"Turn to Acts 3:21," Dad said. "It says the restitution of all things! Restitution means to restore! Now, how can something be restored if it wasn't lost? Joseph Smith restored the priesthood and Christ's church to the earth. I know that more than I know anything!"

He was getting very excited and emphatic. We read the passage together:

> Whom the heaven must receive until the times of restitution of all things, which God hath spoken by the mouth of all his holy prophets since the world began.
>
> —Acts 3:21

I noticed two very important things about this Scripture that I shared with Dad.

"First," I answered, "it says that the heavens must receive Jesus Christ until the restitution occurs. To me that would mean that Jesus would return when the restitution occurs. If the restitution of which Peter was speaking was the restoration of the gospel in 1830, it would seem that Jesus would have returned by now."

I presented the second important point to Dad in the form of a question:

"Could Peter be referring to the *millennial reign* of Christ when the earth will be restored to its paradisiacal glory and everything will be as it was in the Garden, when God first created the earth? That to me would be the *restitution* of *all* things. That would also include doing away with evil and bringing in God's Kingdom instead of this evil system of things. We certainly do not see the restitution of God's Kingdom on the earth now. There is more evil than ever. How could the Mormon Church be the Restoration of all things when so much is not yet restored?"

Condemnation

"I just don't understand what has happened to your mind," Dad said. "You used to understand these things. You were given a spiritual testimony of the gospel. I wish I had some of the letters you wrote home from your mission to remind you. What has happened to you? I don't understand what you have done! What have you done to allow Satan to influence you so drastically and completely?"

His statement was very significant! There it was again—the accusation that I had done something evil and was now under Satan's influence. I knew exactly what had happened to my mind when the blinders came off and I had been set free from the tunnel vision of seeing the Bible only through Mormon spectacles. Not only my mind, but also my spirit had also been set free from powerful, binding spirits—dark, frightening, evil spirits.

I shared with Dad the experience that had dramatically transformed me. My father's reaction was similar to my husband's—the Lord had allowed Lucifer to answer my prayers because I had doubted Joseph Smith. There was no doubt in his mind that my experience had caused me to be under the devil's influence and it was my fault. Dad told me that I had made a mistake in thinking I could show my friend, Tobie, that the church was true.

"You think you are greater than Christ," he said. My dad's words cut deep. "Even Christ couldn't convert everyone," he said. "Why do you think you can?"

Every Member a Missionary

I didn't think I could convert anyone. I knew that was the work of the Holy Ghost. However, I had been taught it was my duty to do all I could to teach and present the gospel. I had heard over and over again the LDS mandate, "Every member a missionary." The Doctrine & Covenants says, "and it becometh every man who hath been warned to warn his neighbor" (Doctrine & Covenants, 88:81).

Also in *Mormon Doctrine* (1958 Edition), by Bruce R. McConkie, we read on page 461: "Every member of the church is a missionary, with the responsibility of teaching the gospel by word and deed to our Father's other children. This responsibility arises through church membership alone, without the receipt of any special call. Church members are under covenant, made in the waters of baptism, 'to stand as witnesses of God at all times and in all things, and in all places that ye may be in, even until death' (Mosiah 18:9)."

As a Mormon I was fully aware of my tremendous responsibility to be a missionary. Because of this conviction I certainly could not in clear conscience just sit back and let my friend become deceived by Jehovah's Witnesses and feel that I was at the same time being obedient to God. Yet now I was being condemned for doing what I had always been taught was my duty. How contradictory and confusing!

Not only was I being condemned, but I was also being told that I had allowed myself to be deceived by Satan because I wanted to teach my friend the truth from the Bible, and secondly, because I had doubts about the church. Was I supposed to deny my questions and pretend I believed, or was I to be honest and admit that I was bothered by problems? Why couldn't my husband and my dad listen and understand instead of condemn? Couldn't they accept the obvious—that God had delivered me from a demonic attack in which the devil tried to make me afraid to question Joseph Smith and the church?

Who Is Deceived?

"Wait a minute," I responded. "How can you say that Father in Heaven turned me over to the influence of the devil when I was filled with love, light, and goodness?" I agreed that I had experienced a demonic attack trying to scare me so that I would not question or continue searching for the truth. However, God had also delivered me in that moment from the devil's oppression. The difference was like night and day!

"Besides," I reasoned, "why would the devil answer my prayer when I was praying to God?"

Dad's answer was quick and emphatic.

"The devil can answer anybody's prayer, and remember, he can appear as an angel of light! He can give us all kinds of good feelings and he does *just that* to lots of people."

"Then how do you know that your experiences were not from the devil?" I asked.

"Well, there's no question about that!" My dad was very absolute. "I know it wasn't the devil talking to me. The Lord is love. My experiences were from God, certainly not the devil. Satan could not make me feel the way I did. However, God let the devil answer your prayer because you doubted. The Lord has already given you a strong testimony of the gospel and you shouldn't have doubted and questioned it. That's the problem! You didn't appreciate what you had. That's why you lost it."

Could my father not see? I had told him how I had been freed from

165

darkness into light and love. I had experienced God's love, peace, joy, and acceptance. Yet my experience was quickly being condemned as "from the devil." It seemed to me that the criteria for judging an experience was a belief in Joseph Smith. If the experience supported Joseph Smith and the church, it was from God. If it didn't, then it was from the devil. That was pretty bizarre. *Do we test everything by Joseph Smith? And what do we use to test Joseph Smith?* I wondered. If the Bible contradicted him, it seemed, it was in error. If an experience contradicted him, it was deceptive. If feelings contradicted him, they were wrong.

What was I to think? All my life I had believed in the church with all my heart and wanted to confirm its truthfulness with objective evidence as well as the subjective evidence upon which my testimony had been based. In my honest attempt to support Mormon theology from the Bible, I had found a lot of leaks and holes. I had wanted to back up my beliefs and doctrines by the Bible, but instead I ended up losing my faith in Joseph Smith and being condemned for it!

I had always been told to believe in my feelings and experiences. However, now I was being told that I couldn't trust an experience, nor my feelings. My experience was quickly judged as a "deception of Satan." But this was highly distressing. If God had allowed Satan to answer my prayer because I was seeking truth and being honest about my questions and concerns, then I could not trust prayer or God. Especially when I was praying so hard that God would not let me be deceived or listen to a deceiving spirit. Wouldn't that be untrustworthy of God? Furthermore, if God did things that way, how could anybody trust any experience? How could members of the church be so emphatic that they knew the truth on the basis of experiences, feelings, and answers to prayers?

Deep Spiritual Conflict

My conversations with Dad were lengthy and intense and lasted for many days. I showed him many things I had learned, but I also listened respectfully. Dad was so authoritative. He had a tremendous power over me and I was getting very confused. When I showed my dad why I no longer could accept Mormon doctrine as biblical, I was not confused, but was convinced that he was confused.

However, there were still several unresolved issues connected with my testimony of the church. What about my testimony of the Book of Mormon? What about that good feeling I got that I thought was the Holy Ghost confirming its truthfulness? Besides, if the Book of Mormon isn't true, where did it come from? Joseph Smith couldn't have just written it! *Could he?* In addition to these questions, how could Mormonism be wrong when it felt so good?

The subject of spiritual experiences, which came up frequently with Dad, was mystifying. Why would God allow my father to have an experience that convinced him that Joseph Smith was a true prophet, and give me an experience that convinced me Joseph Smith was a false prophet? It would seem one of us was deceived by a spiritual counterfeit! While I was convinced it wasn't me, my father was equally (if not more dogmatically) convinced that he was not the deceived one. This was my inner conflict: *Why would a loving God allow Satan to answer our prayers in a way that convinced us it was God speaking truth to us if it was Satan deceiving us?* What was going on? I didn't believe Heavenly Father would do that, yet one of us was deceived. This mystery was causing me to have a spiritual crisis.

As a Mormon, I had several spiritual experiences that had convinced me that the LDS Church was true. Now I was having experiences that reversed my former conclusions. In short, I had either been deceived in the past or I was deceived right now. I had to accept the possibility that I could be deceived. That was part of the spiritual crisis. Why had Father in Heaven allowed me to be deceived in the past when I wanted so much to follow Him and be right with Him?

I remembered the time as a missionary in New Zealand when Father in Heaven had replaced my anxieties and fears with calm and trust. I felt a spiritual presence close to me and it seemed as though a warm hand rested upon my head. Was I to believe that was Satan?

Likewise, it was very difficult for me to believe that my dad was deceived. What about his many experiences? Were they from the devil? It was too difficult for me to make such a judgment. He was a good man. He was very honest in all his business dealings. He loved my mother and was a good example of a husband and father. He definitely had a sincere faith in God and believed in the Savior. I had no reason to doubt Dad's sincerity, honesty, and integrity. *How could I judge his experiences to be from the devil?*

Dad's Testimony

I was hearing what I had heard my dad say many times in my life: "I *know* Joseph Smith is a true prophet more than I know I'm alive. When I was ten-years-old and herding cows in the Ogden Mountains, the Holy Ghost appeared to me—not his Spirit, but Him personally. He was a beautiful man and he conversed with me, and because of what I learned from the Holy Ghost, I *know* Joseph Smith is a true prophet of God. I know that God the Father, and Jesus Christ appeared to him in the sacred grove. I couldn't *know* that any more if I had been in one of those trees and seen the entire event with my own eyes.

"Now, Carma, the only way one can really know these things are true is from a spiritual manifestation! Then other problems don't matter. I know that God the Father, and Jesus Christ His Son, appeared to Joseph Smith and restored the true church to the earth through him. It doesn't matter what Joseph Smith did, or even if he was wrong on certain things. God restored the truth through him, regardless of what he did. I know this because I have been taught by the Holy Ghost. I know the Holy Ghost personally, and I know that when He teaches, you know what He teaches. He becomes a part of you and the knowledge He wishes to impart to you becomes completely you and He combined."

I wanted very much to understand Dad. I was trying to comprehend what he meant by saying that the Holy Ghost appeared to him personally, not his Spirit. Just what had my dad experienced? Was it the Holy Ghost? I did not know of any account written in the Bible where the Holy Ghost was anything but spirit. Angels appeared as men, but not the Holy Ghost. The Old Testament gives a few accounts of the pre-incarnate Christ appearing to certain prophets, such as when God spoke to Moses in the *burning bush* or when Jacob wrestled with the Lord. However, I did not know of any account in the Old or New Testaments that told of the Holy Ghost appearing as a man. Just who or what was that personage my dad saw? Was it the Holy Ghost? Was it in my dad's mind—a dream or hallucination? Was it a *deceiving spirit*? One of us was being deceived because we had opposing conclusions. Or had we experienced something from God and had one or both of us read something into our experience or misinterpreted it?

Not Unique

What about the thousands of other people in the world who claim to have spirits come to them, either as angels, spirits of deceased humans, spirit guides, or even Jesus? Ellen White, the prophetess of the Seventh-day Adventist Church, claimed to have seen the face of Jesus. Sun Myung Moon, the founder of the Unification Church (the Moonies), claims that at the age of sixteen he was visited by Jesus Christ Himself in a vision. It is alleged that Jesus told him He would accomplish a great mission and would establish God's Kingdom on earth.

There are thousands of people making claims to have seen Jesus and to have received messages from Him, yet are they in agreement? Surely if they had all been in the presence of Jesus, or the Holy Ghost, or angels from God, and received messages from them, the recipients of these spiritual manifestations would be united in doctrine and spirit, rather than divided against each other. It was for sure that Dad and I were not united.

Sinking into Spiritual Quicksand

It was all too confusing! *Why did anybody have to be deceived? Why did God allow such deception? Didn't Jesus say that, "if we being evil know how to give good gifts, then how much more would our Heavenly Father give good gifts to those who ask him?" (Matthew 7:11). Was I to believe that Father in Heaven so easily lets Satan answer our prayers and deceive us when we are seeking Him?*

Sometimes nothing made sense! I was not only confused, I was feeling extremely frustrated. I respected my father, and I couldn't easily write his experiences off as demonic—especially since I had done that in the past as a Mormon in regards to spiritual experiences outside the LDS Church. Also, since members of the church were doing that to me now, I didn't want to fall into that narrow-minded, judgmental attitude again. *There must be more to all this than simply accusing each other of being under Satan's influence,* I thought. *Is there an answer to this spiritual enigma?*

Reflecting on My Past

Maybe the answer is what the priesthood leaders and my dad were telling me—that I'm not good enough! After all, I did have struggles in the past trying to do everything I was supposed to do as a faithful Latter-day Saint and be that wonderful example. Then there were the "sins of omission"—all the good things I *wanted* to do but didn't get done—such as genealogy.

In addition to never quite measuring up, I sometimes felt guilty because I was supposed to be happier than others since I had the truth, but I didn't always feel happy. I had many hobbies and interests in life that I enjoyed, and I was generally a happy person; but life had become overwhelming. My husband was gone most of the time and I frequently felt neglected, unloved, overworked, and exhausted. A few times in church when someone spoke on, "the family comes first," I felt like throwing eggs. My husband always sat on the stand while I sat down in the congregation trying to keep our eight kids reverent. (My husband was always on the stand because he was an organist, in addition to a church leader.) Rarely did he sit with us, go to church with us, or help me get the kids ready for church.

Things have changed now since the Mormons have gone to the *block program,* but before the early 1980s the Priesthood-holders always went to church earlier than the wives and children for Priesthood meetings. Charles always had so many commitments on Sunday I felt like he didn't know we existed. It wasn't just Sundays. He was gone a lot during the week, as well. I got to the point where I didn't like hearing, "the family comes first," because it didn't. The church and a man's Priesthood duty came first! I had tried to be the good, submissive, and supportive wife. I hadn't complained out loud, but I had silent resentments in my heart. I was often depressed. That compounded my sadness because I was supposed to be happy that my husband was busy doing his Priesthood duties. I was happy about that, but I couldn't help needing him.

Self-Condemnation

As I reflected back over many years of struggles and as I listened to my father, I started wondering if he was right. Yes, it must be my fault! I must be bad. I guess it was my attitude. I'm just not good enough. The self-condemnation came easy. It had always seemed that no matter how hard I tried I could never attain the level of holiness that I was seeking. I was always falling short! No matter how hard I tried, I could never do enough or be good enough.

Surpassing Experiences

Are the church leaders and my father right? I asked myself. *I guess I'm not as good as they are and not deserving of knowing the truth. I must be bad.* I was sinking fast into spiritual confusion and hopelessness. Why did it have to be so hard? I had only wanted the truth. *I guess I should just forget my quest for truth and trust my dad and his experiences and other church leaders. They were intelligent, spiritual, successful men who held the Priesthood. Who was I to question them or to oppose my father?*

After all I had not seen visions, but my father had! I had not heard the voice of the Lord, but my father had! I had not been spiritually transported to other dimensions and taught spiritual things of which I could not speak. My father had! I had not seen the very person of the Holy Ghost and been taught exclusive, higher knowledge by Him. My father had! He must be right! Yes, I must be bad to even question! I am supposed to "Follow the prophet and the leaders."

Follow the Brethren

"Follow, not question," was being drummed in my head. Follow? Follow whom? I wanted to follow the Good Shepherd. I wanted to be a sheep, not a goat, when Jesus returns and "separates the sheep from the goats" (Matthew 25:31–46). I wanted that more than anything. I not only wanted to follow Father in Heaven and Jesus Christ, but I had made a commitment to do so. I could not ignore that commitment.

I would follow Jesus, but was following the Mormon prophets really following God and Jesus? Was following and believing my dad following Jesus? Was I supposed to trust the church leaders, my husband, and my father? Was I to trust my own past experiences in the Church or my current experiences and the words of the Bible as they had powerfully spoken to me? Still, my father was also a strong influence in my life and his counsel was not to be easily discarded or ignored.

The Raging Battle

That was the whole problem! What could I trust? I was made to feel that I couldn't trust my feelings! I couldn't trust an experience! I couldn't trust my intellect. Dad and other church leaders were more intellectual than I was. The church said I couldn't trust the Bible completely. How could one ever be sure of truth? I thought of Pontius Pilate's question to Jesus, "What is truth?"

I wanted truth; yet, I was so frustrated and weary! I did believe in God and it was very important to me not to be deceived. How could I be sure I was not being deceived by a spiritual power and intelligence far superior to me and not from God? *Was I being deceived now? Had I been deceived as a Mormon?* My dad was so overpowering and positive! *Is he right?* I couldn't be sure of anything at this point. I felt so unsure of everything. I had so many questions—so many unresolved issues. Whom could I trust? Would I ever trust again? There was a raging battle inside of me.

I felt like a tiny sailboat caught in a violent storm on an endless, vast ocean. The horrendous winds and waves were tossing me back and forth and I didn't know how to work the sails. I was lost on an ocean too deep to put down an anchor. How had I gotten in this destructive storm so quickly? Where was my anchor? Recently at times my anchor had held firm, but now I didn't have an anchor. That was the problem. I had lost my anchor and was being tossed to and fro by the winds and waves of religion and religious experiences, especially my dad's.

Feeling Betrayed

How could I resolve this deep conflict within me? I couldn't deny what the Lord was telling me now, but neither could I deny those feelings and experiences of the past. I was more than confused. It was hard to believe that I had been deceived all my life because I had believed in Father in Heaven and Jesus. Was I to believe that the many blessings and spiritual experiences in my life had been deceptions from Satan? Had God deceived me? The thought was blasphemous. Yet I felt as if God had betrayed me.

The storm inside of me was beyond my control. Why does God allow deception? Why does anybody have to be deceived? I felt myself sinking into confusion, despair, and frustration. The conflict of trying to solve this mystery was too much for me. It was easier to give up. Besides, if God had allowed me to believe in a false prophet, then how could I trust Him?

Confusion and Depression

Such thinking plunged me into a terrible pit of darkness. I was miserable. I was really listening to the adversary. The Lord's Spirit of peace was gone and so was the fruit of the Spirit. I was confused, depressed—my faith at an all time low. My spiraling spirit was engulfed in a hopeless depression.

The more I listened to Dad and believed him (as well as believing my husband and other church leaders), the more I questioned God, and the darker my world became. The only answer my father, husband, and other Priesthood leaders had was that Father in Heaven had turned me over to Satan because I doubted the prophet, or I had done some other sin to grieve the Holy Spirit and lose my testimony of the Mormon Church. Such thinking was driving me to the brink of making a shipwreck of my faith.

Saved from Turbulent Waters

The current lack of the fruit of the Spirit in my life was the confirmation I needed to find my anchor again. The more my father said

I had been turned over to Satan because I doubted, the more I realized that giving credibility to that thought was causing Satan to have influence over me. Satan influences us by getting us to believe his lies.

I had returned to my old ways of thinking and grabbed onto my old anchor of trusting others' judgments and experiences, especially my father's. I had also fallen back on my old Mormon influences that I was to follow the Prophet and Priesthood leaders. This lifetime of influence still had a strong hold on me and I realized I currently trusted my dad way too much. In doing so, I had cut the rope to my new anchor that was much stronger and more secure—trusting my new relationship with Jesus and trusting God's Word, the Bible.

Also, I had been listening to Satan's accusation and lie that I wasn't good enough to know the truth. If that were true, who could know the truth? When would "good enough" be good enough? No wonder I had been sinking into spiritual quicksand!

In Revelation we learn that Satan is, "the accuser of our brethren" (Revelation 12:10). I had been listening to his accusations against me and thus been filled with dark despair, hopelessness and confusion. This was all confirmation to me that God was telling me to trust what I was currently learning from the Bible. After all, He had delivered me from Satan's stronghold and confirmed that I belonged to Him.

Jesus and God's Word were now my anchor, but I had temporarily lost them by succumbing to my father's powerful influence and becoming confused by my lack of understanding of his extraordinary spiritual manifestations. I had temporarily returned again to my old Mormon anchor—trusting men, experiences, and feelings more than the Bible. The Lord showed me the folly of this in the book of Jeremiah and the Psalms:

> Thus saith the LORD; Cursed be the man that trusteth in man, and maketh flesh his arm, and whose heart departeth from the LORD.
> —Jeremiah 17:5

> It is better to trust in the LORD than to put confidence in man. It is better to trust in the LORD than to put confidence in princes.
> —Psalm 118:8–9

Come to the Fullness of Christ

I turned to a Scripture that spoke of children being tossed to and fro. That was certainly how I had felt. I had learned part of this Scripture as a Mormon missionary, but had never before understood the meaning of the entire Scripture passage.

> And He Himself gave some to be apostles, some prophets, some evangelists, and some pastors and teachers, for the equipping of the saints for the work of ministry, for the edifying of the body of Christ, till we all come to the unity of the faith and of the knowledge of the Son of God, to a perfect man, to the measure of the stature of the fullness of Christ; that we should no longer be children, tossed to and fro and carried about with every wind of doctrine, by the trickery of men, in the cunning craftiness of deceitful plotting, but, speaking the truth in love, may grow up in all things into Him who is the head—Christ—from whom the whole body, joined and knit together by what every joint supplies, according to the effective working by which every part does its share, causes growth of the body for the edifying of itself in love.
>
> —Ephesians 4:11–16 NKJV

Wow, that was a long sentence! As missionaries, we had used the first part of this sentence to teach the need for apostles and prophets today in Christ's church. Now I could see four teachings in this passage of Scripture: 1) unity in Christ, our head; 2) speaking in love; 3) the reason God gave apostles and prophets, and, 4) the fact that the foundation of apostles and prophets was laid once and does not need to be laid again because we still have that foundation in their writings. Specifically, I saw the principles of:

1. **Unity in Christ**. Christ is the Head, and we are to grow in Him until we come into the unity of the faith . . . the knowledge of the Son of God . . . until we come into the fullness of Christ. If we were growing in Christ and focused on Him, we would not so easily be "children tossed to and fro, and carried about with every wind of doctrine."

I concluded that many of the disagreements over theology

among religious people who read the Bible are a result of people trusting experiences or leaders over the Bible. The lack of unity among Christian religious groups is not the fault of the Bible, it is a lack of submission to the Bible as God's final authority for truth. (See Mind Blocks, Supplemental Material I, p. 293)

As I reflected upon the above passage, I realized that the recent spiritual experiences that had transformed me had definitely brought me to Jesus Christ in a new and living way. By contrast, it seemed evident that Dad's experience committed him to Joseph Smith and the LDS Church. I had heard him say several times that he would not be a member of the church if it were not for his experiences because he had seen too much hypocrisy in the church. Yet his experiences had bound him to Joseph Smith. He had even been told that if he ever turned from the things he had been taught he would be in darkness beyond his comprehension. The combination of these two things held a fearful, binding power over him.

I certainly felt a release from a binding power, but the most important thing was that my new experiences had brought me to Christ and the sufficiency of His sacrifice for me. That was what mattered most. This truth led to:

2. **Love, not Condemnation**: "But speaking the truth in love may grow up into him in all things, which is the head, even Christ." Speaking the truth in love was what I desperately wanted—to be able to discuss what the Bible said without getting upset and arguing so that we could be edified and grow in Christ. However, it seemed impossible. There was a wall between Dad and me because I no longer believed in Joseph Smith, so our conversations usually ended with me being condemned. In Ephesians, chapter four, I also gained new understanding about:

3. **Apostles and Prophets**: The passage was clear that Christ had given apostles, prophets, evangelists, pastors, and teachers so that we would come into unity in Christ and mature in Him. *The important*

thing was to know Jesus and be found in Him. The Bible and our experiences should bring us into unity in Christ. My experience, which Dad had wrongly condemned as from Satan, had definitely bound me to Jesus and brought glory to Him, not to any man or church.

Jesus chose twelve apostles to be His eyewitnesses. Their written accounts have been recorded and transmitted accurately to us today in the Bible. The prophets in the Old and New Testaments also testified of Jesus' coming. The above passage indicates that if we trust the accounts they wrote and that God preserved for us as the Holy Bible, we will, "come in the unity of the faith, and of the knowledge of the Son of God, unto a perfect man, unto the measure of the stature of the fullness of Christ," rather than being children, "tossed to and fro, and carried about with every wind of doctrine."

4. **The Foundation**: This is why we have the Bible—the accounts of the prophets and apostles—to bring us to Christ. The "foundation of the apostles and prophets," (as referred to in Ephesians 2:20) has already been laid. In Ephesians 2:21, Paul refers to the believers as a building in which the apostles and prophets are the foundation and Jesus Christ is the cornerstone. When a building is built, only one foundation and cornerstone is laid. Likewise, we don't need to lay another foundation of twelve apostles today. Paul states in 1 Corinthians 3:11 NKJV: "For no other foundation can anyone lay than that which is laid, which is Jesus Christ."

This is also the main purpose of the Holy Spirit—to testify of Jesus, not any other man. Every truly spiritual experience should bring us to Christ, not puff us up with knowledge. Paul mentions people who worship angels and boast of what they have seen, yet are not connected to Christ, who is the Head (Colossians 2:18–19). Since this is so, we must be very careful to test spiritual experiences and not put our trust in them for truth, especially if the experience in any way glorifies man.

177

Anchored Again

God was teaching me an important lesson—to follow and trust His Word, not influential Priesthood leaders, including my dad, regardless of how much I respected him. As always, when I became focused on the Bible, more answers came. Once again I would be anchored in my relationship with Jesus instead of being tossed by the wind and waves.

The more I thought about Dad's condemnation of me, the more I realized he was not speaking the truth in love. *Was I to believe that God had turned me over to Satan because I wanted to show Tobie from the Bible that the Mormon Church was true? Was I to believe that God had turned me over to Satan because I had been honest about the problems I'd discovered? Not only that, but was I to believe that God turned me over to Satan to answer my prayers when I had been so sincere in my desire to know God's truth and not be deceived? What kind of a God of love would do that, especially since my doubts were about Joseph Smith and I had not doubted God and Jesus Christ?*

No wonder my faith was sinking fast. I had been listening to lies! (This is one way Satan gains power over us since he is the father of lies, says John 8:44.)

Satan Does Not Cast Out Satan

When I turned my focus back to the Bible and Jesus Christ, rather than trusting men, I was no longer confused about my recent experience. As I sought Him in it, a clear answer to my current dilemma came from God's Word. Jesus said that Satan does not cast out Satan:

> And Jesus knew their thoughts, and said unto them, Every Kingdom divided against itself is brought to desolation; and every city or house divided against itself shall not stand: And if Satan cast out Satan, he is divided against himself; how shall then his Kingdom stand?
> —Matthew 12:25–26

I had certainly been delivered from a demonic attack. It had not been Satan that had removed the frightening influence of evil spirits around me and replaced them with love, light, joy, and freedom. If so, he would be, "divided against himself." Gaining this insight from the Scripture, I knew that God had delivered me from Satan's fearful attack and had set me free to worship Him in a new relationship-based manner.

I repented that I had so easily been confused by men and their experiences rather than testing even these by the Bible.

Something Worth Trusting

I was not in a position to judge my dad or his experiences, but I knew I must first and foremost trust God, what I was currently learning from Him, and the Bible. These were my anchors! I must continue to take one step of faith at a time, moving forward in the light I had been given.

I knew my trust had to be in both the Bible and the Holy Ghost, not one without the other, but both confirming and complementing the other. I still believed it was important to seek the guidance of the Holy Ghost in order to understand the Bible, but I also now knew that we could easily be led astray if we did not "prove all things" against the truth given to us in the Bible. That was a major difference between Dad and me. Although Dad loved the Bible and believed it to be God's blueprint for truth, his trust was also in modern-day revelation through the LDS prophets. His trust in them was based on his own spiritual experiences. I now trusted the Bible first and believed that each experience we have, even the "supernatural ones," should be tested by the Bible.

Trusting God as Sovereign Rather than Questioning Why

I didn't have all the answers and I didn't understand why deception had to exist. However, it was enough for me to know that Jesus had told us beforehand that it would be this way, as in this scriptural warning Jesus gave concerning the end times on the earth:

> Then if any man shall say unto you, Lo, here is Christ, or there; believe it not. For there shall arise false Christs, and false prophets, and shall shew great signs and wonders; insomuch that, if it were

possible, they shall deceive the very elect. Behold, I have told you before. Wherefore if they shall say unto you, Behold, he is in the desert; go not forth: behold, he is in the secret chambers; believe it not. For as the lightning cometh out of the east, and shineth even unto the west; so shall also the coming of the Son of Man be.

—Matthew 24:23–27

Jesus made it clear that His Second Coming would not be in a secret place to an individual, but as the lightning, visible to all. Yet, He warned us that many would claim He had appeared exclusively to them. The false prophets Jesus warned about would deceive, "even the elect, if that were possible."

One Scripture I read (Romans 9:20) was very convicting: "Nay but, O man, who art thou that repliest against God?" I repented of my questioning God. It was not for me to ask why God allows deception, but to exercise faith and trust that God allowed the existence of deception for a good purpose that I did not understand.

Also, I knew the end of the story. The deception was temporary. Satan, with all his lies and deceptions, would be destroyed in the end. I just did not want to be under his spell in my life today, neither did I want anyone I loved to be!

Although we now live in a world with a lot of deception, God has not left us defenseless to it. He has given us His word and direction so that we can test all who claim to have had spiritual experiences, visions, or revelations against the writings of the original apostles and prophets. The Word of God must be our anchor!

A Lighthouse for the Simple

"The entrance of thy words giveth light, it giveth understanding unto the simple," says Psalm 119:130. Once again God had given me light from His Word. I was definitely simple. I could not boast of seeing visions, being visited by spirit guides or divine beings, nor had I ever heard an audible voice of the Lord, but I, a simple person, could recognize God's light when He spoke to me by the power of the Holy Spirit through His Word. It was my lighthouse in the midst of the storm of confusion.

> *"Thy word is a lamp unto my feet, and a light unto my path."*
>
> —*Psalm 119:105*

CHAPTER 15

WHO IS WORTHY?

*"Thou art worthy, O Lord, to receive glory and honour
and power: for thou hast created all things, and for thy
pleasure they are and were created."*

—Revelation 4:11

Several weeks after my parents returned home to Utah, mother became very ill. In a few months her condition worsened. Dad called to inform us that she was in the hospital.

"I've never seen your mother this sick before," he said in a very concerned voice. "The doctors have not been able to determine what she has."

As the weeks passed Mom's condition went from bad to critical. I was haunted by the thought, "What if she should die?"

It was time for me to go to Utah.

A Difficult Diagnosis

Finally, after doing all they knew to do, the doctors in Utah sent lab tests to California. These tests revealed that mother had a rare disease called Coccidiomycosis, a highly infectious fungus disease that occurs in two forms, primary and progressive. The primary form, also known as San Joaquin Fever or Valley Fever, is usually a benign, respiratory disease that is self-limiting and disappears within days, like the flu. The progressive form, however, is a chronic, malignant infection that can spread to all tissues and is often fatal. If it enters the spinal fluid, it can paralyze the person and eventually affect their brain. The infection may be dust-borne and is prevalent throughout the Death Valley desert of California, as well as other areas of the American Southwest and western South America. It is possible for individuals to contract the disease by traveling through endemic areas but not develop symptoms until they are in another location.

This is exactly what happened with mother. While traveling from Utah to California on their recent trip to visit my family and discuss religion with me, Mom and Dad had slept at a rest stop outside of Baker, California, one of the endemic areas of this infection (especially when the wind is blowing, which is most of the time). Dad had made a very comfortable bed in his car that he and mother slept in when they traveled. It was their "motel on wheels." A few weeks after they returned home to Northern Utah, mother started to feel strange. She was now extremely ill with the fatal disease.

God's Love—Conditional or Unconditional?

"If mother dies it will be my fault," I said to my sister. I was feeling very sad and blaming myself. After all, she had contracted the disease while they were traveling to my home to "straighten me out." If they hadn't come to California, I reasoned, she would not have gotten sick. If the Mormon Church is true, maybe God is punishing me because I don't believe in it anymore.

I was reverting back to my old lifetime religious programming of seeing God as one who loves conditionally. The LDS doctrine that every blessing from God is earned because of our obedience (D&C 130:20, 21) also leads one to believe that bad things must be our fault when we are not obedient. The result is self-condemnation when things go badly. Without specifically saying it, this philosophy turned God into a demanding judge who rewards us when we do well and punishes us when we do evil. When bad things happen to us, therefore, it must be because we are bad—just as when good things happen to us, it is because we are good. This teaching that God's love was conditional upon my performance was so ingrained in me that I still did not grasp God's grace even though I had experienced it.

Treatment

Mother was moved from the McKay Dee Hospital in Ogden to a hospital in Salt Lake City, where they were more prepared to deal with this rare disease. Fewer than one percent, we learned, of Caucasians that get the common Valley Fever develop the progressive form of the disease. That was the case with mother.

The infection had spread to mother's spinal fluid and was affecting her brain. There was a medicine to treat this disease, Amphotericin B, which had excellent results if administered in the early stages. However, the doctor warned us that this medicine was extremely toxic and that giving her the medicine involved a high risk and could be fatal. Dad took the risk. It was her only hope.

To administer the medicine it was necessary to drill a hole about the size of a quarter in Mother's head and insert a cushion, similar to a pincushion, through which they inserted a needle. It was extremely sad and painful to see mother in this condition. She had always been such a servant, doing so many kind deeds for others and especially for her family. She was truly an example of a loving, submissive wife and a wonderful mother. All the siblings knew that Dad would have a terrible time without her. Of course she was given several Priesthood blessings.

Much to our joy and thanksgiving Mother started to improve. After several weeks she was finally able to go home from the hospital. Months later, the disease went into remission and mother was able to function once again, though not with the strength and energy she'd had before. Still, we were all very grateful she was still with us!

A Visit with a General Authority

While Mother was in the hospital in Salt Lake City, Dad arranged for us to meet with Sterling W. Sill, one of the General Authorities of the Church. He and Dad had been personal acquaintances for many years, and as we greeted one another he welcomed Dad as if they were best buddies. We had a friendly chat, then dad explained to him that I had always been a faithful member of the church and had been given a strong testimony, but that I was currently going through some struggles believing in Joseph Smith. Dad asked Elder Sill to give me a special Priesthood blessing, which he did. He also told me that I had a right to seek answers to my questions, and that it was okay to be honest about my doubts.

He and Dad both reminded me that the Mormon Church was the only church that could possibly be the true church for many reasons, but one very important reason was that it was the only church that held the keys to the Melchizedek Priesthood.

I had already come to the conclusion that there was a silence in the gospels about the Priesthood, and it was also evident to me from the many Christian testimonies of blessings, healings, and miracles I had encountered that God worked in many people's lives without the Priesthood. I believed that the power of God worked in believer's lives through faith in the Name of Jesus, but I certainly was not prepared to discuss the subject of the Melchizedek Priesthood with a General Authority of the Church (at least not at this time).

I was very aware that the book of Hebrews talks about a priesthood, "after the order of Melchizedek." The Melchizedek Priesthood confused me. I did have to agree with Dad and Elder Sill that the Mormon Church was the only church that I knew of that claimed to have High Priests ordained after the Order of Melchizedek.

It became one of my goals to study the book of Hebrews and learn more about the Melchizedek Priesthood when I returned home. Tobie had been encouraging me to read the book of Hebrews, which I had done, and she had pointed out to me some very interesting and new concepts from it. However, there was a lot that I did not understand at this time that I did learn much later. (See Volume Two, *Jesus, Our High Priest Forever*, p. 223.)

Tobie Not Worthy?

While I was in Utah, Dad and I didn't have very many religious conversations because of the circumstance with mother. However, it was practically impossible for the subject not to come up occasionally when we were together. In one of our conversations I had mentioned what a changed person Tobie was after she believed in Jesus, and even more so since she had been studying the Bible with the Jehovah's Witnesses. Before her conversion to Christ she had been guilty of an extramarital affair. In Christ, she had obviously found freedom from her sin, as well as freedom from guilt. She was quick to verbalize her assurance of acceptance with God because of what Jesus had done for her on the cross (only she referred to the cross as the *torture stake*). To me, she was like the woman who washed Jesus' feet with her tears and loved much because she had been forgiven of much (Luke 7:36–50).

As I explained this to Dad, he somehow missed the point. He was shocked that Tobie was guilty of adultery.

"You mean to tell me that Tobie is an adulteress," Dad exclaimed. "Well, that explains why she didn't accept Joseph Smith and the restoration of the gospel when you taught it to her. She isn't worthy."

I was very surprised at his response. However, before my recent experience of being changed by God's love, I would have thought the same way. Now I saw things very differently.

"But Dad," I exclaimed, "she is a new person now that she believes in Jesus. Her past sins should not keep her from truth. Besides, God had revealed the truth about Jesus to her when she was not worthy, so why wouldn't He reveal the truth about Joseph Smith?"

Blessings Earned

I don't think Dad even heard my question. My logic had no impact upon Dad's opinion. His religious mindset had strongly conditioned him that God's love is conditional. Mormon Scripture teaches that all the blessings we receive are because of our obedience. The Doctrine & Covenants, section 130:20–21 says:

"There is a law, irrevocably decreed in heaven before the foundations of this world, upon which all blessings are predicated—and when we obtain any blessing from God, it is by obedience to that law upon which it is predicated."

The Mormon doctrine that any blessing we receive because of our obedience was very different from Tobie's understanding of God. She believed there was a higher standard of God's love in which all humanity reaps from God's blessings of love. On the other hand, all experience evil because Adam and Eve gave Satan power when they believed his lie and they ate the fruit in disobedience to God's command. Therefore, we are all under Satan's influence and attacks. As a result of Satan's influence and God's love, all humans experience a combination of good and evil circumstances that are not always a result of one's obedience or disobedience, worthiness or unworthiness. Good people experience bad things, and bad people experience good things, and vice versa. I silently had to admit that her belief did fit reality.

Tobie reminded me that God makes His sun rise on the evil and on the good, and sends rain on the just and on the unjust (Matthew 5:45).

At this time I didn't get the point; but eventually I came to understand the above verse to mean that God sends certain blessings to both good and evil people without discrimination. Later I learned that theologians refer to this as common grace. It is different from, and not to be confused with, the grace that gives salvation through faith in Jesus Christ. Nonetheless, Jesus' words in Matthew 5:45 make it clear that it is not just the obedient that receive blessings from God.

This higher standard of God's love does not negate the biblical teaching that in this life we reap what we sow (Galatians 6:8). We all reap consequences for our decisions and actions.

The Bible also teaches that God expects obedience and that those who live lawless lives of sin and rebellion against God will be judged and will eventually experience God's wrath. Ultimately, the judgment of God and our eternal destinies are conditional on our relationship with Christ. But is every blessing we receive in our current earthly lives based upon our obedience? Is Father in Heaven a judge ready to punish us every time we mess up and bless us only when we are good? If that were the case, why do so many evil people thrive? Why do many good people suffer?

Joseph Smith's teaching that any blessing we obtain from God is by obedience to a particular law didn't agree with my observation of life nor did it seem biblical. In addition, it made a person feel they were guilty of offending God when bad things happened.

Is Knowing the Truth Contingent upon Personal Worthiness?

The LDS idea that one had to be worthy in order to know the truth was very different from what I read in the New Testament. Wasn't it unworthy sinners who frequently believed in Jesus? Didn't Jesus say He came to save *the lost?* Jesus continually showed unconditional love to these sinners. It was not the sinners he called "whited sepulchers full of dead men's bones," (Matthew 23:27). He rarely condemned the sinner but healed and forgave him and told him or her to "go and sin no more." No, it was the self-righteous, law-abiding religious leaders that Jesus staunchly condemned!

The Worthy Pharisees

Wasn't it the religious scribes and Pharisees (the ones who considered themselves "worthy") who rejected Jesus? These respected religious leaders of the day not only rejected their Messiah, they hated Him—and demanded He be put to death!

After all, this strange man named Jesus, who claimed to be the Son of God, just didn't fit their mold, nor the preconceived mental picture they had of a potential "Savior." He actually disregarded the law (in their minds) by healing on the Sabbath day and neglecting to ceremonially wash His hands. Why, He even associated with sinners!

How could this rebel, who made a whip to drive the moneychangers from the temple, and who called the respected scribes and Pharisees "whited sepulchers full of dead men's bones," be their long-awaited Messiah? No! He didn't fit their preconceived notions at all. He didn't seem to be concerned or impressed with their purity, obtained by strict religious observance of the law. As a matter of fact, He said that unless one's righteousness exceeded the righteousness of the Pharisees and the teachers of the law, one would not see the Kingdom of Heaven (Matthew 5:20).

"Well, they were not righteous because they were hypocrites," we might say. But are we not all hypocrites when we see ourselves as more righteous than we are in God's eyes? The Apostle Paul said, "There is none righteous; no, not one" (Romans 3:10).

Religious Blinders

Isn't it interesting that these religious Pharisees, who were so hung up on the law and seeking to sanctify themselves through a strict observance of *do's* and *don'ts* and religious rituals, were so blind that they missed their Messiah?

They were so religious that they missed a relationship with the Savior of the world—the Author and Finisher of our Faith, the very Creator, the Son of God! Even His miracles couldn't open their eyes since they were so intent on their own traditions. After all, they had to be right! Why, they were the children of Abraham! Yes, their commitment to their religion, their lifestyle, their social prestige and authority blinded them—even in the presence of Jesus.

As I thought about all of this, I also wondered whether, if Jesus came today, many of us might not recognize Him. What would He be like? Would He fit our religious mindset? Would it be possible to be so blinded by our own religious worldview, as the Pharisees were, that we wouldn't even recognize Jesus?

Sinners Recognized Him

Yes, it is very interesting that it was the confessed sinners, not the religious leaders, who could more easily bow before Jesus and worship Him as Lord. Mary Magdalene, from whom Jesus had cast out seven devils (Luke 8:2), was the first to see Him after His resurrection (John 20:1–18)! Yet, the honored, law-abiding Jewish leaders didn't even know what was happening!

Can We Make Ourselves Worthy Enough for God?

My mind reflected on a conversation I'd had with Tobie before the spiritual experience that set me free. Tobie had insisted that if I were so committed to obeying God's laws to earn His acceptance, and especially eternal life, then I had to obey them perfectly. She used two Scriptures to make her point. The first was this:

> For as many as are of the works of the law are under the curse: for it is written, cursed is everyone that continueth not in all things which are written in the book of the law to do them.
>
> —Galatians 3:10

Tobie believed that all humans were cursed because we cannot obey all of the law all the time. The above Scripture did seem to say that. The next Scripture was even more troublesome:

> For whosoever shall keep the whole law, and yet offend in one point, he is guilty of all.
>
> —James 2:10

Those Scriptures were aggravating! Who could keep the law perfectly? I knew I could not. Trying to make myself perfect was futile. That had been one of my burdens—trying to keep all of the laws and commandments of my religion. Besides failing to do all the good things I was supposed to do, I also failed at always being loving, patient, and kind. The harder I tried, the more aware I became of falling short.

One example of my failures that made me feel guilty was keeping Sunday as a Sabbath day of rest. I never could quite get that one together. Before the block program, the men went to church separately in the morning for Priesthood meeting. We went to church twice on Sunday. In addition, Charles had Priesthood responsibilities and choir practice so I didn't see much of him on Sundays. I was left with the responsibility of getting all the children ready for church and keeping them quiet during church. When home I was busy feeding them, cleaning up the kitchen, and keeping eight kids involved in activities appropriate for Sunday (no TV or friends over).

Sundays were very exhausting for me and they were not my idea of a day of rest. I always thought it would be nice to take a family ride up the canyon, or have family activities together, or just plain rest! But Sunday was very busy. Frequently I felt guilty because I didn't know how to make it the day of rest I longed for and needed.

Tobie had known all this, and she was making me feel worse by showing me the above Scriptures. If I stumble at just one point, then I'm guilty of breaking all? *Nobody* could live all the laws and commandments perfectly! If Salvation depended on our ability to perfectly live the law, who could be saved? Nobody!

Of course I told Tobie that I had all eternity to become perfect. She didn't buy that idea, however, because the Bible taught that after this life comes the judgment (Hebrews 9:27), and that judgment is final for eternity.

When Tobie pointed out to me the above Scriptures that stated we had to keep all the law without stumbling at one point or we are guilty, I was insulted. She was guilty of many more sins than I was (including the very serious one of adultery), yet she was pointing out my failure to be perfect! I considered myself a very good Mormon, and she wasn't in much of a position to point out my shortcomings! So, outwardly I ignored her. However, inwardly I could not ignore her. She seemed to have found freedom from guilt and condemnation for her sins.

Under a Curse?

That past conversation with Tobie had been very confusing to me, including the above Scriptures she had shown me that said we were *under a curse* if we didn't obey all of the law. That was one of the instances where the Bible had not made sense through my Mormon spectacles. Even though the idea of being under a curse if we couldn't be perfect sounded unfair and frustrating, silently I knew that was how I had felt many times before my personal encounter with Christ. I had felt under a curse. I had been locked in a spiritual conflict. I believed in Christ and wanted to please Him, yet I felt guilty and condemned because I couldn't be good enough. The stress, guilt, and condemnation were the yoke of religion I had been tied beneath all my life—the curse of failing to live the law perfectly. It didn't matter whether it was the law of Moses or the Mormon laws, or any other religious laws; nobody could live all of the laws perfectly!

But since my experience with Christ, I was beginning to understand.

Freedom from Guilt

Christ had unlocked the yoke of religion and yoked me with Him. Now I no longer felt guilty. Now I no longer felt under a curse. Now I no longer felt stressed trying to do all the things I was told I had to do. I no longer felt *unworthy* of the Kingdom. I no longer felt like one of the five foolish virgins who did not have extra oil for their lanterns. Christ had accepted me the way I was.

At this time, I could not explain this from the Scriptures, that came later; but I knew I had been set free from guilt and condemnation, and that felt wonderful!

A Smoke Screen

After arriving back home in California and attending church with my family, I couldn't help but notice how much personal worthiness was emphasized at the LDS Church. One had to be worthy to do their callings, worthy to be given the Priesthood, worthy to pass the Sacrament, worthy to go on a mission, worthy to go to the temple, worthy to enter the Celestial Kingdom. It was so common for church members to get caught up in doing good that they focused on trying to be worthy through good deeds, church service, obtaining a temple recommend, and attending the temple ceremony. The more I heard "worthy," the more I recognized it to be a smoke screen to blind us to the fact that we are all unworthy.

The Pharisee and the Publican

This was brought home to me even more one day as I was doing my visiting teaching. The lesson I was giving to another member in her home was on Jesus' parable of the Pharisee and the tax collector, found in Luke 18:9–14:

> And he spake this parable unto certain which trusted in themselves that they were righteous, and despised others: Two men went up into the temple to pray; the one a Pharisee, and the other a publican. The Pharisee stood and prayed thus with himself, God, I thank thee, that I am not as other men are, extortioners, unjust, adulterers, or even as

this publican. I fast twice in the week; I give tithes of all that I possess. And the publican, standing afar off, would not lift up so much as his eyes unto heaven, but smote upon his breast, saying, God be merciful to me a sinner. I tell you, this man went down to his house justified rather than the other: for everyone that exalteth himself shall be abased; and he that humbleth himself shall be exalted.

I had always understood this parable as intending to teach the lesson that pride was a sin and we needed to be humble before the Lord. Also, that we should not look down upon others. However, I had always been a little confused as to why the sinner was justified and the one who had done the good things was not. This day the Lord confirmed to me an important truth. The lesson in the manual did not point it out, but the Lord pointed it out to me as I reread the familiar story.

The phrase, "trusted in themselves that they were righteous," spoke mountains to me. Wasn't that sort of the attitude I had all my life in the church? On Sundays while driving to church, hadn't I thought I was more righteous than the neighbors who were doing their yard work? Hadn't I thought I was more righteous than all those Sabbath-breakers at the beach on Sunday? Hadn't I thought I was a little better than the person drinking and smoking, since I obeyed the Word of Wisdom? Hadn't I thought I was "worthy" because I always had a temple recommend and went to the temple? After all, I had been told I was "worthy." These thoughts of worthiness were not conscious but very subconscious. Now I could see that such thoughts had a subtle, blinding affect upon religious people who trusted in their own righteousness. We could not see our self-righteous attitude, but it was there, even though hidden deep within us.

No wonder I had not understood the parable of the Pharisee and the publican. As a religious person all my life, I had been like the Pharisee! I shuddered at the words of the Pharisee's prayer: "I fast twice in the week; I give tithes of all that I possess." Hadn't I considered myself worthy because I fasted and paid full tithing? Yes, I also had the attitude that the Pharisee had—that he was more righteous than the tax collector (the most contemptible traitor to an Israelite). I just had never known I had that attitude. The Pharisee was trusting in his own righteousness.

194

Had I been doing the same?

The parable taught so much more than humility versus pride. It taught me that when we see ourselves as righteous, we are blind to the fact that we are all sinners. That makes us worse off than the sinner who sees his wretched condition and confesses his sin before God. The righteous person is so busy trying to make himself good enough for God that he neglects the first and most important step in coming to Christ— recognizing and confessing his sinful condition. I could see that it was hard for a person steeped in a religion to see his sins, especially if his religion taught that he was righteous and worthy if he (or she) kept the laws and ordinances of that religion. That had been me! I knew I wasn't perfect and that I fell short, but it was hard for me to call myself a sinner. That sounded too much like a Protestant.

All Fall Short

The Scriptures Tobie had shown me came to mind. I read them again in both the King James translation and then in the New International version. James definitely said that if we keep the whole law and yet stumble at one point we are guilty of breaking all of it (James 2:10). In Galatians 3:10–13, Paul definitely said that if we rely on observing the law we are under a curse. He continued to make it clear that no one would be justified before God by the law, but that faith was the important thing.

In verse thirteen of Galatians three, Paul says, "Christ redeemed us from the curse of the law by becoming a curse for us." Obviously everyone is guilty and, if there is no intervening faith, dies in that guilty condition because we are not perfect. All Christians believe in repentance, but how would one know if he had repented of every wrong thing he'd ever said or done? Worse yet, could we all repent of our sins of omission—the good things we should have done but we didn't? Would we even know how many times we'd offended a holy, perfect God? *Probably not!*

When speaking of eternal damnation, Mormon Scripture says, "But if they would not repent they must suffer even as I;" ["I" meaning Christ] (Doctrine & Covenants 19:17).

Another troubling Scripture in the Doctrine & Covenants was section 82:7: ". . . but unto that soul who sinneth shall the former sins return, saith the Lord your God." President Spencer W. Kimball said, "Each previously forgiven sin is added to the new one and the whole gets to be a heavy load." (*Miracle of Forgiveness*, page 170)

No wonder as a Mormon I had been worried about making myself good enough. The only thing "good enough" was perfection. The problem is, we all fall short of this, just like Paul says in Romans 3:23: "for all have sinned and fall short of the glory of God." We have a serious problem because we all sin and are not perfect. According to the Mormon Scripture and prophet quoted above, our former sins return— even forgiven ones. This is more than a heavy load. This is mission impossible!

Worthy, or Guilty?

That was a major difference between my religion and what Tobie and other Christians believed. They each acknowledged that they were sinners, yet they each had confidence in their relationship with Jesus. Even though they were unworthy sinners, they were made right with God because of Jesus and what He had accomplished on the cross at Calvary. My religion had always taught me that I needed Jesus to overcome death, but I had to make myself worthy of Him. I felt like I had to climb a ladder of righteousness— I had to obey the particular laws and ordinances of my religion in order to reach Christ. That is how I had felt all my life, reaching and striving to get to Jesus' level—but never getting high enough. I had lived my life in a spiritual conflict—trying to be worthy but feeling guilty.

Now it was as if a loving Father in Heaven had removed the ladder of religion that I had tirelessly been trying to climb. The ladder had actually been a barrier between Jesus and me because it was too high. Now, instead of me trying to reach Him by climbing the ladder of personal righteousness through obedience to the laws and ordinances of Mormonism, Father in Heaven had reached down to me in my unworthy condition and lifted me to Him through the cross. Even though I couldn't explain it, I knew that it had happened to me.

An Unanswered Question

However, I was confused. What about all the Scriptures I had learned as a Mormon that say we must keep the commandments and do good works? I certainly didn't believe (as I had always supposed Christians believed) that one could merely walk down an aisle at a Billy Graham Crusade and say they believed in Jesus, then continue in their life of sin and be acceptable to God. That was a repulsive idea. Actually, none of the Jehovah's Witnesses or Seventh-day Adventists I knew believed that either. All of them, including Tobie, believed in obedience. How did sin, obedience to God's laws, repentance, forgiveness, and Christ's death on the cross—*God's gift of grace*—all fit together?

Who Is Worthy?

The more I attended the LDS Church and heard the focus on making ourselves worthy through obedience to the laws and ordinances of the church, the more it bothered me. I never forgot Dad's words, "Tobie isn't worthy." The truth of the matter is: no one is worthy. None of us can make ourselves worthy enough for God. To think that we are worthy is to deceive ourselves and to live the life of a Pharisee. We are all sinners in need of Jesus!

He said, "Come unto me, all ye that labour and are heavy laden, and I will give you rest. Take my yoke upon you, and learn of me; for I am meek and lowly in heart: and ye shall find rest unto your souls. For my yoke is easy, and my burden is light" (Matthew 11:28–30).

Jesus had wanted me to come to Him just as I was, admitting my sinful condition and my need for Him. He invited me to bring my brokenness to Him, instead of trying to fix it or cover up my unworthiness through personal righteousness. I never again wanted to be like the Pharisees, who'd tried to make themselves righteous through personal merit and who, consequently, could not admit their inherent sinful nature of pride and self-centeredness, nor could they humbly surrender to Christ.

Condemned by Others

Over the next few years church members would tell me many times that I had lost my testimony because I must not have been able to live the gospel and I wasn't worthy. *Could they live all the laws and ordinances of the gospel and always be loving and kind, without falling short? Did they really think they were worthy? What made them good and me bad?*

In their condemnation of me, none could say what I had done wrong, or what I failed to do that made me unworthy. Through Mormon spectacles, my unworthiness was the only explanation for my disbelief in Joseph Smith. *Was a belief in Joseph Smith the criteria that made us worthy or unworthy?* Apparently so! After all, Brigham Young did say that no one would enter the Celestial Kingdom without the consent of Joseph Smith.[20]

The amazing thing was, the closer I got to Jesus the more aware I became of my unworthiness. I was beginning to understand Peter's words when he fell down at Jesus' knees and said, "Depart from me, for I am a sinful man, O Lord!" (Luke 5:8). When Peter recognized that he was in the presence of the Holy One, he recognized his unworthiness, not his worthiness.

I now understood that no one could make himself good enough for God. We cannot measure up to God's holy standard. I had tried and had fallen short every day of my life.

I also knew that God had now accepted me even though I was not worthy. I was still trying to understand why and how, but I knew it was because of the cross. I no longer had to spend eternity mastering perfection. Jesus had done that for me.

There is only one who lived the perfect life and who is thus worthy—Jesus Christ. He lived the perfect life in my place since I can't do it. Then He died on the cross in my place, so I would not have to spend eternity separated from Him. I had sought God for the truth within His Word, and I was beginning to understand it!

> *"And they sang a new song, saying, Thou art worthy to take the book, and to open the seals thereof: for thou wast slain, and hast redeemed us to God by thy blood*

out of every kindred, and tongue, and people, and nation."

—*Revelation 5:9*

CHAPTER 16

Spirit Manifestations from the Dead: Divine or Deceptive?

"Regard not them that have familiar spirits, neither seek after wizards, To be defiled by them: I am the LORD your God."

—Leviticus 19:31

The reversal of my strong convictions was extremely difficult for me. Sometimes I felt as if I were going to go crazy dealing with my emotions, as well as struggling with all the questions I wanted answered. I wanted to discuss everything I was learning with my family but it was extremely difficult to do so since they didn't want to listen. They wanted only to teach, not to be taught. They knew, based on their knowledge and experiences, that they could not be wrong. My prayer was that God would protect me from Satan's powerful spiritual deceptions and that He would give me true spiritual discernment.

During this period, my life was very busy keeping up with the activities of eight kids, ranging in age from four to seventeen years old, and because I had been using time to pray, study, and seek the Lord's voice, I had not been talking with Tobie quite as often as before.

However, she was very eager to get together and resume our Bible discussions.

She asked if I had read the Bible verses she had given me several months ago concerning communication with the dead. I had always wondered why she wanted me to read them.

"No, I don't communicate with the dead," was my answer.

She acted like she didn't hear me. Before leaving she brought up the topic of spiritism. I remembered that the Seventh-day Adventist evangelist that taught the Revelation seminar had told me that he believed Mormonism was spiritism. That had been several months ago. Since I didn't really understand what was meant by spiritism, I decided it was time I found out.

"What is spiritism?" I naively asked Tobie.

"Look it up in the dictionary," she answered as she left.

What Is Spiritism?

When alone later that day, I got out my *Webster's New World Dictionary*. Under the word, *spiritism*, it referred the reader to spiritualism, which was defined as: a) "the belief that the dead survive as spirits that can communicate with the living, esp. with the help of a third party (medium)", and, b) "any practice arising from this belief."[21]

According to the first part of that definition, Mormonism was spiritism. We didn't believe in mediums, but we did believe that the dead survived as spirits and can communicate with the living.

Now I understood why Tobie wanted me to look up Bible verses about communicating with the dead. Both the Jehovah's Witnesses and the Seventh-day Adventists believe that when a person dies they are unconscious until the resurrection. Therefore, they reject any alleged communication with the dead and consider such to be a deception of Satan.

A Parable by Jesus

I could hardly wait to show her that Jesus believed that the dead were conscious in the spirit realm. The parable of "The Rich Man and

Lazarus," found in Luke 16:19–31, certainly was enough evidence to show that the dead were conscious and that they experienced feelings. Both Lazarus and the rich man died. The beggar, Lazarus, was carried to Abraham's bosom, where he was comforted, while the rich man was in torment in hell.

I thought this would convince Tobie that what she called soul sleep was not biblical. However, as usual, this parable was not new to her. She believed that it was dangerous to take a doctrinal stand based on a parable since these were stories intended primarily to teach a lesson.

"The lesson was to the Pharisees, who loved money," she explained, "and to those who despised someone poor, like Lazarus. Jesus described him as a beggar covered with sores, which the dogs licked. In the opinion of the Pharisees, who justified *themselves* as righteous (verse 15), God would not look on a beggar favorably. This parable was given by the Lord to illustrate to the people, among other things, that what men— and especially the Pharisees—highly esteemed (wealth and honor) was an abomination to God (verse 15)."

A Contradiction

While I found her explanation very interesting and possibly accurate, I still believed that this parable indicated that the dead are conscious. I did not think Jesus would use such an illustration otherwise, even if it were merely a parable and not a true story (although Jesus did give the beggar a name). Aside from that question, this parable did contradict Mormon doctrine that the spirits of the righteous dead went into the realm of the spirits of the wicked (spirit prison) to teach the errant ones there the gospel. According to LDS theology, if a spirit accepts the gospel in the spirit world, and if their baptism and endowment work have been done for them by proxy in a Mormon temple, then this spirit can leave spirit prison and go into Paradise, where the righteous spirits dwell. That is why temple work is so important.

I agreed that if I were going to use this parable to teach that the dead were conscious, then I would also have to accept that the spirits of the righteous in Paradise could not go to the spirits in spirit prison, nor visa versa. The parable was very clear about that:

> And besides all this, between us and you there is a great gulf fixed, so that those who want to pass from here to you cannot, nor can those from there pass to us.
>
> — Luke 16:26

That eliminated the idea that spirits of deceased righteous LDS people go to the spirit prison to teach them the LDS gospel.

Tobie pointed out the figurative nature of the verses; i.e., the rich man's use of the phrase, "dip the tip of his finger in water and cool my tongue; for I am tormented in this flame." This was one reason why the parable was to be taken figuratively, not literally, she insisted.

Another important point was that Lazarus was not allowed to go to the rich man's living brothers to warn them. Luke 16:27–31 NIV, states:

> He answered, "Then I beg you, father, send Lazarus to my father's house, for I have five brothers. Let him warn them, so that they will not also come to this place of torment." Abraham replied, "They have Moses and the Prophets; let them listen to them."
>
> "No, father Abraham," he said, "but if someone from the dead goes to them, they will repent." He said to him, "If they do not listen to Moses and the Prophets, they will not be convinced even if someone rises from the dead."

This was yet another indication that the Scriptures are enough evidence to believe and be saved, even over a visitation from the dead.

Temple Manifestations of the Dead

However, I was aware of many instances where the spirit of a deceased person had appeared to someone. For instance, I remembered attending the Logan temple with my parents many years ago. We had attended a chapel service before going through the temple endowment ceremony. This was the only time I attended a chapel service in the temple where someone spoke. The speaker shared how she had seen her dead sister in the temple on one occasion and how radiant and beautiful she was.

Temple manifestations connected with the spirit world were a part of a Mormon's testimony. Wilford Woodruff, fifth president of the Mormon

Church, delivered a talk in the Salt Lake tabernacle in which he told listeners the following:

> Two weeks before I left St. George, the spirits of the dead gathered around me, wanting to know why we did not redeem them. These were the signers of the Declaration of Independence, and they waited on me for two days and two nights. I straightway went into the baptismal font and called upon brother McCallister to baptize me for the signers of the Declaration of Independence, and fifty other eminent men, making one hundred in all, including John Wesley, Columbus, and others; I then baptized him for every President of the United States, except three; and when their cause is just, somebody will do the work for them.[22]

The purpose of the temple is to do these saving ordinances for the dead, as well as the living. "The dead who repent will be redeemed, through obedience to the ordinances of the house of God." (Doctrine & Covenants 138:58)

Temple work is an important responsibility for Latter-day Saints because baptism into the Mormon Church, temple marriage, and the sacred temple endowment were all requirements for exaltation. These temple manifestations from the spirit world were strong confirmations that the church was true and that the temple is a sacred house of God.

The Thin veil Between Us and Them

Of course, the spirit of a deceased loved person could appear outside of the temple as well. Several weeks before my husband's aunt passed away, she saw her deceased mother at the foot of her bed, beckoning to her. My sister-in-law claimed that she had seen her deceased husband (my husband's brother) sitting at the organ one Sunday when she walked into church a few months after he'd passed away. He had been the church organist before he died. My grandmother claimed she had seen her deceased father come for her son the night her son died. [For a detailed account of this experience, see: D. Appendix to Chapter Sixteen: From *The Autobiography of Nicholas Baker* at the end of this chapter.]

Joseph Smith taught that, "The spirits of the just are exalted to a greater and more glorious work: hence they are blessed in their departure to the world of spirits. Enveloped in flaming fire, they are not far from us, and know and understand our thoughts, feelings, and motions, and are often pained therewith." (*Teachings of the Prophet Joseph Smith*, compiled by Joseph Fielding Smith, page 326)

Viewed in context, there is no question that in the above quote "spirits of the just" refers to deceased, worthy humans, whom Joseph refers to as "spirits of just men made perfect." Joseph makes a distinction between these spirits and the angels. He then continues to talk about Judge Adam, an intimate friend of the Prophet's who had died, and who, according to Joseph Smith, had "gone to open up a more effectual door for the dead."

Mormons believe that the veil between the spirit world and this world is very thin; consequently, the dead are very conscious of the living and capable of appearing and communicating messages to us. Spirit manifestations from the dead within the LDS Church are considered a divine blessing.

A Contradictory Dividing Line

As I thought of appearances of dead loved ones from the spirit world, I suddenly realized how contradictory my thinking had been. Tobie's phrase, "communicating with the dead," had made me think of séances or some bizarre claim on the front page of The National Enquirer, such as "Elvis Returns from the Dead." I had always considered such connections with the dead outside of my church to be from the devil, yet any communication with the dead within my church I considered to be from God. The dividing line had been the church. Within the church, it was divine; outside of the church, it was demonic. Our terminology within the church was different than secular terminology. We spoke of "spirits in the spirit world," rather than, "the dead." But was there really a difference between a spirit visitation within the church and one outside of the church?

It was easy to condemn séances as being the devil's territory, but was it the same to seek any kind of connection with the spirit world? Communicating with the dead was the same no matter what terminology it was given. *Was some of it from God and some of it from the devil, or was it all condemned by God—as the Jehovah's Witnesses and Seventh-day Adventists believed?*

An Undeniable Connection

As time went by and I attended my weekly church meetings, I became uncomfortably aware of the strong connection between my church and the world of the dead. I guess we did communicate with the dead. Joseph Smith said, "The greatest responsibility in this world that God has laid upon us is to seek after our dead."[23] Of course, that was through genealogy and temple work, not séances, but the emphasis on the dead was apparent. Mormon Scripture says:

> For their [the dead's] Salvation is necessary and essential to our Salvation, as Paul says concerning the fathers—that they without us cannot be made perfect—neither can we without our dead be made perfect.[24]
>
> —Doctrine & Covenants 128:15

Saving the Dead

Members of the church are referred to as "Saviors on Mount Zion" when we do temple work for the spirits in the spirit world. My patriarchal blessing stated that the spirits of my dead ancestors were waiting in the spirit world for me to do their genealogy and temple work so that they could get out of spirit prison. This was one of the sources of my guilt. I never seemed to have enough time to get into genealogy and get this important work done!

A strange thought entered my mind. *Wasn't that sort of like Catholicism? Didn't Catholics believe they could pray to get loved ones out of purgatory?* In the past, that idea had seemed so ridiculous to me, but *was that so different from my religious belief that we can get loved ones out of spirit prison by doing temple work for them?*

Apparitions of Mary

I tried to stop thinking about this subject since it was making me uncomfortable, but more thoughts persisted. Didn't Catholics look upon the appearance of the Virgin Mary as a blessed experience? I wondered how many Catholics interpreted the apparitions of Mary as evidence that the Catholic Church was true. I had always been quick to judge such appearances of Mary as deceptive. However, my Catholic neighbor thought differently. Her feelings about the reported appearances of Mary were similar to a Mormon's feelings about a dead relative appearing to them.

Curiosity got the best of me, so I got out the World Book to read about these apparitions of the Virgin Mary. The city of Lourdes, France, is the location of a famous shrine that attracts about two million Roman Catholic pilgrims annually, many of whom are seeking cures for their illnesses. It is believed that at this location, the Virgin Mary appeared to a fourteen-year-old peasant girl, Bernadette Soubirous. Bernadette claimed that the Virgin Mary told her to make known the healing powers of the waters at Lourdes. A beautiful church called The Rosary and a statue of the Virgin stand today where the vision occurred.

There have been literally thousands of appearances of the Virgin Mary claimed throughout history. Another famous one was in 1917 at Fatima, Portugal.

Since 1981, millions have traveled to the farming village of Medjugorje in Southwestern Yugoslavia (now Bosnia-Herzegovina). On a rocky hill overlooking the village, six youngsters claimed to see a vision of a beautiful woman with a shining face, black curly hair, blue eyes, and a gray coat. She told them she was the "Blessed Virgin Mary." For more than five years, she appeared daily to the six visionaries privately and at 6:40 p.m. every evening at the local parish rectory. Reportedly, only these six people could see her, although thousands of pilgrims claimed to see miraculous lights and many claimed to be healed of all kinds of diseases.

I met a Catholic lady who made the pilgrimage to Medjugorje and claimed to be healed of severe stomach problems on the hill where Mary first appeared. She told me that even though none but the visionaries see the Virgin Mary, one knows she is in the church talking to the visionaries because of the phenomena that happens every day when she appears. Flocks of birds fill the trees and certain lights appear in the sky.

A Chilling New Perspective

My curiosity about the apparitions of Mary had caused me to learn some fascinating information, which gave me a chilling new perspective on events in Mormon Church history. The restoration of the gospel was achieved by a series of deceased men appearing to Joseph Smith. Of course, we had always thought of these messengers as resurrected beings who were now angels.

Three years after the appearance of Heavenly Father and Jesus Christ to Joseph Smith, the Angel Moroni had reportedly visited him. This messenger came to Joseph in his bedroom and appeared on the same day, September 21, for four years. Moroni had allegedly lived on the American continent and was the lone survivor of his race, the Nephites. His father, Mormon, had made an abridgment of the history of their people and their brothers, the Lamanites.

During the final battle between the two nations—the Nephites and the Lamanites—the Nephite nation was completely destroyed, except for Moroni. He finished the abridgment written on gold plates and buried them in 420 A.D.

In 1823, 1400 years later, he appeared to Joseph Smith and told him where he had buried these gold plates. After four years, Joseph Smith was allowed to retrieve this historical record from the spot where Moroni had buried them in the Hill Cumorah in upstate New York. Joseph Smith then translated them into the Book of Mormon.

Other Appearances of the Dead

This was only one of several visitations of a deceased person to Joseph Smith during the restoration of the gospel. On May 15, 1829, John the Baptist appeared to him in order to restore the Aaronic Priesthood. Later, Peter, James, and John appeared to Joseph and gave him the Melchizedek Priesthood by the laying on of hands. Two Old Testament prophets—Elijah and Elisha—appeared to Joseph for the purpose of restoring certain keys. Even Moses appeared to Joseph Smith to restore to him the keys for the gathering of Israel. Of course, these men were now resurrected beings and angels, not spirits of dead men.

Noah had become the Angel Gabriel and Adam was Michael, the Archangel.

That was another topic that Tobie had been interested in discussing. She insisted that humans do not become angels, but angels were spirit beings sent from the presence of God as His messengers. She believed that, according to the Bible, God did not send spirits from the dead to communicate with humans.

Now I could see why she had been so intent on discussing this subject! She must have viewed the messengers of the restoration as spirits from the dead. She had never said that, but I was seeing how she could get that idea.

Time to Turn to The Bible

I concluded that it was time to look up the Scriptures Tobie had wanted me to read. *Just what did the Bible say about communicating with the dead?*

> When thou art come into the land which the LORD thy God gives thee, thou shalt not learn to do after the abominations of those nations. There shall not be found among you any one that maketh his son or his daughter to pass through the fire, or that useth divination, or an observer of times, or an enchanter, or a witch, or a charmer, or a consulter with familiar spirits, or a wizard, or a necromancer. For all that do these things are an abomination unto the LORD: and because of these abominations the LORD thy God doth drive them out from before thee.
>
> —Deuteronomy 18:9–12

That sounded like witchcraft to me! That Scripture didn't seem to say anything about spirits of the dead appearing and communicating with us, and Mormons certainly did not do those things mentioned in that verse. I looked up another Scripture she had given me:

> Regard not them that have familiar spirits, neither seek after wizards, to be defiled by them: I am the LORD your God.
>
> —Leviticus 19:31

Defining Terms

As I wondered even further why Tobie wanted me to read these Scriptures, I noticed that they both mentioned "familiar spirits." *What did that mean?* Was this phrase referring to the spirits of deceased persons? The first Scripture did say that a consulter with familiar spirits was an abomination unto the Lord. How could I find out what that meant, and what was a *necromancer?* I got out my *Webster's Dictionary* again. It said:

> Necromancy 1. the practice of claiming to foretell the future by alleged communication with the dead; 2. black magic; sorcery.[25]

I guess the above Scriptures did say *something* about communicating with the dead. As I continued to research this subject, I learned some very penetrating facts. The definitions of *medium, witch, necromancer, divination, and consulter of familiar spirits*, all shared a common foundation—sorcery, magic, fortune-telling, and a connection with spirits of the dead.

All of them were common in the pagan religions of the Chaldeans, the Egyptians, and other nations that surrounded Israel. In Isaiah 19:3, God says, "The Egyptians will lose heart, and I will bring their plans to nothing; they will consult the idols and the spirits of the dead, the mediums and the spiritists."

A *necromancer* was one who consulted the dead. God clearly declares this to be an abomination to Him and says he will drive out the nations that do such a thing. He warned the Israelites many times not to have anything to do with these practices of the pagan nations around them. Because the Israelites compromised and did eventually participate with some of these pagan practices, God judged the nation of Israel and scattered his people among the nations.

A Fascinating "Familiar Spirit" Story

There was another Scripture that Tobie had given me to read—the twenty-eighth chapter of 1 Samuel:

> Then said Saul unto his servants, Seek me a woman that hath a familiar spirit, that I may go to her, and enquire of her. And his servants said to him, Behold, there is a woman that hath a familiar spirit at Endor. And Saul disguised himself, and put on other raiment, and he went, and two men with him, and they came to the woman by night: and he said, I pray thee, divine unto me by the familiar spirit, and bring me him up, whom I shall name unto thee.
>
> —1 Samuel 28:7–8

It was evident from these verses that "familiar spirit" referred to connecting with a spirit from the dead. As I continued to read the story, I learned that Saul asks the woman to raise Samuel from the dead. Samuel was "familiar" to Saul.

Even though Saul knew that God had forbidden seeking out familiar spirits, he did it anyway because he was frightened. The Philistines were making war against him and God wouldn't give Saul any direction or answer him concerning the outcome, so Saul was seeking advice from the prophet Samuel, even though he was dead. The woman at Endor who was a *consulter of familiar spirits* got results! 1 Samuel 28:15 says:

> And Samuel said to Saul, Why hast thou disquieted me, to bring me up? And Saul answered, I am sore distressed; for the Philistines make war against me, and God is departed from me, and answereth me no more, neither by prophets, nor by dreams: therefore I have called thee, that thou mayest make known unto me what I shall do.

Samuel tells Saul that the Lord will turn Israel over to the Philistines, along with Saul and his sons. Samuel then tells Saul that on the morrow both he and his sons will be dead.

What a fascinating story! First of all, Saul has ordered all wizards, witches, and those with a familiar spirit out of the land because they were an abomination to God. Then, he secretly goes to one when he is distressed! Did he think he could hide his sin from God? I soon noticed that "consulter of familiar spirits," "medium," and "witch" are all equal as abominations to God.

Another interesting point was that these kinds of people were not make-believe. They got results! This Witch of Endor (as other translations referred to her) had the power to call up Samuel from the dead— Samuel, or a deceiving spirit that did a credible impersonation of him. That's what Tobie thought. Whether God allowed Samuel to appear in this instance to announce Saul's doom or whether it was a fallen angel (demon) doing a good impersonation of Saul is debatable. However, putting aside that argument, one thing was clear—Saul had done something forbidden by God, and he was destroyed the next day, along with his sons. 1 Samuel 31:2–6 states:

> And the Philistines followed hard upon Saul and upon his sons; and the Philistines slew Jonathan, and Abinadab, and Malchishua, Saul's sons. And the battle went sore against Saul, and the archers hit him; and he was sore wounded of the archers. Then said Saul unto his armourbearer, Draw thy sword, and thrust me through therewith; lest these uncircumcised come and thrust me through, and abuse me. But his armourbearer would not; for he was sore afraid. Therefore Saul took a sword, and fell upon it. And when his armourbearer saw that Saul was dead, he fell likewise upon his sword, and died with him. So Saul died, and his three sons, and his armourbearer, and all his men, that same day together.

A Stern Warning

In Leviticus 20:6, the Lord, warns:

> And the soul that turneth after such as have familiar spirits, and after wizards, to go a whoring after them, I will even set my face against that soul, and will cut him off from among his people.

The Lord had kept His word. I had learned something very devastating: mediums, witches, necromancers, and those who consult a familiar spirit all were in some way connected with communicating with the dead and all were condemned by God! He said that they were, "abominations to Him."

Would God condemn communicating with the dead and then in certain instances condone it? Would God use a method He detested to restore truth? Were all manifestations of the dead an abomination to God? I wasn't aware of any Scriptures in the Bible that supported "seeking after the dead," but there were Scriptures that condemned it.

Should we base truth on spiritual experiences or a visitation from the dead? Scripturally, it seems clear that we are to look to God's Word for guidance, not to the dead. Isaiah 8:19–20 reads:

> And when they shall say unto you, seek unto them that have familiar spirits, and unto wizards that peep, and that mutter: should not a people seek unto their God? For the living to the dead? To the law and to the testimony: if they speak not according to this word, it is because there is no light in them.

A clearer rendition of, "for the living to the dead," would be, "Why consult the dead on behalf of the living?"(NIV)

In the above passage, God tells us to turn to his Word in the law and the testimony (the first five books of the Bible and subsequent writings of the Old Testament prophets) rather than to the dead. If we speak not according to the Bible, there is no light in us. We are not to trust a messenger from the dead, nor seek to communicate with such a one.

Once again it was confirmed to me that the Bible is the cutting-edge sword we are to use to discern truth from error—not feelings or experiences.

Trying to Let Go of Dreams

Several months later, following a stake conference meeting, I sat and listened to my husband play some of my favorite, beloved Mormon hymns, as only he could play them. I loved these Mormon hymns. They had been expressions of my worship, love, and reverence for the Savior. I could not hold back my tears. I was emotionally tied to my church. My mind couldn't believe in it, but my emotions couldn't let go of it. I still loved the church and wanted it to be true, in spite of all I was learning and experiencing.

I loved the church music and had dreamed of my family doing music programs together—something we had started doing. So much more was involved in this than just losing my faith in Joseph Smith and my religion. My goals and dreams centered on my church. My family, my interests, my ties, my sense of value and belonging as an individual—everything, it seemed, was connected with my membership in the church.

As I sat sobbing, a comforting arm wrapped around my shoulder and gave me a hug. I looked up into the compassionate face of Patriarch Hall, a gentle man for whom I had great respect, especially since he was a stake patriarch. (A stake patriarch is considered to be one who lives close to the Lord and is inspired since he gives the members of the church their patriarchal blessings—a unique, inspired blessing and direction for each individual.) Patriarch Hall prayed with me and invited Charles and I to his home for a special blessing.

During the visit to his home, he advised me to go to the temple. I had not renewed my temple recommend because I knew in my heart I could not go through a temple session and still be honest with God or myself. I did agree, however, to visit the temple grounds with Charles.

A visit to the Temple

The following Friday evening Charles drove me to the Los Angeles temple in Santa Monica. Before going, I spent the day in fasting and prayer. We had gone through the temple so many times for our date night, but tonight we were just going to relax on the beautiful grounds outside the temple. Surprisingly, Charles was extremely understanding and accepting about my not wanting to go through the endowment ceremony. We spent some time in the visitor's center and watched a couple of videos. When we left the visitor's center it was almost dark. The lights on the temple made it shine with a bright white, as if it were lit from the inside. This made an incredibly beautiful sight against the navy blue sky. Even more impressive was the well-lit, shiny, gold-plated statue of the Angel Moroni atop the white spire, silhouetted against the deep sky.

Was he an angel or a familiar spirit? I silently wondered. *Was the gold image of Angel Moroni* (a deceased man who appeared to Joseph Smith as an angel) *a representation of communicating with spirits of the dead?* All the things I had learned about communicating with the dead were racing through my mind. There was no denying it. We definitely believed in communicating with the dead! My church was very involved with the dead. The temple was the heart of Mormonism, where vicarious work for the dead was continually performed. Not only did the dead appear in the temple, but every time after the first time we went through the temple endowment, we went as proxy for a dead person. We were given the name, birth date, and death date of a deceased person on a small piece of paper, which was pinned, to our sleeve. We thought of this person and their name as we went through the temple ceremony. We hoped they would receive the sacred endowment so they could be freed from spirit prison and continue on in their eternal progression. We didn't believe in mediums and séances, but we did believe in "seeking after our dead." Did the temple replace the medium?

As I stood in the cool night air, gazing up at the gold statue of Moroni, I couldn't imagine that God would condemn the practice of consulting the dead, then restore His church, the Book of Mormon, His truth, and the Priesthood, through deceased persons—especially since He'd said that communicating with the dead was an abomination to Him!

I also realized how biased I had always been in the past when condemning any appearances of the dead outside of the Mormon Church as demonic, and at the same time considering any such experience *within* the Mormon Church to be a highly spiritual experience from God. Was all this part of a mass counterfeit of Satan's spiritual world? The Bible says he does appear as an "angel of light" (2 Corinthians 11:14–15).

As the sky darkened, I stood staring at the gleaming white temple before me. I had been taught all my life that the temple was the most sacred place on earth. Now it reminded me of the pagan religions of Egypt and Babylon, with their glorious temples and connections with the dead.

Charles noticed the intense look of hurt on my face and suggested it was time to go home. I commented that the Angel Moroni reminded me of a golden image similar to the golden idols of pagan religions. Charles, who usually didn't speak when he was mad at me, obviously didn't like that. We had a very quiet ride home.

"And the soul that turneth after such as have familiar spirits, and after wizards, to go a whoring after them, I will even set my face against that soul, and will cut him off from among his people."

—Leviticus 20:6

C. APPENDIX TO CHAPTER SIXTEEN

From the *Autobiography of Nicholas Baker*, My Father

I remember my brother Berand, who was the first to die in our family. Berand was a very, very fine baby. But through an accident he became an invalid of mind (I guess you would call it). He never grew up mentally. He lived to be about twelve or thirteen years old.

I had nine brothers and sisters and we had a large table downstairs where we used to eat. This table was made of oak by my grandfather. We all used to sit around that table and eat together. One morning at breakfast, Berand spoke to mother. He said to her that he was going to be with us but thirty days and that grandfather, who had died, was going to come and get him. He said that his grandfather was building a beautiful white house for him and when he asked mother if she could see it and she said no, he became a little bit angry.

He said, "Why it is so plain and so beautiful." He told mother that he did not want her to grieve at his death because he would be completely free to go onward and upward and forward in the great eternal plan that our Heavenly Father had for him. The next morning he repeated the very same story, only he said that it was only twenty-nine days now. And so to the very end, each morning, thirty times, he told this story. Finally, on the last day he spoke.

"Now this is the day and tonight my grandfather shall come and get me," said Berand. Again, he asked mother not to grieve or worry, but to be happy with him.

On the back of our home we had a screen porch; the entire east was screened, the south side was screened, and the north side was screened. We had partitions in this porch that went downstairs. There was one bed on the south side of the porch. This is where my dad and mother slept. There were two beds on the north side and we children, some of us, used to sleep there.

Most of my life, or a great part of it, I slept outside in a tent or in an old milk wagon body or something like this. But this night mother and my brother Berand were sleeping in the bed on the south side. Father was sleeping in the bed on the north side, and grandmother was sleeping in the other bed on the north. They were talking back and forth to each other. Mother wished that when her father would come for Berand that the other two would be asleep, and she prayed that this would be. No sooner had she prayed than my father and grandmother fell asleep. Mother then looking to the south through the screen, saw her father standing in the air.

She said, "No, this can't be." She then looked to the east and her father moved to the east, still standing in the air. Then he came right in the porch. He stood beside the bed, north of the bed, in the air and looked at her with a wonderful smile. My brother looked at mother and smiled. My mother saw her father and my brother leave and disappear toward the skies. My mother prepared my brother for burial. None could ever tell her that there was no life after death. (*Autobiography of Nicholas Baker* pages 9–10)

CHAPTER 17

LETTING GO

"Shew me thy ways, O LORD; teach me thy paths. Lead me in thy truth, and teach me: for thou art the God of my Salvation; on thee do I wait all the day."

—*Psalm 25:4–5*

The roller coaster ride had returned and I was on an emotional downhill run. I seemed to plunge easily from mountaintop experiences with the Lord into cavernous lows with myself. Family members, understandably, were confused and frustrated. *What would become of me now*, I wondered.

Time to Resign

I could no longer in good conscience keep serving in my callings at the church. I was not currently serving in a leadership capacity or a teaching position (unusual for me), but I was still doing my visiting teaching, playing the piano for primary and other events, and leading the choir. This had to change now, I realized.

It was hard to quit my callings. I loved leading the choir, but I realized that I was sinning before God to continue serving in callings that I enjoyed when I no longer believed in the Mormon gospel. I was condoning and supporting something I did not believe in and, in so doing, I was being a hypocrite.

Up to this point I had consistently prayed that God would "straighten me out" if I were misunderstanding Him or being deceived in some way. I wanted to remain faithful in serving at church in order to give the Lord every opportunity to show me if I were wrong. But the Lord had put my feet on a new path and I needed to obey.

Taking a Stand Always Caused Trouble

When I resigned from all my callings Charles was very angry.

"I can't believe those Jehovah's Witnesses have messed you up so much," he said. "You don't even want to do a simple thing like play the sweet little primary songs for the children. I forbid you to talk to any of those Jehovah's Witnesses ever again! I don't ever want them in my home again. You call them right now and tell them so!"

It was extremely depressing to me to have my husband be mad at me. This had been a problem in our marriage—that it was always very hard for me to bear his rejection. But I had made a commitment to God. If only Charles and others would hear me when I told them that it was the Holy Spirit working through the Word of God that had changed me! Didn't they understand? They could lock me in a building and not let me talk to anyone and that would not cause me to believe in Joseph Smith again. It was the Lord that had changed me, and only the Lord could change me back if I were wrong. It was He that I was committed to follow. Yes, he had used Tobie and others to open my eyes, but now that my eyes were open, preventing me from talking to them and forcing me to talk only to Mormons was not going to give me back a testimony of Joseph Smith.

Out of respect for him, I did as my husband asked. I was glad, however, that Charles was still letting me talk with Seventh-day Adventists and my best friend, Tobie.

Conclusions about the Watchtower and Tract Society

Even though I was enjoying my discussions with the Jehovah's Witnesses I didn't feel that badly about discontinuing our talks because, in the course of our studies, I had concluded that they were not God's organization, as they claimed. I noticed that they too took Scripture out of context to defend some of their doctrines. Two examples would be the Witnesses' teaching that: 1) Jesus is Michael, the Archangel; and, 2) Jesus is not returning visibly to this earth but will be ruling from the heavens. I concluded that God's organization would not misinterpret His Word. [For a list of other things they teach that I did not think were biblical, see E. Appendix to Chapter Seventeen: Reasons Why I Eliminated the Jehovah's Witnesses as God's One True Organization on Earth.]

In addition to taking some Scriptures out of context, Jehovah's Witness leaders had given many false prophecies concerning the return of Jesus and the end of the world, qualifying them also as false prophets. Another reason I was ready to stop talking with the kind Jehovah's Witness couple that made their weekly visit was that they were very condemning towards the Seventh-day Adventists. When they found out that I was talking with Seventh-day Adventists and even attending some meetings there, they surprised me by turning to the passage that said, "Ye cannot be partakers of the Lord's table, and of the table of devils" (1 Corinthians 10:21b).

Personally, I felt the presence of the Holy Spirit with the Seventh-day Adventist people and I was learning a lot about the Bible from them. I did not appreciate the Jehovah's Witnesses referring to them as "the table of devils," nor did I ever again want to be locked into a religion that condemned all others. That condemning attitude had made me unteachable as a Mormon. Another denomination that promoted the belief that, "We're God's one and only true organization," wasn't for me! At this point I was confused as to just where and what Christ's true church was because they could not all be right. However, I now knew that God's people were not limited to the church membership rosters of one denomination. I also believed that God wanted me to learn about Himself from the people of more than one denomination at this time in my life.

Hence, even though I now saw that they were not God's one and only true organization, God had used the Jehovah's Witnesses to teach me important truths. The first and most significant one was that the Bible

221

in itself contained sufficient truth for mankind to find and obtain Salvation, and that I could trust it. Now, however, it was time to move on.

Telling My Family

Up to this point I had not been able to say aloud that I believed Joseph Smith was a false prophet. Charles knew that I doubted Joseph Smith, but he did not know the extent of my growing conviction that he was a false prophet, nor did my children know. I had decided it was time to tell my family that I did not believe in Joseph Smith. Actually, it was not I that had decided; the Lord laid a strong conviction upon me that I needed to do so. It was extremely difficult for me to verbalize that I thought Joseph Smith was a false prophet. Many people knew I was struggling with my testimony. That was one thing, but to flat out say that I no longer believed in Joseph Smith was something else again. One Sunday morning I woke up with a strong impression of the Holy Spirit. "Today is the day you must tell your family what you believe," He seemed to say.

I put it off all day. That night after church, Charles called us all together for a special Family Home Evening. Guess what he gave the lesson on? "Why Joseph Smith Was a True Prophet." I squirmed all through Charles' talk, silently having a conversation with the Lord in my thoughts.

"Lord, do I really have to contradict my husband and say my true feelings now?" I kept asking. "Isn't there an easier way? You really don't make things easy for me, Lord!"

Charles finished. It was time for treats, but I didn't want any. While everybody was eating, I managed to get it out.

"I'm sorry to disagree, but I don't believe Joseph Smith was a true prophet. I don't believe in him anymore. I believe he was a false prophet. I'm going to continue to go to other churches every weekend. I would like to invite you all to come with me."

There! I had said it! You could have cut the air with a knife. No one moved or said anything for a long moment. That was unusual at our house. I looked at Charles, but he would not look at me. I could see he was very upset. It wasn't news to Charles that I had many doubts and troubles about Joseph Smith, but to hear me say out loud that I did not believe in him, and voice it even to our children, was too much. He stormed out of the room. One by one my eight children left the room, also.

Two younger sons handed me their napkins as they silently left the room. I sat alone with a heavy heart, wondering if we would survive this. Then I noticed some writing on the two napkins my sons had given to me. They had each written that they would like to visit another church with me sometime. It was a ray of light to my burdened soul. I didn't believe for a minute that Charles would let them go to another church with me—but maybe, just maybe, someday.

Charles didn't speak to me for several days. Verbalizing my convictions had definitely erected a sword between us. It seemed too hard to deal with my husband's anger and rejection. I hated rejection. It was one thing I didn't handle very well. It made me terribly depressed.

Going Down

I started to ask that old familiar question that had caused me to go down hill emotionally before—*why? Why did this have to happen to my family? Why, God, do You ask such hard things of me? Hadn't I obeyed when You asked me to give up one-and-a-half years of my young adult life to serve a full-time mission in New Zealand?*

In order to be a missionary I sold my organ, the love of my life at that time, for You. I thought I had learned to let go of other worldly desires for You. I spent fourteen years of my life bearing nine children and providing bodies for Your spirit-children, because I believed that this was my duty as your handmaiden. (Our ninth baby died a few hours after his birth.) *I'm certainly glad I have those eight beautiful children, though, Lord. Thank you. I would not have had the courage to give birth to them if I had not believed I was doing it for You.*

But now I feel like You are asking me to give them up, too! To give up my church is hard enough, but my husband and eight children? This is too hard! This is unfair! All my life I have served you in the only way I knew— through the Mormon Church and my family. Now I feel as if I

223

have done all this for nothing. Now You are taking it all away from me. How could you do this to me, God?

I was convinced Charles was going to divorce me. The Bishop told him that he would be better off without me. How could he stay with me? According to his beliefs, he could never become a god if he stayed married to me. He needed to find someone else who was worthy of being a goddess with him in eternity. I certainly was no longer worthy. Yes, he was definitely justified in divorcing me through a Mormon's eyes. *How could God allow such a gulf to come between Charles and me at a time in our marriage when we were more in love and getting along better than we ever had before?* We had overcome many struggles in our marriage—now this? It was all just too much. Why did it have to be so hard to follow Jesus?

The Battle of the Will

All my life, since I was a child, I had sung the words of a familiar hymn that said, "I'll go where You want me to go, dear Lord; I'll be what You want me to be." Now I wondered if I really meant it. The congregation had sung it at my farewell, many years previous, as I apprehensively left for New Zealand to be a Mormon missionary. I had sung the verses and chorus with all my heart. Now I really wondered: *Was I fully committed to go where God wanted me to go? Could I?* He was calling me to go somewhere else. I didn't know where. I didn't want to leave my comfort zone—my family, my safe social life and friends, my dreams and goals, my lifestyle—my life itself. Could I sing the words, and mean them: "I'll go where You want me to go, dear Lord; I'll be what You want me to be."

It was so easy to feel sorry for myself and want to run from it all. *Maybe I didn't want to try to follow Jesus anymore. Maybe I was too weak to follow God. Maybe I didn't want truth.* I didn't want to admit it, but I was angry at God. *Maybe I would devote myself to worldly pursuits and fulfillments instead of seeking after God. After all, I had been a legal secretary before going on my mission. Yes, I could brush up on some skills, get a job, and make money. There were tangible rewards in pursuing the ways of the world—rewards like prestige, building my self-*

224

confidence, success, and things I'd wanted that money could buy. I could feel, touch, and have these things now, couldn't I?

I had other talents I'd abandoned in my life because I had devoted my time and energies to the church and to my family. *Maybe I'll go to college and study piano. That is what I wanted to do when I was young. Yes, that's what I'll do! I'm through with religion. Maybe if I give up trying to understand God and religions I could find fulfillment in the world and keep my family . . . .*

The more I entertained these thoughts, the darker my world became. The inner light, joy and peace that had filled my soul were being replaced with confusion and despair.

Struggle to Surrender

I was rebelling against God. My anger was a result of not being willing to let go of my family, my church, and my lifestyle. To do so felt like *dying to self.* A well-known Scripture came to mind. It was a declaration of Jesus to His listeners:

> If any man will come after me, let him deny himself, and take up his cross daily, and follow me. For whosoever will save his life shall lose it: but whosoever will lose his life for my sake, the same shall save it.
>
> —Luke 9:23–24

It was obvious that I wasn't worthy of Jesus. Oh, I thought I wanted to follow Jesus and be one of His sheep, but *was I willing to die to self and let go of everything that was my love and security in life?* I thought of my childhood memories and wondered what this would do to my parents. The thought of losing my husband and children was too much to bear!

I thought I had surrendered my life to God, but my will and my emotions were still bound to my flesh. I had asked for the truth and had given a promise to obey it, but now I didn't want to obey. I wanted it my way. It had been easy to surrender to God when I'd felt threatened with destruction by evil forces. I thought of myself as someone who had always wanted to follow Jesus. Now it was difficult to follow because I could see the cost. I wanted to be obedient, but could I be— at the expense of losing my family and everything I loved in this life? I was in a battle for my will, a battle to surrender my will to God's will. He wanted my worship and devotion from all three aspects of my being— not just my mind, not just my emotions, but also my will. As the Scripture says:

> And thou shalt love the Lord thy God with all thy heart, and with all thy soul, and with all thy mind, and with all thy strength: this is the first commandment.
>
> —Mark 12:30

I thought of the individuals in the church who had told me that if they were deceived they didn't want to know it. *Was I any different from them?* I had to be honest and admit it: I was not. I always thought I wanted the truth, regardless of the cost. I wanted to see myself as devoted to God and desirous to obey His will for my life. But now I was seeing and feeling a rebellious side of my nature, and it was manifesting itself loudly and clearly!

I felt like Peter, who had so boldly declared, "Though all men shall be offended because of thee, yet will I never be offended" (Matthew 26:33). That is, until the heat was on. Then, when asked by others, he denied three times that he even *knew* Jesus.

I realized I was just as weak. I had promised God that I would obey Him, but when it came to losing everything I didn't want to do it. I did not have the ability to do it. I was too weak. I was depressed and angry. My future seemed uncertain and terrifying.

The True Nature of the Flesh

My true nature had been exposed. The Lord was confirming a truth to me that I was hearing taught at the Christian churches—the truth that we are all sinners. We want to do it our way. We do not naturally surrender to God's will. I was beginning to understand certain passages in the Bible, such as Romans 3:10–11:

> As it is written, There is none righteous, no, not one. There is none that understandeth, there is none that seeketh after God.

It is easy to obey God when He asks us to do something we want to do, or some good deed for which we expect to be rewarded. However, when we are asked to give up what we love *the most*, our real nature is exposed.

That is why Jesus said, "No man can come to me, except the Father which hath sent me draw him: and I will raise him up at the last day" (John 6:44). The truth of the matter is that none of us has the ability to follow Christ unless the Father is working in us. It is He who gives us the faith, the desire, and the ability to obey and surrender to Him. God wants to be in a love relationship with us, one in which we love Him more than anything else. After all, He loves us so much He gave His only begotten Son to suffer and die for us. Should we not love Him more than all other things?

God's Strength, Not Mine

Paul said, "For when I am weak, then I am strong" (2 Corinthians 12:10). He knew this because the Lord had told him, "My grace is sufficient for you, for My strength is made perfect in weakness" (2 Corinthians 12:9).

What encouraging words! I pleaded with God to forgive me and have mercy on me, and that I may have the power of Christ rest upon me. When asked to surrender all that I loved and held dear, I was too weak to obey and follow God without His empowering strength. Thank goodness for God's grace—His love that we do not deserve! In my struggle, I was to learn an important truth: He gives us His strength when we are weak.

Broken

My strong, self-centered will was broken by the power of God's Word. Jeremiah 23:29 says, "Is not my word like as a fire? saith the LORD; and like a hammer that breaketh the rock in pieces?"

I had resisted and rebelled, but I soon realized I needed to surrender all. I had no choice. I knew that from now on life would be horrible and dark if I didn't. Jesus had been tugging, now pulling, on the strings of my soul and I could go no other way but towards Him. I wanted to keep my promise to obey God. *How could I not obey Him?* If I did not, I would be miserable in this life, as well as face a fearful judgment in the resurrection. I realized I couldn't live in rebellion to God. The pursuit of worldly wealth and pleasures could never make me happy without Him. At the same time I realized I could not obey God in my own strength. I could only obey and surrender to Him by the power of His strength working in me. Yielding to this process in prayer, I was a rock broken in pieces, and then put back together by God's power. Jesus' words describe it best:

> Abide in me, and I in you. As the branch cannot bear fruit of itself, except it abide in the vine; no more can ye, except ye abide in me. I am the vine, ye are the branches: He that abideth in me, and I in him, the same bringeth forth much fruit: for without me ye can do nothing.
> —John 15:4–5

Convicted

Christ's words convicted me even more as I read:

> He that loveth father or mother more than me is not worthy of me: and he that loveth son or daughter more than me is not worthy of me.
> —Matthew 10:37

That was a strong Scripture for one who had always been taught that Father in Heaven expected me to put my family first—especially since I had been taught all my life that the family was an eternal unit and was necessary for my exaltation. *Did this Scripture really mean what it seemed to say? Was I required to give up my family, if necessary, to follow Jesus and be His true disciple?*

Yes, His Word was breaking me. Another passage of Scripture convicted me still more:

> And Jesus said unto him, No man, having put his hand to the plough, and looking back, is fit for the Kingdom of God.
> —Luke 9:62

"Lord, please forgive me for being so selfish and wanting things my way," I prayed. "Please forgive me for being so stubborn and resisting

You so much. Thank you for allowing me to be in darkness when I was
turning from You. Thank You for disciplining me and not letting me fail
to keep the promise I made to You. Please help me to let go. I can't do it
on my own! I need You to do it through me. I am too weak. I love my
family too much. I don't want to live without them. Please help me to
give them to You. I am weak, but You are strong. I can only do what
You are asking of me with Your strength. Help me to not look back, but
to walk the path upon which You have set my feet. I want You, Jesus, to
be Lord of my life. Help me to walk in Your light and to let go of the
things that I am hanging onto so tightly. Give me the ability to lose even
that which is dearest, that which is my life, in order to follow You. In
Jesus Name, Amen."

Surrender Brings Peace

Because of God's grace working in me I was finally able to
relinquish my family and become willing even to lose them. Struggling
in deep prayer, when the time came that I was really able to give them up
in order to follow Jesus, the Holy Spirit flooded me with a calm peace
and love. I was comforted by an inward voice that spoke encouragingly
to me.

"I will take care of you," He said. *"What is required of you is
patience and trust. Trust Me!"*

I was comforted. Once again the Lord had forgiven me for my
rebellious attitude and filled me with His grace, His love, and His light.
In His mercy, He'd pulled me out of the darkness into which my
rebellion had plunged me.

Holding On to Promises

I did not know what the outcome to all this was going to be. I could
not see any light at the end of the tunnel. However, I knew that God was
with me and that He had once again given me *enough* light to walk in, as
well as His strength in order to move forward one step at a time. The
light didn't shine very far ahead, but it shone far enough for me to take
steps of faith, sometimes very tiny steps. The Lord gave me the strength

not to give up but to look to Him. I knew I needed to get my focus on Jesus and His promises:

> And every one that hath forsaken houses, or brethren, or sisters, or father, or mother, or wife, or children, or lands, for my name's sake, shall receive an hundredfold, and shall inherit everlasting life.
>
> —Matthew 19:29

God had called me onto a new path and a new walk with Him—a path that assured me of eternal life, but one that also required I let go of my tight grasp on this life.

> *"For whosoever will save his life shall lose it: but whosoever will lose his life for my sake, the same shall save it."*
>
> *—Luke 9:24*

D. APPENDIX TO CHAPTER SEVENTEEN

Reasons Why I Eliminated the Jehovah's Witnesses as God's One True Organization on Earth

1. The Jehovah's Witness organization teaches that Jesus is Michael, the Archangel.

2. They deny that Jesus ascended into heaven with a physical body. They do not believe that He was resurrected with His own personal body, but that He temporarily materialized and dematerialized a body on the occasions that his disciples saw him after the resurrection. They state that He did this in order to convince His disciples He had risen from the dead.

3. The Jehovah's Witnesses teach that the second coming of Jesus will not be visible, but will be invisible. He will not reign on this earth physically but will rule from the heavens as a spirit. Acts 1:9–11 says Jesus, "will so come in like manner as you saw Him go into heaven." In spite of this Scripture, they still insist we will not see Him. Also, Revelation 1:7 says, "Behold, He is coming with clouds, and every eye will see Him, even they who pierced Him." The Witnesses believe "see" means to comprehend with the "eyes of understanding," but not with literal eyesight. The founders of the Watchtower Bible and Tract Society (now Jehovah's Witnesses) taught that Christ's second coming (invisible) occurred in October, 1874. Therefore, Jesus is now present, and His Kingdom is being established through their organization (*Studies in the*

Scriptures, Volume 4, p. 621.)

4.   In Witness theology the saved are divided into two groups. Only 144,000, who have a special anointing, will go to heaven. They will rule with Jesus from heaven. The rest of the saved will be on Paradise Earth and will not live in the presence of Jesus. (Alex, the Jehovah's Witness gentleman who visited our home *claimed* to be one of the 144,000. He was convinced that he had been called through a spiritual experience. I tried to get him to give me the details, but he never did.)

In Revelation 7:2–8, we are told that the 144,000 will be Jews— 12,000 from each tribe of Israel. Also, John's Revelation tells us that these will be sealed during the Tribulation period, which hasn't happened yet.

5.   Witnesses believe that Satan is in control of all governments. This they determine from some of the wording of Christ's temptation: "Again, the devil took Him up on an exceedingly high mountain, and showed Him all the Kingdoms of the world and their glory. And he said to Him, 'All these things I will give you if You will fall down and worship me' " (Matthew 4:8–9).

Even though Satan claimed to have the power to give the kingdoms of the world to Jesus, we need to remember that he is a liar. It is true that Satan was given temporary rule over this current system of things when Adam and Eve obeyed him rather than God. However, God is still sovereign. Daniel 4:31b says: "Seven times shall pass over you, until you know that the Most High rules in the Kingdom of men, and gives it to whomever He chooses." Also, Romans 13:1 says, "Let every soul be subject to the governing authorities. For there is no authority except from God, and the authorities that exist are appointed by God."

6.   The Witnesses say that saluting the flag is worshiping it, and they quote the second commandment to support this belief. I don't believe that saluting, or *showing honor to*, the flag is the same as making a graven image and bowing down and worshiping it.

7.   *Watchtower* founder Charles Taze Russell and other leaders have set different dates for "end time" events that have failed to take place, particularly predictions concerning the year 1914, which can be summarized as follows:

   a.   According to Russell, the great battle of God Almighty, as spoken of in Revelation 16, was to end in 1914, resulting in a complete overthrow of earth's present rulership. (*The Time is at Hand*, 1889, p. 101.)

   b.   In 1917, Russell changed this prophecy to say that 1914 became the year for the beginning of the "Day of God's Wrath" or the Battle of Armageddon. (*Pastor Russell's Sermons*, 1917, p. 676.)

   c.   Then, 1925 was the year set for the time when the world would end. Also, Abraham, Isaac, Jacob, and other prophets of old were to return. (*The Watchtower*, September 1, 1922, p. 262; *The Watchtower*, April 1, 1923, p. 106.)

   d.   In 1940 the group believed that Armageddon was very near and that the glorious reign of Christ would immediately follow. (*Informant*, May, 1940; July, 1940; *The Messenger*, September 1, 1940, p. 6.)

   e.   Then, World War II was thought to be Armageddon. (*Consolation*, October 29, 1941, p. 11.)

f.   In 1968, since the predicted events had not happened, they taught that the Kingdom of God went into operation in 1914. (*The Truth that Leads to Eternal Life*, 1968, p. 92, 93.)

[I extracted the above references from photocopies of these predictions from *Witnessing to the Witnesses*, by Jerry & Marian Bodine, pages 12, 14, 17–19, 25, 26. Also, a devout, knowledgeable Jehovah Witness friend affirmed the statements and references as accurate.]

CHAPTER 18

TIME TO REREAD
THE BOOK OF MORMON

*"And ye shall seek me, and find me, when ye shall
search for me with all your heart."*

—*Jeremiah 29:13*

Since I had verbalized my disbelief in Joseph Smith, Charles was
very hurt and angry. His decree that I could not speak to the Jehovah's
Witnesses soon included a ban on communication with my friend, Tobie,
as well. Charles was getting desperate. He stated that I could not see
Tobie or talk to her—not on the phone, nor through letters. Absolutely no
contact! My friend and I were both extremely saddened by this. Of
course, Tobie thought it was ridiculous.

"How long is this going to last?" she asked me.

"I have no idea," was my answer. "But I think it is important that we
oblige Charles. Maybe he will realize that it is not people that have
changed me, but the Lord."

"Well, I'll go along with it, although I don't want to," Tobie
responded. "I hope it will not be for very long."

We expressed our love to each other, gave one another a hug, and
said goodbye. Little did I know what it would take for Charles to let me
see Tobie again.

Time to Be Influenced Only by God

I felt sad that I could not see Tobie anymore. However, I knew God was with me and I treasured time alone with Him. My life was extremely busy with my large family and I needed more time to be with God, uninfluenced by others. I still had many questions and so much to learn, but one unanswered question bothered me deeply: What about the Book of Mormon? Was it of God, or not? It was time to get alone with the Lord and seek His truth about the Book of Mormon. After all, as a young missionary I had once gotten that good feeling that I'd interpreted to be the Holy Ghost confirming its truthfulness. If Joseph Smith were not a true prophet, as I now believed, what about the Book of Mormon?

I needed to read and pray about the Book of Mormon, the Doctrine & Covenants, and the Pearl of Great Price. After all, these LDS Scriptures were the fruit of Joseph Smith. Jesus had said that we would know a true prophet from a false prophet by his fruit (Matthew 7:15–20). It was time to prayerfully study the fruit of Joseph Smith.

The Key to a Testimony

The Book of Mormon is the foundation of a testimony of the LDS Church. If the Book of Mormon is true, then Joseph Smith is a true prophet and the LDS church is true. That is what we were taught. That is how it worked, without question. That is why it was now so important for me to read the Book of Mormon and pray about it again. When that good feeling comes, you (as a Mormon) know it is the Holy Ghost confirming the truthfulness of the Book of Mormon. Therefore, one does not doubt Joseph Smith or the church after receiving that witness, lest he be sinning against the Holy Ghost.

Subjective Experiences with the Book of Mormon

I had gotten "that good feeling" when I'd prayed about the Book of Mormon as a young missionary in New Zealand over twenty years earlier. I still remember that morning. I was kneeling by my bed, praying for a confirmation from the Holy Ghost that the Book of Mormon was true. While reading in the Book of Mosiah and meditating on its message of serving others, a unique, good feeling came over me. It was a happy, rather euphoric feeling. I even felt a little dizzy as I rested my head on the side of the bed. I had gotten what I'd wanted, had asked for, and been anxiously awaiting.

Even now I had not forgotten that experience and I wasn't going to deny it. But now I realized more than ever that Satan's falsehoods are often accompanied by good feelings and experiences that seem beautiful. A subjective experience was not a sufficient test for truth. For the past twenty plus years, I'd believed that that feeling was the Holy Ghost confirming the truthfulness of the Book of Mormon to me. Was it?

I also remember that I needed that testimony of the Book of Mormon so I could say publicly that, "I know Joseph Smith was a true prophet and that the LDS Church is the only true church on the face of the earth today." Missionaries didn't say, "I *believe* Joseph Smith was a true prophet." They said, "I *know* . . . ."

There were places in our missionary discussions where we were supposed to bear strong testimony to the investigators that we were teaching. This had presented a problem for me as a new missionary in New Zealand because I wasn't just going to say, "I know these things are true," without that confirmation from the Holy Ghost. The first few months in the mission field I was feeling rather frustrated because I had not received that special witness from the Holy Ghost about the Book of Mormon. I was intensely seeking some kind of spiritual manifestation about the truthfulness of the book. Each morning as I read in the Book of Mormon I expected something to happen. After several weeks I was getting anxious and asking Father in Heaven when He was going to give me that special witness that I was fully expecting, and I *did* get it— a unique spiritual sign I had been seeking! Now as a missionary I could say, "I know Joseph Smith is a true prophet, the Church is true, and the Book of Mormon is true." And I did for the next two decades.

Looking at the Book of Mormon Objectively

In addition to the subjective reasons for believing in the Book of

Mormon, I believed in it because it did not seem logical that Joseph Smith could have just written the Book of Mormon. That seemed unreasonable. Could an unschooled twenty-three-year-old write such a book? The Book of Mormon was more than a religious book; it claimed to be a history of the ancient inhabitants of America—the descendants of which are the American Indians. I also believed in the Book of Mormon because it said so many good things about Jesus.

Remembering a Second Experience with the Book of Mormon

I read in the Book of Mormon frequently, but I had only read it from beginning to end as a personal study twice. Church leaders, of course, stressed reading the Book of Mormon in order to get closer to God. Joseph Smith had said:

> I told the brethren that the Book of Mormon was the most correct of any book on earth, and the keystone of our religion, and a man would get nearer to God by abiding by its precepts than any other book.
> —*History of the Church*, 4:461

The leaders of the church also promised that we would reap family blessings from reading the Book of Mormon. We did read from the Book of Mormon as a family and we faithfully held our Family Home Evenings every Monday night. We were told that these activities would help to bring peace and harmony to our homes. Still, we had too much contention in our home, and I was going through some depression at that time (around 1979, about fifteen years after serving my mission and five years prior to the current time). So, I reread the Book of Mormon, believing it would bring peace and love to my family and help me feel closer to God.

I was disappointed, as well as bewildered, that upon finishing the Book of Mormon I did not feel any better—nor did it ease my depression, nor did it help the sibling rivalry and spirit of discord in our home. Because I had not received the spiritual blessings I had been promised from reading the Book of Mormon at that time, I wondered what was wrong with me. The answer to this question also did not come.

Now, since I was trying to understand my Mormon testimony, as well as my dad's, I knew it was time to reread the Book of Mormon and pray about it for the third time. It was very important for me to be open-minded and to seek the truth.

A Brief Summary of the Book of Mormon

According to the account written in the Book of Mormon, ancient prophets on the American continent wrote this history, covering a thousand years (from 600 B.C. until 421 A.D.). Mormon, the final leader of the Nephite armies, abridged this history, engraved it on gold plates, and called it the Book of Mormon (Mormon 1:1). (However, the first part of the Book of Mormon is not an abridgment, but the original writings of Nephi and some brief writings of others.)

These people originated from a family living in Jerusalem. Lehi, the father, was commanded to take his wife and sons and leave Jerusalem. Ishmael's family left with them and his daughters provided wives for Lehi's sons. They were commanded to build a boat and cross the ocean to a new Promised Land.

After arriving in the Promised Land (somewhere in the Americas, possibly Central America), they were divided into two nations—the Lamanites (descendants of Lamon and Lemuel, two sons of Lehi), and the Nephites (the descendants of Nephi and the other sons of Lehi). The Nephites were basically good. The Lamanites were rebellious and wicked and were thus cursed with a dark skin.

In the end, the Lamanite Nation annihilated the Nephite Nation. Moroni, Mormon's son, was the sole survivor of the Nephites. He finished the record on gold plates that his father Mormon had abridged. Before he died, he buried these gold plates in the ground, in about the year 421 A.D. Fourteen hundred years later, Moroni appeared to Joseph Smith as an angel and told him that he had buried this ancient history recorded on gold plates in the Hill Cumorah, not far from Joseph's home in New York State. The Angel Moroni visited Joseph Smith once a year for four years. Then Joseph Smith was allowed to retrieve the gold plates from their burial spot. Joseph then translated them from Reformed

Egyptian into English.

One part of the Book of Mormon, the Book of Ether, is the record of another nation, the *Jaredites*. They, it said, had migrated across the ocean to America from the Old World at the time of the building of the Tower of Babel.

One or the Other?

The Book of Mormon definitely was a challenge to the world. It didn't seem possible to me that Joseph Smith could have just made it up claiming it to be a history, and had millions of people (including myself) take it so *seriously*. If it were not a true history of the inhabitants of the American continent written by God's prophets and translated by Joseph Smith, then what was it and where did it come from?

When it comes to the claims of the Book of Mormon, there is no in between: It is either a true history inspired by God, or it is not!

Remembering Questions from My Youth

Although I had gleaned many good teachings from the Book of Mormon in my life, there had been many times (especially as a teenager) that I had been intellectually troubled with questions about the Book of Mormon for which I had never received satisfactory answers. However, once I'd had my subjective experience, I no longer allowed these questions to bother me. I buried them and didn't allow them to surface again. I focused on the positive teaching, especially about the Savior and salvation. After all, I knew the Book of Mormon was true because I had prayed about it and had received my answer.

Now, however, these questions were looming up like giants, and I could not just stuff them down anymore. Following are a few of my questions:

1. If the Book of Mormon is a history, where is the historical evidence for it? There is an abundance of historical evidence outside of the Bible to support it as a true history of the Jews. On the contrary, there is no historical evidence for the existence of the Nephite, Lamanite, or Jaredite nations.

The same could be said for scientific and archaeological evidences. Despite great efforts of LDS scholars to uncover archaeological findings to support the account given in the Book of Mormon, no substantial evidence exists.

For years Mormon scholars have suggested the location of the Book of Mormon lands to be in South and Central America, and have tried to make some connection with the Incan and Mayan ruins in these areas. However, no parallel with any names, places, dates, or religious practices that would link these civilizations with the Book of Mormon has been found.

As a matter of fact, Charles and I had been blessed several years previously to visit the archaeological site of the Pre-Columbian city of Chichen Itza in the Yucatan Peninsula. We were on a company trip to Cancun and we were very excited to take the expedition to the site. We believed the famous ruins of Chichen Itza were evidences of the existence of the Book of Mormon civilization. Years before as a missionary, I had an LDS published book compiled by Milton R Hunter (a General Authority) which contained pictures of these amazing structures in Chichen Itza. This book strongly indicated that these were ruins from the Book of Mormon civilization. I had shown this book to investigators to hopefully convince them of the truthfulness of the Book of Mormon. Needless to say, Charles and I thought we were going to see archeological evidences that would validate the Book of Mormon. However, we were shocked to learn that the Mayan civilization was completely pagan and idolatrous. They were as far removed from Christianity as they could be. The Book of Mormon is about Jesus Christ. We saw no connection with their culture and the Book of Mormon—not historically, geographically, archeo-logically, or religiously.

You can see a picture of Charles and I in front of the famous El

Castillo Pyramid in Chichen Itza if you visit my website, MormonismToGrace.com

2. If the Book of Mormon is a history, where are the maps? Where are the towns and rivers? Where are the Book of Mormon lands? Geographically speaking, no one has ever been able to pinpoint the location of these two great nations that thrived for a thousand years. One can go visit Jerusalem, the River Jordan, the Sea of Galilee and other New Testament places, as well as Old Testament places much older than the Book of Mormon lands. Bible locations are real places that exist and are represented on the maps of today. Where are the towns, rivers, and places mentioned in the Book of Mormon; and where is the "narrow neck of land" that divided the Sea East from the Sea West, and connected the land northward with the land southward? (Alma 22:32)

LDS scholars have speculated that the Isthmus of Panama or the Isthmus of Tehuantepec could be the "narrow neck of land" and the location for the Book of Mormon story. However, both of these locations present serious problems and are not compatible with the description of the "narrow neck of land" in the Book of Mormon. For example, if the Isthmus of Panama is the "narrow neck of land" connecting the Land Northward with the Land Southward we have a problem. This isthmus that connects Central America with South America is 300 miles in length. Alma 22:32 states that a Nephite could cross the "narrow neck of land" by foot in a day and a-half.

We were told that Father in Heaven wanted us to accept the Book of Mormon by faith, not evidence. Yet, He left plenty of evidence to help us believe in the Bible.

[It was a few years after this time that I did learn of a geographical area that does fit the Book of Mormon description of the "Narrow Neck of Land." It was quite an eye-opener. This discovery and many other surprising discoveries including writings of Joseph Smith's day were confirmation that the Book of Mormon was not history, but was a product of Joseph Smith's environment - which is something that I did not learn about until later. See Volume 2, Chapter 16 for more details.]

3.   If these people lived in Central and South America, how did the gold plates end up getting buried in upstate New York? That was a long way for Moroni to travel by himself without modern transportation!

4.   Joseph Smith claimed the engravings upon the gold plates were written in *Reformed Egyptian*. Why is it that no one has ever heard of the existence of a Reformed Egyptian language? Also, why would these Hebrew prophets who came from Jerusalem in 600 B.C., be writing their sacred record in any form of Egyptian writing rather than their own Hebrew language?

5.   I had other questions that related to the secrecy of the gold plates and their translation. Why did Joseph Smith always have a curtain between himself and his scribe as he dictated the words of the Book of Mormon? Why did Joseph Smith have to always have a scribe? Why couldn't he write the translation in English himself as he read the engravings on the gold plates? Why was no one ever allowed to see the plates when he was translating them or at any other time that they were in his possession? Even his wife was never allowed to see them. Only the witnesses were allowed to see them after the translating was finished. The Angel Moroni had taken them to heaven, but he returned to show them to the witnesses. However, one of them referred to this experience as a vision, and said that they saw the plates with their spiritual eyes.

I had been taught in my high school seminary class that Emma Smith, Joseph's wife, stated that Joseph could translate even when the plates were hidden in a log in the woods. Was Joseph

Smith really translating from an unknown language, or was the Book of Mormon given to him as inspiration?

6. Why was the Book of Mormon so much like the Bible—written in the King James language with many quotes taken from the Bible?

I had stuffed and ignored these and many more questions for years.

Earnestly Desiring the Truth

Yes, it was time for me to read the Book of Mormon from cover to cover for the third time and earnestly and sincerely ask God to enlighten me about it. *Was it really a translation of an ancient record of history in the Americas? Was it really written by prophets of God two thousand years ago?*

Was the Book of Mormon the most correct book on earth—even more correct than the Bible? Was it translated by the gift and power of God (as the introduction to the Book of Mormon stated?)

I knew God had the answers about the Book of Mormon, and I wanted the truth from Him and trusted that He would reveal the truth to me. Also, one thing was different this time from the other times I had read and prayed about the Book of Mormon. This time my mind was not already made up as to what I wanted God to tell me. I really wanted God to speak to me about the truthfulness or falsehood of the Book of Mormon. This time I asked God to help me to recognize the truth about the Book of Mormon, rather than asking "to know that it is true," as I had done twenty years earlier as a missionary.

A True History?

I was amazed as I read through the book prayerfully from cover to cover. I had never noticed so many problems before. Actually, it read more like a novel than a history covering a thousand years. For instance, in the second chapter of Helaman, we are introduced to Gadianton who becomes the leader of a band of robbers and murderers. We read more about these Gadianton robbers in Third Nephi (1:27, 29; 2:11, 12, 18) and also in Mormon's own ending history account (Mormon 1:18; 2:27–28). This may not appear to be strange until we realize that approximately four hundred years of history lapsed between the events of these books within the Book of Mormon. Four hundred years is a long time for a band of robbers to be functioning, even if it was comprised of descendants or a group carrying the same name. Think about it. In today's terms, the same group of murderers and thieves that existed in the 1600s (when the Pilgrims landed at Plymouth Rock) would still be committing crimes today!

Mormon affirms that this is the same band of Gadianton robbers and murderers. In his abridgment of the Nephite record, he introduces Gadianton and his band of robbers and murderers in the book of Helaman (chapter 2:4, 11) which takes place in 50 B.C. (noted on the bottom of p. 371, 1981 edition). On the next page, Mormon inserts the following personal note:

> And more of this Gadianton shall be spoken hereafter. And thus ended the forty and second year of the reign of the judges over the people of Nephi. And behold, in the end of this book ye shall see that this Gadianton did prove the overthrow, yea, almost the entire destruction of the people of Nephi.
>
> —Helaman 2:12–13

Mormon then clarifies that he does not mean the end of the book of Helaman, but the end of his Nephite record he is abridging (the Book of Mormon). Mormon lived in the fourth century A.D. and finished his record of his people around 350 A.D. (Book of Mormon, Mormon 2:17,18; 1981 ed., p. 471). Then he writes his own account of current history (the end of the Nephite nation) which includes the Gadianton robbers still alive and well.

Spurious Stories

Following are two more examples of unusual events that I noticed as I read the Book of Mormon:

1. **Laban and Nephi**

   In 1 Nephi, chapter four, Nephi is going to Jerusalem, to Laban's house, to obtain the plates of brass from Laban in order to take them on their journey to the new Promised Land. Nephi and his brothers had already tried to get the brass plates, but Laban had refused to give the plates to them. Instead, Laban confiscated their property and tried to kill them. However, it was very important that they obtain these brass plates because they contained the record of the Jews and the law. So Nephi returns to Jerusalem with faith that God will help him obtain these records. As he enters Jerusalem and comes near to Laban's house, he finds Laban lying on the ground, drunk with wine. He is prompted by the Spirit of the Lord to take Laban's sword and cut off his head, which he does. Nephi states, "I did obey the voice of the spirit, and took Laban by the hair of the head, and I smote off his head with his own sword." (1 Nephi 4:18)

   Now the story gets rather questionable. Again I quote the words of Nephi: "And after I had smitten off his head with his own sword, I took the garments of Laban and put them upon mine own body; yea, even every whit; and I did gird on his armor about my loins." (1 Nephi 4:19)

   After decapitating Laban, he removes Laban's armor and clothes, then puts them on himself. My question is, "What happened to the blood?" Would it be possible to undress someone (including his heavy armor) who'd just had his head chopped off without getting blood all over his clothes and armor? That doesn't seem to be a problem for Nephi because he goes into the treasury of Laban wearing the king's clothes and armor! Then, in the voice of Laban, he fools Laban's servant into thinking that he is Laban. Zoram, the servant, gives Nephi the brass plates and then follows Nephi out of the city, thinking he is Laban. I should think that Nephi would have looked rather conspicuous dressed in Laban's bloody clothes!

2. **The Story of Shiz**

In a battle between Shiz and Coriantumr, Shiz faints for lack of blood. Coriantumr cuts off the head of Shiz, then, "Shiz raised up on his hands and fell: and after that he had struggled for breath, he died." (Ether 15:29–31) How does one rise up on his hands and "struggle for breath" without a head? This is even more incredible since Shiz had fainted for lack of blood first!

Doctrinal Challenges

There were also doctrinal problems that jumped off the pages of the Book of Mormon as I prayerfully read it. It is not my intention to list them all here, but I will mention a few:

1. **One God, or Three Gods?**

In several places, the Book of Mormon says there is only one God and refers to the Father, the Son, and the Holy Ghost as one God (2 Nephi 31:21, Alma 11:44, Mormon 7:7, as well as at the end of the testimony of the three witnesses in the introduction of the Book of Mormon.) This is a contradiction to Mormon doctrine. Joseph Smith clearly taught that the Father, the Son, and the Holy Ghost are three gods.[26] (See endnote on pages 357-358 for this statement by Joseph Smith and for passages from the Book of Mormon.)

The passages from the Book of Mormon listed above do not just say that the Father and Son are one, which I had been taught meant that they are one in purpose, but these verses state that *they* are one God. Three of these four passages even use the singular verb "is," which indicates one, singular God. It seemed strange to me that I had read the Book of Mormon twice before and never noticed this contradiction.

2. **Is Jesus Both the Father *and* the Son?**

A significant doctrine in the church that was demonstrated by the first vision of Joseph Smith when both the Father and the Son appeared to Joseph Smith, was that they were two distinct personages. Yet, Mosiah 15:1–5 in the Book of Mormon implies that Jesus is both the Father *and* the Son. Specifically, it says: "And now Abinadi said unto them: I would that ye should understand that God himself shall come down among the children of men, and shall redeem his people."

I noticed that this verse refers to Jesus as "God himself." But the next few verses became even more explicit that Jesus is both the Father and the Son. "And because he dwelleth in flesh he shall be called the Son of God, and having subjected the flesh to the will of the Father, being the Father and the Son— the Father, because he was conceived by the power of God, and the Son, because of the flesh; thus becoming the Father and Son—they are one God, yea, the very Eternal Father of heaven and of earth. And thus the flesh becoming subject to the Spirit, or the Son to the Father, being one God, suffereth temptation, and yieldeth not to the temptation, but suffereth himself to be mocked, and scourged, and cast out, and disowned by his people." (Mosiah 15:2–5)

This passage was not new to me. I'd first had it pointed out when I was a missionary by an investigator. It confused me at the time, but my mission president explained that it meant that Jesus was our father in a spiritual sense because He overcame death for us, but it did not mean that he was God, the Father. He then turned to Mosiah 5:7, which says: "And now, because of the covenant which ye have made ye shall be called the children of Christ, his sons, and his daughters; for behold, this day he hath spiritually begotten you."

I had always been taught that I was spiritually begotten by Heavenly Father and was His child, but I'd never really heard the teaching in the church that I was spiritually begotten by Christ.

Anyway, I'd tried to accept my mission president's explanation and stuff down the fact that the verses in Mosiah 15:1–5 still bothered me. After all, I had gotten that good feeling about the Book of Mormon, so it was not appropriate for me to doubt or question.

However, it now appeared clear to me that whoever had authored the Book of Mormon believed that Jesus was both the Father and the Son, and that they are one God. Ether 3:14 says: "Behold, I am Jesus Christ. I am the Father and the Son."

This was definitely not Mormon doctrine and I could no longer accept explanations that seemed to deny what the Book of Mormon really said.

3. Does God the Father Have a Body of Flesh and Bone, or Is He Spirit?

The Book of Mormon contradicted another foundational LDS doctrine that was a result of Joseph Smith's first vision. This was the Mormon doctrine that the Father and Son both have bodies of flesh and bone. Through modern-day revelation Joseph Smith had said: "The Father has a body of flesh and bone as tangible as man's; the Son also; but the Holy Ghost has not a body of flesh and bone, but is a personage of Spirit." (Doctrine & Covenants 130:22)

Yet the Book of Mormon contradicts Joseph Smith. It never teaches that God the Father has a body of flesh and bone, but it does say God is a Great Spirit:

"And Ammon began to speak unto him with boldness, and said unto him: Believest thou that there is a God? And he answered, and said unto him: I do not know what that meaneth. And then Ammon said: Believest thou that there is a Great Spirit? And he said, Yea. And Ammon said: This is God. And Ammon said unto him again: Believest thou that this great Spirit, who is God, created all things which are in heaven and in the earth?" (Book of Mormon; Alma 18:24–28)

4. Was God Once a Man Who Changed and Became God, or Is He a God Who Never Changes?

I knew that only one of these could be true. Joseph Smith had said: "God himself was once as we are now, and is an exalted man, and sits enthroned in yonder heavens! That is the great secret." (*Teachings of the Prophet Joseph Smith*, p. 345)

The Book of Mormon says: "For do we not read that God is the same yesterday, today, and forever, and in him there is no variableness, neither shadow of changing?" (Mormon 9:9)

Joseph Smith said: "In order to understand the subject of the dead, for consolation of those who mourn for the loss of their friends, it is necessary we should understand the character and being of God and how he came to be so; for I am going to tell you how God came to be God. We have imagined and supposed that God was God from all eternity. I will refute that idea, and take away the veil, so that you may see." (*Teachings of the Prophet Joseph Smith*, p. 345)

The Book of Mormon says: "For I know that God is not a partial God, neither a changeable being, but he is unchangeable from all eternity to all eternity." (Moroni 8:18)

5. Does God Dwell Within Believers, or Does He Not?

Through modern-day revelation Joseph Smith had said: "John 14:23. The appearing of the Father and the Son, in that verse, is a personal appearance; and the idea that the Father and the Son dwell in a man's heart is an old sectarian notion, and is false." (Doctrine & Covenants 130:3)

The Book of Mormon says: "And this I know, because the Lord hath said he dwelleth not in unholy temples, but in the hearts of the righteous doth he dwell . . ." (Alma 34:36)

I cannot here mention the numerous other problems I became aware of as I read the Book of Mormon with a sincere desire to know God's truth about the book. I'd surrendered my life to Him, and now He had opened my eyes to discrepancies in the text that before I could not see, or maybe did not want to see. One thing was evident: the Book of Mormon did not teach Mormon doctrine—and even contradicted some of Joseph Smith's revelations.

1 Corinthians 14:33 says, "For God is not the author of confusion." Joseph Smith and the Book of Mormon made it seem as if God were confused about Himself.

The Absence of a Witness

The greatest impact on me, however, at this time was the spiritual aspect of the book. I had received no witness that it was true, in spite of the promise in Moroni 10:4.

> And when ye shall receive these things, I would exhort you that ye would ask God, the Eternal Father, in the name of Christ, if these things are not true; and if ye shall ask with a sincere heart, with real intent, having faith in Christ, he will manifest the truth of it unto you, by the power of the Holy Ghost.

I certainly had a sincere desire in my heart to know the truth about the Book of Mormon. I certainly had real intent, and my faith in Christ was stronger than ever. I trusted the Holy Ghost to open my eyes to the truth about the Book of Mormon. I was not influenced by any other source now. It was the Book of Mormon, the Lord, and me.

Nevertheless, I received no witness from the Holy Ghost that it was true. Quite the contrary, after reading the text through again, I was convinced that it was *not* a sacred, true, historical record. In summary, the Book of Mormon did not appear in any way to be an ancient history book. It seemed more like a fictitious novel to me, with many quotes from the King James translation of the Bible. In fact, I could see how someone in the nineteenth century with a good imagination, some knowledge of the Bible, and some confused theology could have written the Book of Mormon.

God had opened my eyes to numerous evidences that it was of human origin, rather than inspired. (It was later that I received convincing evidence that confirmed this conclusion. See Vol. 2, Chapter 16) It was an insult to put it above the Bible, especially since the Book of Mormon discredits the Holy Bible as the inerrant Word of God (1 Nephi 13:20–29). [See Chapter Eight]

Yes, I had asked to know the truth about the Book of Mormon and I was seeing it in a new light. It was not easy to accept that a book I had reverenced as Scripture all my life was not true. I myself had testified to its truthfulness many times.

The Difference

If it were not true, why had I received a witness as a missionary over twenty years ago that the book was true? The answer was clear. I had not received a witness from the Holy Ghost. Yes, I had experienced an unusual, euphoric sensation as a young missionary while reading the Book of Mormon and praying for some kind of experience to know that it was true. But was that experience the Holy Ghost confirming the entire Book of Mormon and everything associated with it, including Joseph Smith, to be true? In my zeal to experience some kind of spiritual manifestation about the Book of Mormon, had I become vulnerable to a deceptive, spiritual feeling that I misinterpreted to be the Holy Ghost? I certainly had been expecting and needing some kind of manifestation about the Book of Mormon. All my life I had been taught that a good feeling that I felt at church or while reading the Book of Mormon was the Holy Ghost confirming them to be true. But now I was acutely aware of many devout Christians in other denominations that had good feelings and experiences that confirmed their faith.

Besides, my Book of Mormon experience was completely different from my recent life-changing experience when I surrendered all to Jesus and was filled with light, love, joy and the fruit of the Holy Spirit! When I was born again, Jesus had flooded my soul with His peace and given me an assurance of my eternal inheritance with Him in His Kingdom. There was no comparison between that and the temporary, emotional experience I had when seeking a testimony of the Book of Mormon. One was fleeting; the other changed me forever. One bound me to Joseph Smith; the other bound me to Jesus.

My Book of Mormon experience bound me to religious expectations that made me feel I could never be good enough. My born-again experience set me free from that burden. I knew I was accepted just as I was because Jesus had lived the perfect life (I could not live) in my place, paid the penalty for my sins through His sufferings, died in my place, and rose victoriously over sin and death to the Glory of God!

Yes, I could undeniably recognize an irrefutable, huge difference between my Book of Mormon experience and my born-again experience—two different spirits! My Book of Mormon experience was very different from the quiet peace that transforms that is a result of the indwelling presence of the Holy Spirit.

Another Significant Difference

The most significant point I understood from all of this was that when I got that good feeling as a missionary, I was seeking a good feeling or some spiritual sign to convince me that the Book of Mormon was true. I wanted that witness. I *needed* that witness to continue in the path of my choosing. It was as if my mind was already made up and I was just waiting for God to give me what I expected.

Jesus did say, "A wicked and adulterous generation seeketh after a sign; and there shall no sign be given unto it, but the sign of the prophet Jonas." (Matthew 16:4)

Isn't seeking a good feeling or a "burning in the bosom" to know that the Book of Mormon is true the same as seeking a sign? *Do we subject ourselves to a counterfeit spirit when we seek a sign to confirm what we want to believe?* I wondered.

There was a major difference in my desire and motives now and when I got my testimony of the Book of Mormon. Then, I had wanted and expected a witness of the Book of Mormon so I could testify that I knew it was true. That is what I was sent out to do as a missionary. The pressure was on me to say, "I know the Book of Mormon is true and that Joseph Smith is a true prophet." Now, however, with no external pressure prompting me, I sincerely wanted to know the truth about the Book of Mormon. My mind was open, not made up. I was committed to God's truth only, rather than committed to my church and to being a good missionary. That had made all the difference!

Somewhere along the way I had learned another important lesson: The only truth that matters is God's truth, not what I want to believe!

Does God Turn Us Over to Our Desires?

I now believe that God had never given me a testimony of the Book of Mormon and Joseph Smith, but He had allowed me to believe what I wanted to believe. In other words, He turned me over to the desire of my heart and gave me what I wanted.

Does the Bible confirm this idea? God gave the Israelites what they wanted, even when it was not His perfect plan for them. They wanted a king, so God allowed them to have a king in King Saul.

Jesus told the Pharisees that Moses permitted the Jews to write a certificate of divorce because of the hardness of their hearts, but from the beginning it was not God's will for man (Mark 10:2–9).

Another example of God giving the Israelites what they desired when it was not good for them is when they were discontent with the manna God provided for their food in the wilderness after He had miraculously delivered them from bondage in Egypt. Many of the Israelites complained about eating only manna. They craved meat, leeks, garlic, and other fresh foods they had eaten in Egypt. The story is told in Numbers 11:18–20 NIV:

> Tell the people: Consecrate yourselves in preparation for tomorrow, when you will eat meat. The LORD heard you when you wailed, "If only we had meat to eat! We were better off in Egypt!" Now the LORD will give you meat, and you will eat it. You will not eat it for just one day, or two days, or five, ten or twenty days, but for a whole month— until it comes out of your nostrils and you loathe it—

because you have rejected the LORD, who is among you, and have wailed before him, saying, "Why did we ever leave Egypt?"

The story continues in Numbers 11:31–34 NIV:

Now a wind went out from the LORD and drove quail in from the sea. It brought them down all around the camp to about three feet above the ground, as far as a day's walk in any direction. All that day and night and all the next day the people went out and gathered quail. No one gathered less than ten homers. Then they spread them out all around the camp. But while the meat was still between their teeth and before it could be consumed, the anger of the LORD burned against the people, and he struck them with a severe plague. Therefore the place was named Kibroth Hattaavah, because there they buried the people who had craved other food.

They were not satisfied with God's provision for them, so God gave them what they wanted, even though it meant death for them.

In reference to the Israelites behavior, the Psalmist said:

But craved intensely in the wilderness, and tempted God in the desert. So He gave them their request, but sent a wasting disease among them.

—Psalms 106:14–15 NASB

In the New Testament, Paul makes it clear that God does turn people over to the desires of their hearts. He doesn't just state this once, but three times. (Romans 1:24, 26, 28)

Do we open ourselves to Satan's deception when we seek something we desire rather than being fully surrendered to God's will? Paul says that God even sends a strong delusion to those who do not love the truth:

And for this reason God will send them strong delusion, that they should believe the lie.

—2 Thessalonians 2:11 NKJV

For what reason? The answer lay in the verses just preceding this one.

The coming of the lawless one is according to the working of Satan, with all power, signs, and lying wonders, and with all unrighteous deception among those who perish, because they did not receive the

255

> love of the truth, that they might be saved. And for this reason God
> will send them strong delusion, that they should believe the lie.
> —2 Thessalonians 2:9–11 NKJV

This Scripture sounded so harsh! It was hard to apply this verse to myself, as well as the Mormons I loved, because I thought we loved the truth. Or did we?

Confirmation from the Mouths of Mormons

My answer that God allows people to be deceived because that is what they want was confirmed to me in more ways than in Bible Scriptures. I was surprised how many times I heard comments such as, "If I'm deceived, which I'm not, then I don't want to find out. I'll just be deceived."

My stake president was the first one to make this statement to me, but many others had expressed the same attitude. Even a member of my family gave me a similar answer when he said, "If the Mormon Church is not true, I don't want to know."

"Why?" I asked. "Is it because the price you would have to pay is too great?"

"Yes," he answered.

Another family member told me, "I am not at all interested in what you have learned. I love what I have." (meaning all she had in the Mormon Church)

Many times the "I-don't-want-to-know" mentality was repeated as I frequently heard such statements as, "I don't care what the Bible says! If Joseph Smith said it, that's good enough for me." The old adage, "Don't confuse me with the facts; my mind is made up," seemed to say it all.

Of Far Greater Worth

Even though this "closed-mind mentality" frustrated me and made me sad, from a human standpoint I could understood their point of view. Besides being a fantastic community of support, the Mormon Church offers such a wealth of good teachings and programs to help us have good families and live clean, productive, quality lives. It also teaches many truths about Jesus from the Bible that give many of them a desire to follow Jesus. Because Mormonism is such a combination of truth and error, and one is blessed by living the principles of righteousness that it teaches, it is hard to imagine that it is deceptive. It is also hard to give up all those benefits received from applying righteous principles in ones' lifestyle. However, now I understood that salvation was not obtained through human merits of righteous living. Since the veil had been lifted from my mind when I was transformed, I could understand the Apostle Paul's epistles. In Philippians chapter three, he reiterates how righteous he had been and even says that according to the law he was blameless (vs. 4-6). But then he says he counts all of that as dung (manure) in comparison to the surpassing greatness of knowing Christ Jesus his Lord (vs. 7-8). Now I could relate to Paul's writings. I never wanted to hang onto the beautiful aspects of life that my LDS religion and culture had given me (no matter how much I loved them) at the expense of missing out on "knowing" Jesus and being with him forever in the Kingdom of God. It wasn't my righteousness that was going to get me there, it was His righteousness credited to me through faith. I love what Paul has to say next in verse 9:

> And be found in him, not having mine own righteousness, which is of the law, but that which is through the faith of Christ, the righteousness which is of God by faith:
>
> —Philippians 3:9

Jesus had brought me to His righteousness "which is of God by faith." Not that I was righteous enough, but God accepts me as righteous (made right with Him) through faith in Jesus and all He did for me.

There was another reason I understood my Mormon family and friends desire to hang onto their religious comfort zone. I had learned that it isn't easy to follow Jesus. To truly trust in Christ is to surrender everything—to die to self, take up ones' cross daily and follow Him. Not easy, but so worth it!

257

A Clever Combination of Truth and Error

Even though I no longer believed in the Book of Mormon, I did believe that God had used the truths it contains about Jesus to increase my faith in Jesus. However, He never confirmed the untruths. I had learned when God is calling us into His light, He will use truth for His purpose wherever we encounter it. This does not necessarily validate the entire message or book, nor the messenger as being from God, nor does it validate a religion. Since the Book of Mormon contains many biblical passages, it stands to reason that one would get a good feeling reading them and even grow as they seek God. (The Sermon on the Mount in the Book of Mormon is a good example of this.)

Father in Heaven had given me a faith in Him and a desire to follow Jesus as a Mormon. He used many truths in my religion to bring me to a point of faith sufficient to follow Jesus out of the Mormon Church. The problem was that I believed when God worked in my life (which He did many times) it meant that my religion was true. I swallowed the untruths with the truth. As a committed, active, temple Mormon I could not discern between three strong feelings and experiences that were part of my life and that permeate the Mormon experience: 1) positive emotions of the soul that are a result of many good acts and disciplines; 2) deceptive spiritual experiences that seem good to humans--after all Satan does appear as an angel of light (2Cor. 11:14); and 3) God pouring out His love on me through truths I believed as He was drawing me by the Holy Spirit into a saving relationship with Himself.

As a Mormon, any of the three above types of experiences confirmed my religion. Now however, I had been given discernment to see the difference. Once again, I was reminded how easy it is to be deceived, and how important it is to test and prove all things by the Bible—God's double-edged sword.

A Clear Answer

As I looked back over my life as a Mormon I could see that many times God had pricked me with questions about problematic aspects of

Joseph Smith's teachings and the Book of Mormon. However, I had ignored them, stuffed them down, and never admitted that they bothered me. Had I loved my lifestyle and all the wonderful things my religion had provided for me more than I loved the truth?

Now these problems were piling up into one big giant that would not be stuffed down anymore. I could see that God had certainly not betrayed me. As a matter of fact, in His mercy and love for me He had been pricking me all my life. I now understood what Jesus meant when He appeared to Saul, who became Paul, on the road to Damascus and told him, "It is hard for thee to kick against the pricks" (Acts 9:5b). I had ignored and brushed off the "pricks" of the Holy Spirit all of my life. God had not betrayed me; I had betrayed Him—and myself. I had not listened with an open heart and an open mind. I had been taught that it was a sin to doubt and that doubts came from the devil. Now it was clear that the problems and questions that had bothered me as a teenager were true, legitimate problems that God had been using to get my attention and draw me to the truth.

I had been guilty of focusing on information that confirmed my church while rejecting any information that might discredit it. My life had been lived in an environment that required me to have a testimony, besides the fact that I wanted a testimony. I was taught that my feelings were witnesses of the Holy Ghost. In ignorance, I bought into the system. Once I started saying, "I know the Book of Mormon is true and Joseph Smith is a true prophet of God," I certainly wasn't going to change that position. Especially since all my life I had believed my good feelings were the Holy Ghost. *How could I dare to change that position?* Once committed to my testimony, the problems faded away and I hadn't let them bother me after that. The more I publicly spoke my testimony at Church meetings (which I did often), the stronger my testimony became.

It became all the more imperative to only take in information that supported the accepted position and ignore all else. I had to protect my testimony above everything else. I wonder what kind of judge would listen only to the defense and leave out the prosecution. Yet that was what I had done all my life. Now I recognized that others were doing the same thing.

I now had my answer as to why God had allowed me to believe in the Book of Mormon if it were not true. I had been deceived for two basic reasons:

1. The foundation of my testimony of the Book of Mormon was based on the false premise that a good feeling was a witness of the Holy Ghost confirming the Book of Mormon to be true and that, therefore, Joseph Smith was a true prophet and the church is true.

2. I had wanted a testimony of the Mormon Church more than I wanted to know the truth about the Book of Mormon.

A Scary Thought

I was still wrestling with recent discussions with my father and wanting to understand his experience, which bound him to Joseph Smith. I couldn't forget his trying to convince me that my experience was from Lucifer. Dad was explaining that Lucifer sometimes appears as an angel of light, a beautiful angel, an intelligent angel, a desirable angel. Even though these things are true, it almost seemed that Dad had an unusual respect for Lucifer (the name Dad chose to call him) as he continued to impress upon me Satan's powers and appealing nature. He said that in the pre-existence Lucifer was known as the Star of the Morning and that he was smart enough that in the presence of our Heavenly Father, our heavenly mothers, and all the great spirits, he managed to take one-third of our Heavenly Father's children away from our Heavenly Father. Then Dad said something I had heard him say several times in my life. But this time it gave me the shivers.

"He is so intelligent that I would love to sit at the feet of Lucifer and be taught by him," Dad said. "However, I would want the Holy Ghost right beside me."

I shuddered at the thought. Had my father been given what he wanted?

"And no marvel; for Satan himself is transformed into an angel of light. Therefore it is no great thing if his

ministers also be transformed as the ministers of righteousness; whose end shall be according to their works."

—2 Corinthians 11:14–15

A MISSING PUZZLE PIECE PUT IN PLACE

"For we wrestle not against flesh and blood, but against principalities, against powers, against the rulers of the darkness of this world, against spiritual wickedness in high places."
—Ephesians 6:12

Over two years had passed since Mother had contracted Coccydiomycosis after she and Dad had come to California. Little had I known that would be mother's last visit to our home. She and Dad had not come to California since then because of her illness. The disease had gone into remission, but mother was never quite herself again. At her best she was limited in her energy and she didn't stay well for long periods.

Even though it was an up-and-down struggle for her during this time she was able to come to our first Baker family camping reunion in Southern Utah in the summer of 1984. After the reunion her disease flared up again and she was hospitalized for several months.

This time the disease paralyzed mother's body. Eventually she could not even speak. She lay in bed, unable to move. It was a true love story to see Dad tenderly care for her. The hospital sent her home, saying they could not do anything more for her. Dad bought a hospital bed and put mother in the front room. He refused to put her in a nursing facility. Determined that there was no place for her except home, he announced that he would take care of her. He even made a bed for himself on the front room floor where he slept by her side for months instead of in his own bed. He never left her alone.

If Dad did have to go somewhere he made sure someone would be there by her side, and he wasn't gone very long. He blended food for Mother and fed her with a syringe. He rolled her over from side to side regularly since she could not turn herself over. He would talk to her lovingly, and even though she could not speak he insisted that she answered him with her eyes. I do not doubt that. They had such a beautiful relationship that he seemed to read her eyes and know her thoughts without her speaking.

A Painful Loss

To have mother completely paralyzed was hard on all of us, especially Dad. Taking care of her wasn't hard for him, but knowing that she still had all her feelings and emotions inside but was not able to communicate or do anything was the hard part. Mom was coherent and knew what was going on around her but she couldn't respond. She was helpless.

Of course Dad prayed with her morning and night, as family prayer was a daily occurrence in his home. Many prayers were being offered for Mother. One morning he knelt by her bedside and poured out his heart to Heavenly Father. He expressed to God that it was too painful to continue to see her like this—and realized the agony that she herself must feel. For her sake, he was ready to let go of her.

"Please take Dorothy home now," he prayed. About ten minutes later mother passed away. It was February 21, 1985.

I knew I would miss Mom very much. Mother's death was a painful loss for all of us. In my opinion, she was the best. Mom had very high standards and lived an excellent, LDS life. She was kind, caring, very talented, and a hard worker. She was devoted to her husband and family and had a submissive and gentle spirit.

264

Difficult Years

The next few years were lonely ones for me. Mother was gone, and I also missed my best friend Tobie very much. I had never had a friend like Tobie, and no one could replace the empty spots in my heart that my mother and she left. In addition to these losses, Charles' hurt and frustration with me caused him to withdraw from me. At times he would not speak to me at all. The tension between us was very painful. One day he threatened to get his own apartment as he angrily slammed the door and left. I didn't know if he would come back or not, but he did.

Every day I thanked the Lord that Charles had not divorced me yet, even though he had been counseled by the bishop and others that he would be better off without me. Sometimes I would get brave and tell him I would wait for him to become a Christian.

"You will wait until I'm dead, then," he would angrily respond. "I will never leave the church."

It seemed impossible to penetrate Charles' thick, Mormon walls. He was faithful to the office of High Priest, which he held. After all, according to the Oath and Covenant of the Priesthood, if he ever turned from his Priesthood he would never be forgiven in this life or in the life to come.[27] That definitely was a fearful stronghold!

I was still attending the LDS Church every Sunday, but it was difficult because I no longer believed in it. Also, I was no longer a part of the sisterhood, as I had always been. This was very hard for me. I knew that members of the church were talking about me and wondering what was wrong with me. Most of them thought I was in a midlife crisis or had had some kind of breakdown and needed a long rest in the hospital. Some of my friends would talk to me to express their views, but when I would respond with my views from the Bible they would get upset and didn't want to talk to me anymore.

Although going to other churches without my family was lonely, I was drawn to them like a moth to the light. I had an insatiable hunger to be taught from the Bible.

Setting Me Straight

Charles was determined to show me the error of my ways, without engaging in religious combat. He preferred to take me to every "Know Your Religion" lecture, symposium, and meeting in the area, hoping that the BYU professors, other respected lecturers, and church leaders who led them would straighten me out. However, the more I listened to them and spoke with them, the more I could see the vast difference between Mormonism and the Bible. Biblical Christianity was making more and more sense, and Mormonism was becoming more and more contradictory. This was all quite depressing for Charles.

I was frequently told to *cleanse my hands and purify my heart* so I would believe rather than doubt the church. Some told me that I was doubting Joseph Smith because I couldn't live the gospel. Others concluded that I must not have had a testimony of the church to begin with. The bottom line in these conclusions made by others was always that it was my fault if I doubted Joseph Smith. I just wasn't good enough!

An Unsettling Experience

At one of the large regional meetings in Anaheim to which Charles took me, I saw an old friend that had moved out of our area. She was very excited to see me.

"I want to tell you something that happened to me," she said. "But it will probably upset you." She knew I had been struggling with my testimony before she'd moved. She acted almost afraid to continue, so I encouraged her to tell me what was on her heart.

"Well, several months ago when I was going through the temple endowment, I heard a baby crying. It was very spiritual; it was in my mind. I knew it was Nicholas."

I was stunned, as well as speechless. Nicholas was our ninth baby, who had been born early and had lived only a few hours. He was born and died on November 13, 1980. It was now five years later and I had not even seen this friend or heard from her for a couple of years. Why would she hear my deceased baby crying?

She continued with her story.

"I knew why he was crying. He was weeping for you. He was weeping for you because you no longer believe the church is true. I know it was your baby. Besides, I never did know what you named him, but through the spirit I knew his name was Nicholas."

I was taken aback. *Was my baby in the spirit world crying for me?* I could tell she was not making this up. She really had experienced a spiritual connection with *something*.

Similar kinds of supernatural phenomena and spirit manifestations in the church were powerful and binding. They had always been strong evidences to us as Mormons that the church was true. It certainly was a strong evidence of that to her!

"The church just has to be true," she confidently said. "Besides, since I've moved to Corona, I feel like I've finally found the true church because the people in my new ward are so friendly."

My heart was flooded with sorrow. I was already trying to deal with a tremendous burden of loneliness and rejection. She seemed so happy and confident. Besides, this was my deceased baby she was talking about. Her story deeply affected my emotions. This was another one of those times when it was easy to become confused by a personal experience. But it was also a reminder that one should not form positive conclusions based on feelings, an experience, or incomplete knowledge.

Before I could respond my friend continued.

"I know when we moved away you were starting to have some struggles with Joseph Smith. I'm so glad that I saw you today, because I've wanted to tell you about this experience so you would not have any more doubts about Joseph Smith."

I knew she wanted me to be convinced, but the things I had learned about communicating with the dead were running through my mind. Still, in spite of what I now knew the Bible said, my emotions were confusing me. *Why had that happened to her? I doubt she had been seeking to communicate with my deceased baby! Why would she have been thinking about him? He died five years ago.* That overwhelming intimidation of the Mormon experience of spiritual phenomena was taking over in me.

I felt so left out and lonely. I missed the sisterhood and the feeling of

267

belonging and being needed that the church had so wonderfully provided for me all my life. *If only the church were true, I thought to myself and, if it is, I truly want to believe in it.*

Before I had a chance to tell her that the Bible forbids communicating with the dead she said she had to go and left as quickly as she had appeared. I was left standing in a Mormon Church, feeling bewildered and sad. Somehow my friend's experience had penetrated me deeply. *Had she really heard my baby weeping for me in the temple?* I needed to know whether it was real or deceptive. Also, I wanted to know why God had allowed that to happen. All I could think at the moment was, *"Father in Heaven, please don't let me be wrong! I feel like a jar of clay— easily broken. Please don't let me be deceived."* It was my continual prayer not to be deceived by spiritual phenomena, deceiving spirits, or my own emotions.

It was these types of experiences that made me very cautious about forming an absolute opinion. There were just too many supernatural experiences in the LDS Church. *I have to be so patient and thorough*, I thought. I could not risk making a mistake that would have eternal consequences. Even though I was convinced from the Bible and my own current experience that Joseph Smith was a false prophet, I knew that I must continue to seek God's truth with an openness to have Him change me if I were wrong.

No In Between

As I saw it, my friend's message to me was either evidence that the church really was true, or that it was a powerful counterfeit to the truth with its roots deep in spiritism. There is no gray area for such type of experiences: Either they are from God, or possibly hallucinations of the mind, or they are deceptions of deceiving spirits under the influence of the devil, whom Jesus referred to as the "prince of this world" (John 12:31, 14:30, and 16:11). In speaking of the *man of sin* (or Son of Perdition) who will be revealed in the end times, Paul says:

> Even him, whose coming is after the working of Satan, with all power and signs and lying wonders...
>
> —2 Thessalonians 2:9

Certainly Satan has power to deceive with signs and lying wonders. Paul refers to the devil as the "prince of the power of the air" (Ephesians 2:2). A few chapters later Paul tells us how to stand against the devil's schemes and says that, ". . . our battle is against principalities, against powers, against the rulers of the darkness of this world, against spiritual wickedness in high places" (Ephesians 6:10–12).

There is no in between for Joseph Smith, the founding prophet of Mormonism! Either he was the great prophet of the restoration who had done more for the salvation of man than anyone who had ever lived except Jesus Christ, (Doctrine & Covenants 135:3) or he was influenced by the powers of darkness, headed by the devil, who is the "prince of the power of the air" and the "prince of this world."

Joseph Smith was not an ordinary man. He definitely had spiritual powers. The Mormon Church could not be so spiritual if an ordinary man had started it. I needed to learn more about Joseph Smith. Just what kind of a man was this prophet that millions of Mormons honor and hold in reverent respect? Where did his influence and powers come from?

However, even if Joseph Smith was a false prophet and the LDS Church was Spiritism and not the true church of Jesus Christ, God had worked in my life through that which was true in my religion to draw me to Him. I could not deny that God had given me a love for Jesus and a desire to follow Him as a Mormon. God had also answered many of my prayers. But was that confirmation that everything my religion taught was true? I realized now it was not.

Suppressing My Curiosity

Around this time, the Seventh-day Adventist Church in Beaumont, California, was having another Revelation seminar. It had been a few years since I'd attended the first Revelation seminar in Calimesa and a different evangelist was teaching this seminar, so I decided to go. Much to my surprise Charles went to a few meetings with me. I think he was curious and wanted to know what I was learning. He seemed to enjoy the Seventh-day Adventists, although he was still very positive that the Mormon Church was the only true Church.

The Seventh-day Adventist evangelist who was teaching the classes started coming to our home to visit with us. He tried to visit when Charles was available, but that did not always work out. During one of his visits the evangelist mentioned a notebook he had about LDS Church history. The next time the evangelist came to our home, he again mentioned the notebook and said he would loan it to us if we were interested. He said it was very well-researched and documented, and that the author used to be a Mormon.

I had been extra curious about church history all my life, and especially now. However, for the past three-and-one-half years since I had lost my testimony of Joseph Smith, I had resisted studying LDS Church history because I had heard many times in my life that it was riddled with problems. My focus had been on understanding the Bible and on studying the four standard works of the church. I really didn't want to read anything that would cause me to have more problems believing in Joseph Smith, even if it was published by the church. I had been even more determined not to read anything that could be classified as anti-Mormon literature. I was not interested in reading anything written by someone who had left the church. So I told the evangelist I was not interested.

Secretly, however, I was very interested. For several weeks I wondered what was in this book about LDS Church history, but I suppressed my curiosity. I was not going to read it.

The Salamander Letter

Meanwhile the evangelist mentioned a document called the Salamander Letter. He was surprised that I had not heard of it since several news articles had been written about it. Charles was on the high council of the church at the time and had not heard of it either. In any case, I decided to read his news article about this Salamander Letter.

The Salamander Letter was alleged to have been written by Martin Harris (one of the initial witnesses to the Book of Mormon). It talked about a spirit that turned himself into a salamander. This was one of the spirits that appeared to Joseph Smith. According to the news article, a young man named Mark Hoffman discovered this old document. This letter linked Joseph Smith with the occult, and some BYU professors had affirmed its authenticity. Church leaders had paid thousands of dollars for it and tried to keep it quiet.

This was all very strange and curious. A spirit turning himself into a salamander? I decided it was time I found out about something else that this article mentioned: the occult. Just what was the occult?

I decided to look it up in the World Book Encyclopedia.

What Is the Occult?

According to the World Book, occult means secret or mysterious. The term is usually applied to knowledge of a supernatural type or that which is not bound by the exact laws of modern science. A person claiming to know the occult claims to know things that cannot be known by ordinary men—things outside the field of ordinary science. A fortune-teller, for instance, claims to know the occult when he tells a fortune, because he says he can foretell things that people generally cannot know.

During ancient times people in many countries believed in the occult sciences, including astrology, alchemy, necromancy, and magic. Many people guided their lives by such studies. At a time when the rigorous methods of modern science had not been far developed, people were easily influenced by those who claimed to have unusual knowledge and easily accepted any convincing idea. Several branches of the occult sciences are still practiced today.

I noticed that *necromancy* was part of the occult sciences mentioned in my *World Book*. I certainly had learned what that was all about—seeking information from the dead! Out of curiosity I decided to look up the first word on the list—alchemy. The following definition is from *The World Book Dictionary*, 1969, page 52:

> 1. a combination of chemistry and magic, studied in the Middle Ages, especially the search for a process by which cheaper metals could be turned into gold and silver; . . . 2. a magic power or process for changing one thing into another.

I learned in other definitions that the alchemists desired to find the elixir of perpetual youth. Also alchemy was believed to be a power of transmutation or a miraculous change of a thing into something better. The Salamander Letter mentioned the belief that spirits can transform themselves into salamanders and visa versa. This was getting intense. Apparently, people really believed in the mystical, magical power of transmutation of spirits into salamanders. Is that why the leaders of the church paid a lot of money to buy this old document? It all seemed pretty strange to me. However, I had already realized that Joseph Smith was connected with necromancy. If the Salamander Letter was authentic, Joseph Smith was also involved in alchemy, which would connect him with two branches of the occult.

What Is a Cult?

Something else was really bothering me. For quite some time, I had been aware that certain misinformed people had accused the Mormon Church of being a cult. I had always been highly offended by the term. I didn't know exactly what it meant, but I believed it was in some way connected with Satan. *What was the difference between cult and occult?* I decided to look up cult in *The American College Dictionary* and read the following:

> Cult 1. A particular system of religious worship, esp. with reference to its rites and ceremonies. 2. An instance of an almost religious veneration for a person or thing, esp. as manifested by a body of admirers: a cult of Napoleon. 3. The object of such devotion. 4. Sociol. A group having an exclusive sacred ideology and a series of rites centering around their sacred symbols.

I was certainly surprised. There was no mention of anything of a satanic nature. As a matter of fact, the LDS Church fit the definitions. I was very surprised to learn that Mormonism was a cult. I could no longer be angry or offended at others who referred to the LDS Church as a cult. They were not misinformed. I had been the misinformed one.

Even though all this was very fascinating, it was extremely sobering to say the least. I had just learned what a cult was and what the occult was, and Mormonism, it seemed, had a connection with both.

The Big Blue Book

I had not forgotten the notebook containing LDS Church history the evangelist had mentioned, and my need to read it was getting stronger and stronger.

What am I afraid of? I finally asked myself. I called the Seventh-day Adventist evangelist and said I was interested in seeing the book. He was cordial and said he would bring it to the meeting that night at the Seventh-day Adventist Church.

After the meeting I was amazed to see that he had a large, hard-bound, four-hundred-page book in his hand. Before offering the book to me, he spoke cautiously.

"Now, I value our friendship. Are you sure you want to read this? I mean, I don't want you and your husband to get mad at me and not speak to me anymore."

I drew a deep breath, assured him that this would not happen, and took the book home. Before I opened it I spoke frankly to Charles.

"I want you to be my witness that this is the first anti-Mormon book I have ever read," I told him. "I have not believed in Joseph Smith for three and one-half years and during that time I have not read any anti-Mormon literature. I don't want anyone ever to say I lost my testimony of Joseph Smith because I was reading anti-Mormon literature."

Charles sighed and nodded his head in agreement. He knew that this was the truth so he couldn't disagree. I was very surprised that he wasn't angry with me for bringing the book home. I think down deep he was a little curious but he couldn't admit it.

I was amazed to learn that what I had always thought was "anti-Mormon" was really Mormon history, documents, and writings that were kept hidden in the church archives. At least that is what this book was comprised of. It was simply the rest of the story that most members of the church did not know—and was it surprising! I didn't have to read much of this book to understand why the church leaders kept these well-documented writings hidden from the membership.

The book was a compilation of quotes from early journals, histories, speeches, and the writings of many people who were family, friends, and acquaintances of Joseph Smith and Brigham Young (including statements from them). It was very comprehensive. Most of all it was incredible! I couldn't believe there was so much written about incidences and happenings in the earliest days of the Church, of which I knew nothing. These accounts were so fascinating that I couldn't resist reading some of them to Charles. I expected him to get mad, but he didn't.

"You don't really believe that stuff, do you?" was his only comment, as he shook his head in disbelief.

I really didn't blame him for shrugging it off as ridiculous. If I had not already concluded from my studies in the Bible that Joseph Smith was a false prophet I probably would not have believed what I was reading either. As a matter of fact, I wasn't sure I could believe this book anyway. After all, I didn't want to be gullible and led astray again. I didn't know anything about the Tanners, the authors of the book, so I didn't know if I could trust them or the quotes in the book, even though they gave complete references from well-known figures in Mormon history. Also, it just didn't make sense that they could quote such a vast amount of information and be lying. The amazing thing was that the Tanners claimed the information came out of the LDS Church archives. Nevertheless, I could see why Charles didn't want to believe it.

I started wondering what kind of people the Tanners were. I'd read that Sandra Tanner was a direct descendant of Brigham Young. It was very important to know whom I could trust. *Were Jerald and Sandra Tanner liars, or were they honest? Were they anti-Mormons with an evil intent, or were they sincere people wanting truth to be known?*

A Significant Turn of Events

This book had so much information in it that I knew it was going to take considerable time to read all of it, so I ordered my own book. I also requested to be on the Tanner's mailing list. It wasn't long before I received my first newsletter from *Utah Lighthouse Ministry*, the Tanner's ministry. I was surprised to find out that the newsletter was all about the Salamander Letter.

The Tanners told how Mark Hoffman, the young man that had found the Salamander Letter, had come to them with the Salamander Letter in hopes that they would endorse it as authentic. Of course, if anyone would want this document to be authentic the Tanner's would, because it would add credibility to the quotes in their book that linked Joseph Smith to the occult. However, I was very surprised to learn from their newsletter that they did not validate the Salamander Letter as authentic. The Tanners gave several reasons why they considered it to be fraudulent. They rejected Mark Hoffman and his Salamander Letter, even though a BYU professor had validated it as authentic, as had church leaders.

A few weeks later, I got a phone call from my dad.

"Carma, you know that Salamander Letter that you were concerned about? Well, just today it has been found to be a fraud. Mark Hoffman produced it himself, along with other early church history documents."

My dad was very eager to let me know that the Salamander Letter was not for real. However, what Dad did not realize was that his phone call provided a tremendous amount of credibility to the Tanners and their ministry. I had wanted to know who to believe and who not to believe when reading about LDS Church history. *Could I trust the Tanners' research or were they just anti-Mormons out to destroy the church with lies, as Charles and my dad believed?*

This incident was an answer to my prayer to know whom to trust. The Tanners had been honest and trustworthy in their response to the Salamander Letter. They had not run with sensationalism in order to validate their beliefs and writings. On the other hand, the leaders of the LDS Church had tried to cover up information that they didn't like, even though they thought it was authentic. Other fraudulent documents from early LDS Church history were thought to be authentic. They ended up in the Church's possession, and Mark Hoffman received thousands of dollars for them.

Truth Made Known

The rest of the story about Mark Hoffman was told later in the news media as events unfolded. A Mormon Bishop was killed when he picked up a package containing a pipe bomb that was left at his office with his name on it. A second package was left at the front door of another Bishop's home. It was intended for this second Bishop; but when his wife picked up the package, a second pipe bomb exploded and she was killed. It seems that Mark Hoffman had not only been busy making fraudulent church history documents, he had also been busy making the pipe bombs. Hoffman was eventually convicted of both murders. He was also guilty of many other counts including stealing thousands of dollars from LDS Church leaders and other individuals through the sale of forged or nonexistent documents.

This was extremely significant to me. The Tanners had been proven to be right. This con artist had not fooled the Tanners, but he had deceived the Prophet and apostles of the LDS Church. Very interesting! *Where was their divine inspiration?*

Prophet of God or Prophet of the Occult?

The Tanner's book, *Mormonism, Shadow or Reality*, answered a critical question I had been asking for over three years: Just what kind of a person was Joseph Smith? I wanted to know the source of his powers, and the book answered that question. Joseph Smith was involved in divination, fortune-telling, necromancy, magic, and spiritism—all of which are branches of the occult and all of which are condemned by God in the Bible. If true, which I had no reason to doubt that it was, the book was irrefutable evidence that Joseph Smith was a prophet all right, but a prophet of the occult, not of God. No wonder spiritual phenomena were so common in Mormonism!

The Bible's teaching had been evidence enough to expose Joseph Smith as a false prophet. He not only contradicted the Bible, but he also *changed* the Bible. The big blue book was simply confirmation of what God had already shown me. It put the final piece of the puzzle in place regarding Joseph Smith. He was a very powerful, influential, charismatic man—but so are many other false prophets. Jeremiah tells us how to discern the difference:

> I have heard what the prophets said, that prophesy lies in my name, saying, I have dreamed, I have dreamed. How long shall this be in the heart of the prophets that prophesy lies? Yea, they are prophets of the deceit of their own heart. Which think to cause my people to forget my name by their dreams, which they tell every man to his neighbour, as their fathers have forgotten my name for Baal. The

prophet that hath a dream, let him tell a dream; and he that hath my word, let him speak my word faithfully. What is the chaff to the wheat? Saith the LORD. Is not my word like as a fire? Saith the LORD; and like a hammer that breaketh the rock in pieces? Therefore, behold I am against the prophets, saith the LORD, that steal my words every one from his neighbour. Behold, I am against the prophets, saith the LORD, that use their tongues and say, He saith. Behold, I am against them that prophesy false dreams, saith the LORD, and do tell them, and cause my people to err by their lies, and by their lightness, yet I sent them not, nor commanded them; therefore they shall not profit this people at all, saith the LORD.

—Jeremiah 23:25–32

Through the Prophet Jeremiah, the Lord let us know that we can test a false prophet by God's Word. The Lord compares the prophet's dreams to chaff, and God's Word to wheat. His Word is the fire and hammer that exposes (breaks in pieces) even the spiritual manifestations that can accompany false prophets and their followers. If they discredit God's Word or contradict what God has already revealed in the Bible, then they are false prophets.

False prophets helped to contribute to the downfall of Israel. The Israelites thought they could combine Baal worship and other pagan rituals with their worship of Jehovah. Because God is a jealous God and He would not accept their participation in false religions, He allowed both the Northern Kingdom (Israel) and the Southern Kingdom (Judah) to be taken captive by heathen nations (Syria and Babylon). God also allowed King Nebuchadnezzar to destroy Jerusalem and the temple in order to show the Israelites that He would not allow them to compromise their worship of Him with false religions and pagan worship that involved the occult.

Spirit Manifestations and False Religions

I learned just how prevalent spiritual encounters were in other religions. They certainly were not unique to Mormonism. The Hindus have plenty of spiritual experiences. Does that mean their religion is true? We can say the same for Buddhism and the ancient pagan religions of Egypt and Babylon. Did not the wise men and magicians of Egypt turn their rods into serpents, just as Moses did? (Exodus 7:11) In addition, the modern religion known as *New Age* religion has many spiritual manifestations and encounters with spirit guides and the spirits of deceased people speaking through human mediums. Some of these people in the New Age Movement claim to have seen Jesus. Yet this religion teaches that we are all *little gods*. Therefore, it must be false. We are not gods; we are humans created by God to worship Him, not to seek to be worshiped someday and glorify ourselves.

False religions seek to bring glory to man. The devil knows that men are self-centered and he tempts us by telling us we can become like God. Isn't that the very temptation that he used to get Eve to disobey God and partake of the forbidden fruit? Didn't he tell her in Genesis, chapter three, that if she ate the fruit she would become, "like God, knowing good from evil?" She took that bite and did realize the difference between good and evil, but the half-truth Satan lured her with didn't turn out as she expected. She wanted to be like God, but that's not what happened. Isn't that the sin that caused Satan himself to fall from heaven? He wanted to exalt himself and be like God. The Bible tells the story:

> How art thou fallen from heaven, O Lucifer, son of the morning! How art thou cut down to the ground, which didst weaken the nations! For thou hast said in thine heart, I will ascend into heaven, I will exalt my throne above the stars of God: I will sit also upon the mount of the congregation, in the sides of the north: I will ascend above the heights of the clouds; I will be like the most High. Yet thou shalt be brought down to hell, to the sides of the pit.
> —Isaiah 14:12–15

Yes, Satan said, "I will be like the most High." Even though he has fallen from heaven, apparently he hasn't learned his lesson because he still seeks to exalt himself above the throne of God and to instill that desire in men. To affirm this, Paul says that before the day of the Lord, the final antichrist will be empowered by Satan with this desire:

> Let no man deceive you by any means: for that day shall not come, except there come a falling away first, and that man of sin be revealed, the son of perdition; Who opposeth and exalteth himself

above all that is called God, or that is worshipped; so that he as God
sitteth in the temple of God, shewing himself that he is God.
—2 Thessalonians 2:3–4

Satan wants to be worshipped as God. He wants to take the throne
and Kingdom away from Jesus. He is the enemy of Jesus and wants
humans to worship him, not the Father and Jesus. One of his tactics to
control the hearts of men is through the vicious lie with which he is still
tempting men—that they can become like God. He was successful with
Eve and is still successful through the same lie today. Only he is now
even bolder. Instead of tempting humans by telling them they can
become like God, knowing good from evil, he tells them they can
become gods. He has deceived millions in the Mormon religion with that
temptation. The ultimate destiny in LDS theology is to be exalted as gods
and goddesses. (Doctrine & Covenants 132:20, 37) Now he is even
bolder in the New Age Religion. Many in that religion believe they
already are gods. Some of the pharaohs of Egypt and Emperors of Rome
believed that they were gods, also. *Did that make it true?* God has made
it very clear in His Word that there is no other God besides Himself
(Isaiah 43:10; 44:6, 8). Anybody that teaches we can become gods or that
we are gods is not sent from God. It's that simple.

The Battle against Principalities and Powers

False prophets and false religions do manifest spiritual powers
because Satan and his hosts are behind them. There are good angels who
are God's messengers, but there are also deceptive spirits under Satan's
dominion who can appear as good angels. If they appeared as demons
they wouldn't be able to deceive very many. Paul warns us that "Satan
masquerades as an angel of light and his servants as apostles of
righteousness" (2 Corinthians 11:13–15). That is why we cannot test the
validity of a prophet or a religion by virtue of our spiritual experiences—
or even a spiritual manifestation of a deceased loved one.

Satan and his demons *hate Jesus.* They are doing everything in their
power to destroy Jesus and His Kingdom. As Paul says, the spiritual
battle is real:

279

> For we wrestle not against flesh and blood, but against principalities, against powers, against the rulers of the darkness of this world, against spiritual wickedness in high places.
>
> —Ephesians 6:12

This verse was very impactful to me! When Charles and I were married in the Salt Lake Temple, part of the closing words for our marriage ceremony were, "I seal upon you principalities, powers, and dominions." These were not just words the temple sealer chose to use. These words are part of the temple-sealing ceremony and are repeated at all marriage sealings performed in LDS temples (unless they have changed this in recent years). Joseph Smith supposedly received this sacred temple ceremony as a divine revelation. It was so sacred that we were not to discuss it outside of the temple. As a matter of fact, we were sworn to secrecy in the temple and put under solemn oaths never to reveal what we learned in the temple.

I was literally stunned when I read Ephesians 6:12 (quoted above) and realized that Paul associated "principalities and powers" with "the rulers of the darkness of this world" and "spiritual wickedness in high places."

Wow! My heart was heavy-burdened. I could see it clearly. How could I get those I loved to see it? I knew that only God could show them, as He had shown me.

Solid Ground

I no longer had to be emotionally influenced by my friend's experience of hearing a spirit crying in the temple. I was very certain that she had not heard my deceased baby crying. If God condemns communicating with the dead, He certainly is not going to send us messages through the dead—a practice that He condemns. If He did, then He would be a contradictory and untrustworthy God. Necromancy—communicating with the dead—is clearly forbidden in the Bible. Since the Mormon temple is closely associated with the dead, is it any wonder that a spirit was able to deceive my friend while she was in the temple.

I also now understood where Joseph Smith had gotten his powers. His involvement in occult practices that are condemned by God was convincing evidence that he was heavily influenced by spirits under the influence of the "prince of the air," "principalities and powers," the "rulers of the darkness of this world," and "spiritual wickedness in high places."

Puzzled No More

I had found the missing puzzle piece that explained the commonplace nature of spiritual phenomena and encounters with the spirits of the deceased within Mormonism. My eyes had been opened. These experiences were not evidence that the church was true and that Joseph Smith was a prophet of God. On the contrary, these experiences confirmed that Mormonism was *spiritism*. These types of spirit-encounters also linked Mormonism with the occult and other false religions.

Now I understood what the occult was and I recognized how prevalent and widespread it was in our lives—from entertainment to religions. I also became aware how easily humans are attracted to the unknown and mysticism of the occult. No wonder the Bible warns us that "the whole world lies under the sway of the wicked one" (1 John 5:19 NKJV).

A large part of my new-found puzzle piece was the sad but true realization that there were two common threads between Mormonism and the ancient pagan religions of Egypt and Babylon—the belief in the deification of man, and a connection with the dead.

I was doing some research in a book Tobie had given me entitled *Aid to Bible Understanding*. A picture on page 668 caught my attention. It depicted the three symbols of the Babylonian triad (three main false gods)—the sun, a crescent moon, and a star. They caught my attention because there was a resemblance in them to the carvings in granite of the sun, moon, and stars on the outside of the Salt Lake Temple. In Mormonism they symbolize the three degrees of glory—the sun represented the celestial kingdom, the moon the terrestrial kingdom, and the stars the telestial kingdom. It seemed more than coincidence that they would have such an uncanny resemblance to symbols of pagan religious deities. It was much later that I learned the dark significance of the

281

inverted pentagram (the upside down five-pointed star) that is carved in granite above the doors of the Salt Lake Temple.

Following Mother's death, dad made the comment, "I could kiss the ground the temple sits on." I knew his devotion and love for the temple was because of his belief that he would be married to Mother in eternity because of his temple sealing. I wished with all my heart that he had said, "I could kiss the feet of Jesus," instead of, ". . . the ground the temple sits on."

Yes, I had found a missing puzzle piece—the answer to my question, *Where did Joseph Smith get his powers?* But the answer intensified another missing puzzle piece: *How could my religion that had seemed so good, have its roots in something so opposed to God?* Finding the answer to that puzzle was one of my biggest struggles.

In time, the following answers did come:

First of all, I had believed in many truths that were entwined with the falsehoods of my religion. I could not, nor did I ever want to deny that I had received a love for Jesus and a desire to follow Him from the numerous teachings, songs, and quiet moments of prayer and meditation on His sacrifice that had been so much a part of my religion.

In rejecting the errors of Joseph Smith, I was not rejecting the biblical truths that I loved and that had been my connection with God and Jesus Christ. These truths were in the Bible and Christianity long before they were in Mormonism. Neither was I losing any of Jesus; I was gaining much, much more of Him. Now Jesus was removing, little by little, any hindrances between Him and me. The more I surrendered to Him alone, the more of His love and peace permeated my soul. Jesus had given me complete faith and trust in Him instead of partly in Him and partly in religious ordinances and my own righteous efforts! Now I understood why I had never felt close to Jesus in the temple. It wasn't my fault or because I wasn't spiritual enough. On the contrary, it was because Jesus had His hand upon me all my life and had been calling me to Himself. Now, He was separating out religious beliefs and practices that had been a barrier between Him and me. He had used truths that I had believed as stepping stones to bring me to the point of surrender and being born again, so I would have eternal life in His Kingdom. However, He had never confirmed the untruths.

The second answer that came to me was that I had not known about Joseph Smith's involvement in the occult. I had been in ignorance regarding the origins of Mormonism. For this reason, God had shown me mercy. In 1 Timothy 1:13b Paul writes: "...but I obtained mercy, because I did it ignorantly in unbelief." But now that God had shown me the truth, I needed to obey.

Oh, to understand the width, length, depth, and height of the love of Christ, which passes knowledge. (Eph. 3:18) God is so rich in mercy and He loves us so much, He will use truths taught about Jesus wherever it is taught or by whomever is speaking it. But this does not validate the source. (Philippians 1:15-18) Yet it is so easy for us humans to jump to conclusions about our religion and religious leaders when they speak truth, and consequently we accept deceptions as truth also. That was the faulty foundation upon which my testimony of the Book of Mormon, Joseph Smith and the LDS Church had been based! After all, all my life I had been taught that good feelings confirmed my church and leaders to be true. Now God was sorting the lies from the truths for me in so many ways I can only put a small portion of them in this book.

In summary, in-spite of the black and white dichotomy of my religion, my loving, merciful God had not ignored or abandoned me. No! Instead, He drew me out of my religion into His Grace through the truths that are part of that religion. He built my faith in Jesus so I would leave my religion that I had loved and love Him and Jesus with all my heart.

"And when they say to you, "Seek those who are mediums and wizards, who whisper and mutter," should not a people seek their God? Should they seek the dead on behalf of the living? To the law and to the testimony! If they do not speak according to this word, it is because there is no light in them."

—Isaiah 8:19–20 NIV

CHAPTER 20

THE CALL

*"Every word of God is pure: he is a shield unto them
that put their trust in him. Add thou not unto his words,
lest he reprove thee and thou be found a liar."*
—*Proverbs 30:5–6*

The irony of it all! All my life I had prayed that my children would grow up to go on missions and get married in the temple, but now I was troubled and heavyhearted at my prayers becoming a reality. Our oldest son, Lance, would soon be nineteen years old, the age at which the young men in the church are expected to go on a mission. Lance was working hard, saving his money, and preparing to receive his mission call, and I was deeply burdened.

This paradoxical situation created a severe struggle and intense anxiety within me. I had learned many things, none of which my family wanted to hear. I felt concerned that Lance would be indoctrinated by the clever and powerful missionary training program and be denied the freedom to investigate truth for himself. Yet every time I tried to tutor him he became angry and the discussion deteriorated into a heated argument. Lance would get very upset and there was a definite lack of God's Spirit when we argued. (This was what usually happened when I tried to show my family or friends the important things I was learning.)

It seemed impossible to have a rational, calm talk about religion with my family, with the exception of our daughter, Linda. She had been watching me over the past four-and-a-half years. There had been Sundays that I'd had to leave the LDS sacrament meeting and go to the car and sob. It was very emotional and difficult for me to sit in church and listen to everybody give testimony that they knew Joseph Smith was a true prophet, in light of the things I had learned. Others did not know these things, nor did they *want* to know them. In fact, trying to tell them anything I'd learned about the Bible was like trying to communicate with a roaring jet engine. They just couldn't hear it. I loved my Mormon friends and family and wanted them to learn the truths I had discovered and it was extremely frustrating to me that I could not communicate with them. They *knew* they could not be wrong, no matter what!

It was also very difficult sitting in church remembering all the good feelings and good times yet knowing I didn't belong anymore. So, on those occasions that my emotions couldn't handle any more, I would leave the meeting. Sometimes Linda would follow me out and want to know why I was crying. She was a very compassionate teenager with a mature and understanding heart. Because of this, over the course of the past four years, she had begun to question and seek answers herself. She still loved the Mormon Church and was a Mormon, but she was more open-minded than the others.

Still Learning to Let Go

Because of the struggle I was having communicating with Lance, I felt a deep impression that I was to back off and trust God in this situation. After all, that is what He had told me to do a few years ago. Besides, the Bible says not to quarrel. I had given my family to God. Maybe I just needed to be quiet and trust Him.

This was very difficult for me. I longed to openly discuss these critical issues about Joseph Smith, the Book of Mormon, and the teachings of the church with my family. If only the doors of communication weren't so tightly closed! If only they wanted to hear what I desperately wanted to share! But they didn't. They knew they were right, and needed no more additional instruction or discussion.

It is useless to pour water into a cup that's already full. In the same way, it is useless to teach a person another perspective when they are absolutely sure that they are right and don't want to learn anything else. One way Satan can deceive us is to make us so positive *we have to be right* that our minds become closed and we are no longer teachable. I never wanted to be that positive and unteachable again. There were so many things my family didn't know, but I had to accept the fact that they didn't want to know these things. This seemed to only widen the walls that were already forming between us.

Late one night when I was in bed, Lance burst into the room and said, "Mom, I want you to tell me all the reasons why you don't believe in Joseph Smith."

My mind thought, *Wonderful! Where do I begin,* but out of my mouth came something quite different.

"Lance, there is plenty of information about Joseph Smith that is readily available. As a matter of fact, there is a book on my dresser you are welcome to read for yourself. But the most important book for you to read is the Bible. You don't need to read anything besides the Bible right now. You need to ask God to show you the truth about Joseph Smith. We must test all prophets or people claiming divine revelation by the Bible. A true prophet of God will not teach anything that would conflict with God's truths in the Bible. I am not going to influence you. I want God to influence you."

Lance walked out of the room. He never touched the book on my dresser. It was really hard for me to not show Lance all the biblical and historical reasons why I no longer believed in Joseph Smith, but I felt a "check" in the Spirit about doing so. I silently prayed.

"Lord, is this what you want—for me to be quiet?"

The quiet but penetrating answer that came from the Spirit was, "If you show him, you will be blamed for his decision. If I show him, it will be a testimony that will produce fruit and will be to my glory."

From that point on I knew I had to let go and trust God. This proved to be one of the most difficult challenges of my life.

The conflict of having to be obedient and silent when there seemed a critical need to discuss things was causing an emotional trauma for me. It just didn't make sense to sit back and let Lance go to the Mormon temple where he would be placed under serious and fearful, life-threatening oaths. It didn't seem fair. I felt that Lance needed more time to understand the Bible, as well as the whole picture of the church, and see both sides before being locked into such powerful commitments. I couldn't help recoiling at the thought of him being under pressure to say that he knew Joseph Smith and the Book of Mormon were true, with only one side of the story told to him.

There were times now when I wanted to run from it all because I couldn't understand why it had to be so hard. I reminded myself that I needed more faith and needed to trust God. The battle between my spirit wanting to trust God and my flesh wanting to intervene wasn't easy. However, I had learned enough to know that God had spoken to me and I needed to stay out of His way. He would take care of this situation.

A Difficult Decision

Lance, too, was struggling and in turmoil. He had been programmed all his life that he would go on a mission at the age of nineteen. It was his Priesthood duty to go! A decision not to go would be unacceptable in his LDS world. He would be thought of as a failure. He believed in the church. Having been taught all his life about its authority, it was hard for him to comprehend how the church could be anything but true. Still, he did not know it was true deep inside himself. He had a desire to do right and to fulfill his duty, yet he had not personally received that call from the Holy Ghost that told him he should go on a mission. He also knew that he would bring great disappointment and sorrow to his father if he didn't go. These conflicting forces within him were building into a colossal pressure, but he valiantly tried to conceal his emotional turbulence.

One Saturday night these pent up emotions came to the surface. Lance was scheduled to play a trumpet solo for the Pass Chorale Concert, which I was accompanying that night. Just prior to leaving time he angrily told me he wouldn't do it, slammed the door, and left. I was sure he would show up anyway. He could always be counted on. *Even if he had threatened not to show up, he won't let us all down*, I thought.

But this time he didn't show up. He had gone hiking in the foothills not far from our home. He needed to sort everything out, he later said. Sunday morning I was in too much turmoil to go to church. I never missed church, unless I was very sick, but today I couldn't go. Lance didn't go either. Instead, we had a good long talk. He'd expected me to be angry with him for not playing in the concert. Much to his surprise, I wasn't angry, just very disappointed and concerned.

He confided in me that he did not want to go on a mission, but it was hard for him to say so. I told him that he needed to be honest with himself. He also needed to express his true feelings to his father.

That night he told his dad he didn't want to go. The air was so thick you could have cut it with a knife. My heart went out to Lance because I knew it was very hard for him to verbalize his decision. His father's reaction cut him to the quick.

"This is the most disappointing day of my life," Charles said. "I have always wanted a son that would go on a mission."

Those words hurt and stung deeply and were a vivid illustration of the lack of freedom to be honest about your true feelings as a nineteen-year-old Mormon male, or to make your own decision about a mission. The pressure was on every one of them to fulfill an honorable, full-time mission for the church.

Two days later our son-in-law to be, who was a returned missionary, had a long, private talk with Lance. I have no idea what he said to Lance but Lance changed his mind and decided to go on his mission.

The Big Brown Envelope

The proceedings started—interviews, filling out forms, physicals, tests, and shots. Finally everything was ready and he turned his paperwork in to the bishop. Everyone at church was proud of Lance and he was flooded with congratulations and compliments.

After several weeks of waiting, the big brown envelope from church headquarters in Salt Lake City arrived. My stomach, as well as my emotions, felt sick. The envelope represented final decisions that I knew Lance was not ready to make—not just a decision about a mission but also a serious decision of eternal consequences. As I looked at the big, brown envelope with orders about where he would be going, I prayed to God to please teach my son the truth. Please don't let him be indoctrinated into something deceptive.

I didn't want to give the envelope to Lance until the entire family was together, so I waited until that night at dinner time.

Trusting God

For four years I had been praying that the right thing would happen concerning this mission. I was convinced that God had shown me in many, many ways that the church was wrong, yet I had to leave room for the possibility that I could be misunderstanding something. When it comes to comprehending the greatness of God, I realized, I actually knew very little. I felt somewhat like an ant trying to comprehend a computer.

"No one can fathom God," King David had declared; and God said, "His ways are not our ways." Therefore, I was cautious to not become *absolute* in my own thinking and thereby close the door to learning more of the whole picture of God's ways. For forty years of my life I had been closed-minded in defending what I believed as a Mormon. Now I realized that *that* kind of attitude had stifled my wisdom and understanding of God.

All I could do in this delicate situation with my son was to trust God. I fervently prayed that He would somehow use this to help my family and me not to be divided and at least to come to the point where we could openly discuss doctrine and feelings without tension and anger. I longed for us to have a loving, open atmosphere in which all desired to know and would be willing to search for the truth rather than be controlled by the fear of being wrong.

I prayed if God were speaking to me, as I believed with every fiber of my soul that He was, and my perceptions and conclusions were correct, that He would use Lance's mission in a powerful way to show Lance and my family the truth, especially my husband.

If the church were true then I wanted Lance to go out and be a great missionary. On the other hand, if it was deceptive, as I was now convinced that it was, I pleaded with God to save Lance from its powerful and clever strongholds. I understood the controlling power of the Mormon mindset and the power behind its Priesthood oaths. Thus I knew that only God could save Lance from this influence. I knew I was powerless to do so, and that God had let me know that I was to entrust Lance to Him.

My advice to him was to be very careful not to simply repeat what he had heard or what he was taught to say but to keep his ability to reason and question. I encouraged him to think for himself rather than to repeat what he was expected to say when the pressure was on. I also encouraged him to pray to God and to have faith in Him alone, not blindly follow men. Most of all I wanted Lance to be able to be honest with himself and God, rather than feel trapped in a binding, premature commitment that at some point would be very difficult to reverse.

I realized this kind of advice was going to be extremely difficult for him to apply. Searching for God, with the freedom to question and think for yourself, is not the atmosphere of the Mormon mission field. On the contrary, it is one of obedience without questioning. Since it is believed that the leaders of the church are called and inspired by God, a strong emphasis is placed on the oft-repeated injunction, "Follow the brethren." A missionary is expected to obey strict rules and to closely follow the study guides and outlined discussions he is given. He is sent to, ". . . teach, not to be taught."

"Teach, Not Be Taught"

Joseph Smith said: "Again I say, hearken ye elders of my church, whom I have appointed; Ye are not sent forth to be taught, but to teach the children of men the things which I have put into your hands by the power of my Spirit . . ." (Doctrine & Covenants 43:15).

The LDS mission field is not the place to openly search, study, and seek for truth. Rather, it is an environment of *bearing* strong testimony of: 1) the truthfulness of the Book of Mormon and, 2) the fact that you *know* (not simply believe) that Joseph Smith is a true prophet and that the church is true. It is interesting that the majority of the young men and ladies who leave home to go into the mission field do not have that kind of testimony. Yet it is expected of them that they start bearing that testimony when they arrive as a missionary.

One of the strong teachings of the church is that you get a testimony by *bearing* your testimony. There are specific places in each missionary discussion where it states that the missionary is to "bear his testimony." I have come to the conclusion that what the ear hears the mouth say often enough, the brain will believe.

A Lack of Peace

Lance's mission call was to Des Moines, Iowa, and he was to enter the Missionary Training Center on October 1, 1986. Lance took his call seriously and was studying every chance he could get. Obviously, he was caught between my rejection of Mormonism and his father's strong, valiant, and unquestioning commitment to it. But, once he was committed to go, he felt a strong responsibility to be the best missionary ever so that if the LDS Church were the true church he could help me.

The more he studied, the more pensive he became. He expressed anxiety over not being able to learn the discussions that were to be memorized. At times Lance indicated to me and me alone, that he wasn't at all sure about going. One time he became angry and said he wasn't going. I ignored him and said nothing, knowing he had an intense conflict going on inside of him. It was obvious he did not have peace about his decision. I remembered what the still, small voice had told me about not interfering with God's work and tried to be obedient. I knew it was not my place to tell him what to do (even though I wanted to!) I kept simply encouraging him to be honest.

The Ordination

I remember well the Sunday Lance was ordained as an elder and given the Melchizedek Priesthood. I guess I believed that in some way God would intervene and stop it from happening, but He didn't. The Bishopric came to our home. Before laying hands on his head with these three men to ordain him, my husband read the Oath and Covenant of the Priesthood, found in the eighty-fourth section of the Doctrine & Covenants. Members of the church believe these revelations to be the very words of Christ speaking through the Prophet Joseph Smith, and they are accepted with the same authority as if Christ personally spoke them to you:

> Therefore, all those who receive the priesthood, receive this oath and covenant of my Father, which he cannot break, neither can it be moved. But whoso breaketh this covenant after he hath received it, and altogether turneth therefrom, shall not have forgiveness of sins in this world, nor in the world to come.
>
> —Doctrine & Covenants 84:40,41

The words pierced me deeply, as if a knife had just stabbed me. I felt that this was such an injustice. Here was my nineteen-year-old son, seeking and searching, still uncertain and not-at-all sure of his position on truth, yet sincerely desiring to do the right thing . . . and at this crucial, questioning point of his life he was being told that if he ever changed his mind after receiving the Priesthood and turned from it, he would never, ever be forgiven for his sins. Not only did this limit his free agency to choose what he wanted to believe, but it also did away with the need for Christ's atoning blood, which was shed for him on the cross.

1 John 1:7b says, "the blood of Jesus Christ his Son cleanseth us from all sin." How could these men tell him he would never be forgiven for his sins if he turned from the Priesthood? He wasn't even sure what he believed, and this oath seemed so absolute, so final, and so scary. Every motherly instinct within me wanted to cry out: "No, no, no! You can't do this to him!"

Somehow I was unable to speak, unable to move, glued to the organ bench, my mouth sealed. *How can I just sit here, and let them do this to him,* I thought to myself.

Lance's deep, intense eyes stared at me and I desperately wanted him to stand up and say, "Stop, I'm not ready for this." But he didn't! He trusted. He trusted his father, the church, and the leaders he had been reared under. He trusted what he had been taught for nineteen years. He was ordained an Elder in the Melchizedek Priesthood.

While preparing dinner, a flood of tears helped only a tiny degree to relieve the explosion that was going off inside of me. I had been so calm and quiet throughout the entire ordination, but inside I was ready to burst.

Lance became very quiet and thoughtful. Later that day, he privately expressed his opinion as to why I had lost my testimony of the Church.

He believed it was because he had not been good enough. I couldn't believe that he was blaming himself so harshly and unfairly. Satan is the *accuser of the brethren* (Revelation 12:10). He loves to wrongly blame us, and then taunt us with that misplaced sense of personal guilt that he has authored.

I assured Lance that my beliefs were not contingent upon his worthiness, or anyone else's worthiness. Truth was found in the Bible, and my beliefs were a result of both my experiences with God and what I had learned from God's Word. It was very apparent to me that Lance needed to be set free from guilt trips laid on him by a religious system.

Sharing Lance's Birth at His Farewell

When it came time for Lance's farewell two of my sisters, my brother, and dad drove down to California from Utah. Our family sang "How Great Thou Art," and Charles, I, and Lance all spoke. I shared the story of Lance's birth. He had been born over two months early and was not expected to live. However, when the doctors informed me that I would not take my baby home, an inner voice spoke to my heart louder than the doctor's voice in my ear. I had an assurance that our baby boy was going to live and that God had a mission for him. For ten days, he struggled and fought for every breath he took, while in an incubator with needles inserted into his tiny body. What a joy for us, as well as the intensive care nurses, the day he was placed in my arms and we were able to take him home.

One nurse said to me, "Remember when President John F. Kennedy's baby died? He was born with the same lung disease your baby had. They moved him to the best hospital in the country to provide him with the best care available. Well, if the Kennedy baby would have been given the same care that your baby has received, he probably wouldn't have died." It wasn't by chance that we were close to the only hospital in the nation that had recently developed the most modern methods and equipment to treat this disease, as well as a staff of pediatricians and nurses with the most up-to-date knowledge of infant care. We were on vacation at the time, over four hundred miles away from home. Lance would have never lived if he had been born in the tiny hospital in Panguitch, a small town in Southern Utah, located thirty miles from the miniature town of Circleville, where we lived at the time.

No, it wasn't a coincidence that we were in the right place at the right time. I was convinced that it was an act of God that had led us to be there and had saved our baby's life. Yes, Lance did have a special mission—I'd always known it. This mission that he was leaving on now wasn't an ordinary mission; it was going to be very significant. God had preserved his life for a reason, and I believed He would use him now to witness to his family and others. I had given him to God, and I trusted that God would use him for His purposes.

The farewell service was followed by an open house at our home in Lance's honor. Many friends came to wish him well on his mission as I silently wondered how the future would unfold.

A Noticeable Change

On Friday I drove to Utah with my sister. Lance was going to the temple on Saturday with his father. There he would take upon himself even more binding and serious oaths than the one he made at the time of his ordination to the Melchizedek Priesthood. It was hard for me not to interfere and prevent him from going to the temple. To minimize the turmoil and stress I was going through, I needed to leave. Lance was still occasionally expressing negative feelings about going on his mission to me, even doing so on the day before going to the temple. I felt it would be easier for all if I were not around when he went.

The next day I met Lance at the Salt Lake airport. He had gone to the Los Angeles temple in Santa Monica that morning, then caught a plane at the Los Angeles International Airport. When I met him at the Salt Lake airport, he looked very dazed. He told me that he didn't understand the temple ceremony.

My father took us out to dinner and Lance mentioned several times that the temple ceremony had been confusing to him. He was in deep thought and very spacey. My dad reassured him if he kept going that over a period of time the temple ceremony would become more meaningful and he would understand it.

It was as if Lance were under some kind of a spell. I knew the temple ceremony had affected him strongly. Even though we could not discuss it because of the secret nature of the temple I understood why Lance was bothered. The first time I went, it was very strange and foreign to me. (Please note: in 1990, significant changes were made in the temple ceremony and they no longer do some of the things we did before that time.)

Dad owned a timeshare at Snowbird, a ski resort in the canyon at Salt Lake. It happened to be his week in October to be at his timeshare. Since Lance did not enter the Missionary Training Center (MTC) until the following Wednesday, this was perfect timing for us to spend the next few days with Dad at Snowbird. So there we were—up in the beautiful Rocky Mountains in a condominium for three days. You can guess what we talked about. Dad had a tremendous zeal to save me from what he considered to be the devil's influence over me.

Bible Interpretation

Dad insisted that I didn't believe in the Bible anymore because I didn't believe in the apostasy and restoration, and the necessity of the LDS Priesthood. As we turned to Bible Scriptures concerning these subjects, I tried to show him that my interpretation fit the context of the Bible more than his interpretation did.

Dad responded in a strong, very annoyed voice, "You don't *interpret* the Bible! I don't like the word interpret. You just read it and accept what it says!"

How paradoxical, I thought. Dad could not see he was reading a lot into the Bible Scriptures we discussed, because he was so accustomed to seeing them through his Mormon mindset. An example was Hebrews 5:4:

> No man taketh this honour unto himself, but he that is called of God, as was Aaron.

To Dad, "called of God, as was Aaron" meant that one had to be given the Aaronic and Melchizedek Priesthoods by the laying on of hands by one whom already had been given the priesthood. An LDS priesthood holder can trace his priesthood authority all the way back to

296

Joseph Smith, who supposedly received it from Peter, James, and John, who received it from Christ. Dad believed that Aaron was ordained to be a high priest by having Moses lay his hands upon his head and ordain Aaron to the priesthood. Therefore, anyone serving God must trace his authority back to a prophet who received it from God.

My first thought was that God validated Aaron's call to be high priest by causing a detached, dry branch to bloom with buds overnight. Certainly that has never happened to any LDS priesthood holder. However, I knew that Dad was referring to receiving the priesthood through the laying on of hands from one who has the priesthood already, so I kept my thought to myself.

However, I did suggest that we read about Aaron's ordination in the Old Testament. The twenty-eighth and twenty-ninth chapters of Exodus give the details of this lengthy and very unusual ordination for Aaron and his sons. After being washed, shaved, and dressed in specific clothing, they took the blood of certain animals that they had killed, and put it on themselves and their clothing.

This ordination process took several days and had no resemblance to Dad's interpretation of "called of God, as was Aaron." There was one similarity, however, and I couldn't wait to point it out to dad. The "laying on of hands" was a part of Aaron's and his sons' ordination, but not the way Dad thought. Nobody laid hands on the heads of Aaron or his sons. On the contrary, they laid hands on the heads of the animals before they killed them. This act was not just part of slaying the animal. It was a deliberate act of placing their hands on the head of each animal, as they were specifically instructed to do before it was killed and sacrificed. I'm sure they were not giving the animals the priesthood. (For this discussion with Dad, including the Scriptures, and the explanation of why they laid hands on the animals, please read Supplemental Material, V. *Discussing the Aaronic Priesthood with Dad* at the end of this book.)

It was obvious that the LDS ordination to the Aaronic Priesthood had no similarities to Aaron's and his sons' ordination in the Old Testament.

A Religious Mindset

I learned a lot about the biblical priesthood much later, but at this

297

time of discussing Aaron's ordination with Dad I certainly didn't have all the answers. That night at Snowbird as I lay in bed reflecting on our conversation, I was struck with a very interesting observation. Dad insisted that he did not "interpret" the Bible, yet he certainly had an interpretation of "called of God, as was Aaron" (Hebrews 5:4). The incredible part of all this was that nothing had phased Dad. He still believed that, "a man must be called of God, by prophecy, and by the laying on of hands by those who are in authority, to preach the Gospel and administer in the ordinances thereof." That is the fifth Article of Faith given by Joseph Smith.

That Article of Faith was so programmed in Dad's mind that whenever he read the phrase "called of God" he automatically thought, "called of God by the laying on of hands by those in authority." It was so automatic with him that he didn't realize he was putting that interpretation into Hebrews 5:4 and insisted that he did not interpret the Bible. To him that was what it said, but it actually does not say that at all.

This is only one example of what I call *religious programming*, or a religious mindset. It is very difficult to see beyond that kind of mindset. It is like looking through a window of the mind that is a computer monitor that only displays interpretations of the Bible that have been programmed into it. There seems to be a blockage (or mind block) in seeing beyond that computer window of the mind.

Is Adam the "Ancient of Days?"

The second day at Snowbird, Dad and I discussed several different subjects that led into a discussion of two contrasting views about Adam. The biblical Christian view of Adam is that he was the first man created by God and he was a sinner.

The Mormon view is that Adam was a god who stepped down from his exalted state and brought one of his wives, Eve, with him to begin the generation of human life on planet earth (Journal of Discourses, Vol. 1, p. 50; Conference talk delivered on April 9, 1852). Joseph Smith taught that Adam is Michael, the Archangel, and helped Jehovah create the world. He is also the Ancient of Days.

Dad had his *standard works* with him, so we looked up some LDS

Scriptures about Adam. The first one was:

> Among the great and mighty ones who were assembled in this vast
> congregation of the righteous were Father Adam, the Ancient of Days
> and father of all. (Doctrine & Covenants 138:38)

Next we read D&C 116:1:

> Spring Hill is named by the Lord Adam-ondi-Ahman, because, said
> he, it is the place where Adam shall come to visit his people, or the
> Ancient of Days shall sit, as spoken of by Daniel, the prophet.

We also looked up D&C 107:54:

> And the Lord appeared unto them, and they rose up and blessed
> Adam, and called him Michael, the prince, the archangel.

"Yes," Dad said, "Adam is the Ancient of Days as well as Michael,
the Archangel. As such he holds the keys of the first dispensation and
also the keys of salvation."

He confirmed his statement by reading Doctrine & Covenants 78:16:

> Who hath appointed Michael your prince, and established his feet,
> and set him upon high, and given unto him the keys of Salvation
> under the counsel and direction of the Holy One . . .

I was appalled at the enormous gap between the Christian view of
Adam and the LDS view of him. We had just read an LDS Scripture that
stated that Adam held the keys of salvation. I was thinking of Acts 4:12,
which says salvation is found in no other name but the name of Jesus. I
was highly offended as we read the above Mormon Scriptures because
my eyes had been opened to the biblical truth that salvation was only in
Jesus and was made complete *through* Jesus. I was quite sure that Jesus
did not need the help of Adam. But before I could say anything, Dad
continued to explain his view.

"Adam is Michael, who helped to create the earth. You know that,
Carma!"

Yes, I had definitely been taught that. The temple endowment clearly
teaches that before Adam was created as the first man he was Michael,

who helped Jehovah create the world. Also, several verses in the Doctrine & Covenants refer to Adam as Michael, the Archangel (D&C 27:11, 107:54, 128:21).

Section 27:11 calls him both Michael and the Ancient of Days: "And also with Michael, or Adam, the father of all, the prince of all, the ancient of days."

I remembered reading about the Ancient of Days in the Book of Daniel. I found this passage now and read it to Dad:

> I beheld till the thrones were cast down, and the Ancient of Days did sit, whose garment was white as snow, and the hair of his head like the pure wool: his throne was like the fiery flame, and his wheels as burning fire. A fiery stream issued and came forth from before him: a thousand thousands ministered unto him, and ten thousand times ten thousand stood before him: the judgment was set, and the books were opened.
>
> —Daniel 7:9–11

"That sounds similar to John's description of Jesus in the first chapter of Revelation," I said. "It also sounds like judgment day and Adam certainly is not our Judge, God is."

Then we read the next few verses of Daniel. In his vision of God's judgment, Daniel sees the Son of man, who is Jesus, coming in the clouds and is brought before the Ancient of Days and was given an everlasting dominion and Kingdom.

> I saw in the night visions, and, behold, one like the Son of man came with the clouds of heaven, and came to the Ancient of days, and they brought him near before him. And there was given him dominion, and glory, and a Kingdom, that all people, nations, and languages, should serve him: his dominion is an everlasting dominion, which shall not pass away, and his Kingdom that which shall not be destroyed.
>
> —Daniel 7:13–14

"Why would Adam give Jesus dominion, glory, and His Kingdom?" I asked. "It sounds to me like the Ancient of Days is God."

Dad responded with firmness.

"Carma, I spent much time seeking true knowledge about Adam. I heard the voice of the Lord tell me that he was a god before he became the father of all humans born to this planet. He had created his own world that he had populated with his own spirit-children. He stepped down from his high position temporarily, to get the ball rolling on planet earth. I know that is true. I have been taught these things by the voice of the Lord! I was also told that was all I was going to be taught about Adam."

Adam: a God or a Sinner?

"Dad," I pointed out, "the Bible never gives such honor and glory to Adam. As a matter of fact, the Bible says he disobeyed God and brought sin, condemnation, and death to the human race." I was getting bold.

"Besides all that, the Bible says there is only one God. So how could Adam be a god?"

I pointed out that in Isaiah 44:6 God says there are no gods besides Him. He repeats it two verses later: "Is there a God beside Me? Yea, there is no God; I know not any" (Isaiah 44:8).

"If Adam were a god, wouldn't God know about him?" I asked. Dad was getting very excited and intense.

"Carma, Carma, Carma!" he said. "You know that means God is the only god of this world. Everything in the Bible is just for the family of Heavenly Father's children on this planet. You've got to look at the big picture. I know you know all this. I am amazed how thoroughly Satan has confused you!"

"But Dad," I responded, "you always said not to add words to the Bible. We are supposed to take it for what it says. In order to interpret the many passages that say there is no god but one, we would have to add the words 'for this world.' The Bible does not say 'for this world.' It says, '. . . there is no god formed before me, neither will there be after me' " (Isaiah 43:10). I thought of a Bible verse I had read recently in an article, but I couldn't remember where it was, so I didn't show Dad. I found it later and read it:

> Every word of God is pure: he is a shield unto them that put their trust in him. Add thou not unto his words, lest he reprove thee and thou be found a liar. —Proverbs 30:5–6

I guess it was just as well I didn't show it to Dad. He was getting upset. He insisted all those passages about one god meant for this world only. It didn't mean there were not other gods of other worlds, according to his worldview. In a stern and loud voice, he addressed me.

"You need to understand these things by the Spirit. A testimony is from the Spirit. I have been taught personally by the Holy Ghost! I have heard the voice of the Lord! Have you heard the voice of the Lord?"

Dad was getting pretty intense. He continued: "I personally heard the voice of the Lord tell me that Adam was a god! I know that! Now you are getting all messed up reading the Bible and talking to all these other people. You need to stop reading the Bible for awhile. The only way you can know the truthfulness of the gospel is by a spiritual manifestation. What have you done to become the *devil's henchman*?"

I knew I had pushed too far and that it was time to let my father have the last word. I apologized for upsetting him. Then I remembered Lance. Dad and I had been so engrossed in our conversation most of the day that we had forgotten he was there. I had mixed emotions as I wondered how our conversation had affected him. I knew he was already stressed enough, and I did not want to add to his anxieties. I had deep concern for him, but I also hoped the conversation would possibly cause him to change his mind about his mission. I turned around to see if he was still present. He was sitting behind me, looking straight at both of us. His eyes were as big as saucers. I suggested we go for a walk and get some fresh air. We did so, but he didn't have much to say.

Does the Bible Contradict Itself?

The next day Dad was ready to demonstrate that sometimes the Bible contradicts itself. Dad believed the Bible and was convinced that Mormons believed and followed it more than anyone else. But he was trying here to make the point that the Bible was not sufficient.

"Now, don't get me wrong," he said. "I love the Bible and there is a lot of truth in it. But the fullness of the gospel was restored through Joseph Smith. We need modern-day revelation in addition to the Bible because the Bible has too many translation errors in it."

Then he showed me that Matthew, Mark, and Luke all recorded in their gospels that Jesus was on the cross at the sixth hour, when darkness came over the entire land until the ninth hour (Matthew 27:45, Mark 15:33, Luke 23:44). The three gospels are in agreement about the sixth hour, but John contradicts them. In his gospel he recorded that at the sixth hour Jesus was sitting in a place called the Pavement, where Pilate was saying to the Jews, "Behold, your King!" (John 19:14).

"Now, which one is right?" Dad asked. "Was Jesus on the cross, or was He being tried before Pilate at the sixth hour? You see, the Bible contradicts itself. That is why the Bible is not sufficient. We need modern-day revelation in addition to the Bible."

Over the past four years, I had been challenged many times by members of the church trying to show me that the Bible contradicted itself. I had purchased a book entitled *Encyclopedia of Bible Difficulties*, by Gleason Archer. In this book I found answers for many of these alleged contradictions, plus many more so-called problems that critics use in their efforts to discredit the Bible. When understood correctly, these alleged contradictions and so-called problems really verify the inspiration of the Bible.

I was prepared with an answer for Dad.

"Matthew, Mark, and Luke were using the Jewish method for reckoning time that started at 6 a.m. (the first hour). John was using Roman time, which started at midnight. Therefore, in Roman time Jesus was before Pilate at 6 a.m. (the sixth hour) as John records. The crucifixion started at 9 a.m.—the third hour in Jewish time, as recorded in Mark 15:25. Jesus hung on the cross at the sixth hour, noon in Jewish time, as Matthew, Mark, and Luke recorded," I explained.

There was no contradiction. It all made complete sense and fit together beautifully, since there was six hours' difference between Jewish and Roman time.

After we discussed a few more examples of what seemed to him to be contradictions in the Bible, I remembered something Tobie had said: "If it seems that the Bible contradicts itself, it is our understanding and interpretation that is in error, not the Bible."

I had found that to be true.

Many times in my life I had heard Dad quote an old Indian saying: "White man speak with forked tongue." Then Dad would say,

"Sometimes the Mormons speak with a forked tongue."

That was definitely true when it came to their belief about the Bible. One moment they believed it, the next moment it was erroneous. My Dad was demonstrating this quite well. He had taught me all my life that the Bible was the blueprint for truth. Now he was showing me that it contradicted itself. God certainly would not contradict himself; therefore, if the Bible is His Word, it would not contradict itself either. Seeing contradictions mean that we have the wrong (or an incomplete) understanding of what we are reading.

The bottom line seems to be that one eventually needs to discredit the Bible in order to defend Joseph Smith, I thought to myself, sadly. But I didn't say it aloud.

The Final Farewell

On Wednesday Lance and I went to the Missionary Training Center in Provo, Utah. All the missionaries went there for three weeks of training (or for a couple of months if they were going to a country where they had to learn a foreign language) before being sent to their specific places of service. Lance had relaxed a bit, but he was still extremely pensive. My real desire was to talk him out of going, but I reminded myself that I had given this situation over to God. I must trust Him and not let my own emotions interfere with what I felt God had told me to do—which was to *wait on the Lord* and not take matters into my own hands.

As we entered the main entrance of the MTC my eyes focused on a large picture of Joseph Smith hanging next to a picture of Jesus. I felt sick. How could I be leaving Lance here? I silently prayed.

"Lord, I hope this is your will."

It was so hard for me to think that Lance was going to go out and teach that Joseph Smith was a true prophet, but all I could do was pray. "Father in Heaven, Please don't let him be deceived. Please teach him the truth, whatever it is that You know is right— your way, dear God— not my way, nor anybody else's way, but your way."

I had given Lance to God as Hannah in the Old Testament had given her son, Samuel, to God. The difference between Hannah and me was that she'd left her son at God's house. I felt like I was leaving my son with a pack of wolves. I realized that Lance had a very strong constitution and a strong will, but he was a sheep among wolves here at the Missionary Training Center. I realized it was going to be stressful for him. I continually prayed for God to protect him and teach him the truth. All I could do was trust that God was going to do something to save him—something that would be a testimony to the rest of the family and me. I prayed and trusted.

Lance seemed so troubled. He asked for a special blessing from the Priesthood leader at the MTC. We attended the parent/missionary meeting, after which we were to say our final goodbye. George P. Durrant, president of the MTC, conducted the meeting. He welcomed everybody, and then spoke.

"The opening prayer will be given by . . ." He paused, looked around the room, and then quickly pointed to a young elder on the front row. I felt a sting of fear and relief for Lance and every other new missionary in the room as they realized they could be called on extemporaneously to pray or bear testimony.

I remembered how it was mandatory in the mission field to bear one's testimony at each bimonthly zone meeting when the missionaries got together. This wasn't voluntary; it was done row by row, missionary by missionary, as your turn came up.

I knew Lance was deeply searching for God and for answers, as were probably the majority of the other new, unprepared, and nervous missionaries in the room. This was not the place to seek and search for God and truth. It was now time to be a teacher and to be sure of yourself. It was now time to say and speak what was expected of you to say and speak. It was now time to give your testimony.

My instructions to Lance had been: "Do your own thinking, seek God and don't just say and do what you are told." Given the expectations here, how could he do that? Once again I asked Father in Heaven to please help my son.

The main emphasis of the meeting was that we (family members) were not to have any contact of any kind except by letter. The missionary was not allowed to telephone home and we were not to call him or come and see him. His sister Nancy, who was attending Brigham Young

University which was located just next to the training center, couldn't even see him. If any serious problems arose, or the missionary got sick while on his mission, we were assured that the mission leaders would contact his parents. Under no circumstance was the missionary to call his home or friends. The president of the MTC pointed to a door on his right as he spoke.

"You see that door? After telling you goodbye, your son or daughter is going to walk through that door and that will be the last you will see him for two years. All parents are to walk through the door on my left and there will be no more communication with each other except by mail."

We were committed to the first mission rule, which was to write to each other weekly. It was extremely difficult to leave Lance at the MTC. I was fully aware of the intense pressure he would be under to articulate a testimony that he knew Joseph Smith was a true prophet, that the Book of Mormon was true, and that the church was true. Nonetheless, I was not at all prepared for what was to come!

Don't Miss **Book 2**!

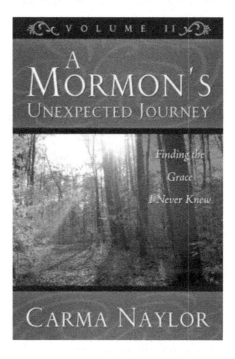

A MORMON'S UNEXPECTED JOURNEY
Finding the Grace I Never Knew   **Volume 2**

Carma Naylor continues her compelling story, as she compares Mormonism to the true gospel of Jesus Christ. Here is a **brief segment** from Volume 2:

Leaving our son, Lance, in the Missionary Training Center was one of my most difficult steps of faith. I trusted I was acting in God's will and that He was going to do something. I returned home to California and waited anxiously for a letter from Lance. Over a week passed. No letter. I was extremely eager to hear how he was doing. Early Friday morning the phone rang. It was Nancy, our oldest daughter. She was attending Brigham Young University, located next to the Missionary Training Center (MTC) in Provo, Utah. Her soft, cautious voice suggested something was wrong. She had gone to the MTC early that morning with some homemade cookies and a card for Lance. Knowing that she would not be allowed to deliver them personally, she was waiting at the front desk when a missionary happened to walk up and notice Lance's name on the envelope. The unknown missionary looked at Nancy and spoke.

"Lance isn't here."

Thinking he was teasing, Nancy responded cheerfully. "Oh, do you know Lance?"

With over nineteen hundred elders in the MTC, it was rather amazing that she would meet one at 6:30 a.m. who was acquainted with Lance.

"Yes," the missionary said. "I was his companion. As I told you, he isn't here."

His expression and tone of voice stunned Nancy as she realized he wasn't joking.

"But my mom left him here ten days ago. What do you mean, he isn't here?" she asked with surprise.

"He's in the hospital. He's been there since Monday night," was his answer.

As Nancy told me this over the phone, my heart sank. Why hadn't we been notified there was a problem, as they had told us we would be? I had been so concerned about him since we parted at the MTC.

"What happened? Is he sick? What has he got?" I impatiently asked my daughter.

Nancy's voice was subdued and slow.

"Mom, he's in the psychiatric ward at the hospital. I called to find out if he was really there, like his companion said he was."

"What!" I felt myself getting sick and angry at the same time. I could hardly speak; my thoughts were racing so. What had Lance been going through? My heart hurt for him. Why hadn't someone called from the MTC to let us know there was a problem? We should have been notified

308

that Lance was struggling! Why had everything been kept a secret? Why couldn't he have called us and talked to us? How could they just put him in the hospital, the psychiatric ward no less, and not even ask our permission, or, even worse than that, not even inform us!

Read more in **Volume 2** of
A MORMON'S UNEXPECTED JOURNEY
available at bookstores and online book retailers worldwide

SUPPLEMENTAL MATERIAL

I.   Mind Blocks

II.   The Stick of Judah and the Stick of Joseph

III. Three Degrees of Glory

IV.   The Holy Bible: God's Double-Edged Sword

V.   Discussing the Aaronic Priesthood with Dad

I. Mind Blocks

"Nevertheless when one turns to the Lord, the veil is taken away."
—2 Corinthians 3:16

Overcoming Spiritual Mind Blocks

Bible interpretation is not always an easy matter; otherwise, everyone would be united in doctrine. The world is full of many sincere people who are convinced that they are following God and yet believing contradictory doctrines. What is the problem? Is it the Bible? Is it a matter of the Bible being too difficult to understand, or is it a matter of a lack of desire to truly understand the Bible?

The first step in overcoming spiritual mind blocks is to desire truth. An example is baptism by immersion. The Bible says that when Jesus was baptized, he "went up straightway out of the water" (Matthew 3:16). John the Baptist baptized in the Jordan River (Mark 1:5). The word baptize comes from a word that means "to immerse." In spite of these and other biblical evidences to support baptism by immersion, there are Christian churches that baptize by sprinkling or by touching one's forehead with water. In order for a person who believes in sprinkling to accept baptism by immersion, they would first need to want to know the truth about baptism, then read the Bible and accept what it says. Then they'd have to swallow their pride and admit they could be wrong. They need to want the truth more than they want to be right.

Is the Bible unclear, or is our understanding of it unclear because of a biased mind? Are we all guilty, at times, of ignoring facts that disagree with what we want to believe while over-emphasizing information or ideas that support what we want to be true? Probably. Interpreting the Bible thus becomes a matter of desiring God's truth rather than wanting to be right because of a pre-conceived mindset.

Conforming Our Beliefs to the Bible

Secondly, we need to be willing to conform our beliefs to the Bible rather than conforming the Bible to our beliefs. That seemed to be the whole issue here. First, be willing to find out what the Bible really says, and then secondly, be willing to accept what it says without coloring it. In order to do that, we need the Lord to show us that we are coloring it. Peter tells us that we have the prophecies of the prophets which are sure, and it is up to us to read them and not put personal interpretation into them:

> "And we have the word of the prophets made more certain, and you will do well to pay attention to it, as to a light shining in a dark place, until the day dawns and the morning star rises in your heart. Above all, you must understand that no prophecy of Scripture came about by the prophet's own interpretation. For prophecy never had its origin in the will of man, but men spoke from God as they were carried along by the Holy Spirit."
>
> —2 Peter 1:19–21 NIV

The above Scripture indicates that God's interpretation and viewpoint are in the Bible and we should be able to understand His viewpoint if we are willing to submit our wills and viewpoints to His own. There is really no reason to have so many interpretations of what God said. He knows what He meant, and I firmly believe He will reveal to us the correct meaning of His Word if we are surrendered to Him. He had inspired holy men to write it so that we need not be confused if we are willing to let go of our preconceived, predetermined, religious views.

The problem of their being so many different religious views is not the fault of the Bible. Rather the fault is in men trying to conform the Bible to their beliefs instead of conforming their beliefs to the Bible. To correct this error, we must be willing to surrender our will to God's will and submit to the Bible as God's written Word to us. Erroneous interpretations of the Scriptures occur because of preprogrammed mindsets and a lack of submission to God's mind and will.

Removing the Veil

A religious mindset can be a veil over our mind and heart. The opening of my mind and heart was nothing short of a miracle of God. He removed the veil over my mind, with all its preconceived ideas and spiritual mind blocks when I fully surrendered to Him. From that time on, I prayed daily that God would also remove the veil from my Dad's, my husband's, and my family's minds, as He had done for me.

When speaking of the Jews, Paul said, "But their minds were blinded. For until this day the same veil remains unlifted in the reading of the Old Testament, because the veil is taken away in Christ. But even to this day, when Moses is read, a veil lies on their heart. Nevertheless when one turns to the Lord, the veil is taken away." (2 Corinthians 3:14–16 NKJV)

II. The Stick of Judah and the Stick of Joseph

"Moreover, thou son of man, take thee one stick, and write upon it, For Judah, and for the children of Israel his companions: then take another stick, and write upon it, For Joseph, the stick of Ephraim, and for all the house of Israel his companions: And join them one to another into one stick; and they shall become one in thine hand."
—Ezekiel 37:16–17

• Mormon Interpretation

The word stick refers to a book, since anciently they wrote books on scrolls rolled up on sticks. The above Scripture refers to two different books. The first book (or stick) is for Judah and his companions and is interpreted to refer to the Bible. The second book (or stick) is to be written for Joseph and his companions, and is interpreted to refer to the Book of Mormon—allegedly the descendants of Joseph, son of Jacob.

Verse 17, above, states that they would be joined together, "and they shall become one in thine hand." This is interpreted by the Mormon Church to imply that the Bible and the Book of Mormon would be used together as one Scripture by God. They go hand in hand with each other. They are separate books, but both books of Scripture are used together to clarify God's Word. Today they are bound together in one book, but still recognized as two different books.

• Biblical Christian Interpretation

The word "sticks" literally means two sticks, not scrolls, that Ezekiel holds, one in each hand, and they symbolize the divided Kingdom of

Israel. Looking back into Israel's history, we see that God divided the nation of Israel after King Solomon's tenure. The Northern Kingdom (ten tribes) was referred to as the Kingdom of Israel. It was also called Ephraim (Joseph's son) because Ephraim was the most prominent and influential tribe of the Northern Kingdom.

The first king of the Northern Kingdom (Israel, or Ephraim) was Jeroboam, an Ephraimite who established calf-worship. This idolatrous worship was never reversed. As the dominant tribe of the Northern Kingdom, Ephraim came to stand for the entire ten-tribe Kingdom (2 Chronicles 25:7, Jeremiah 7:15). The Southern Kingdom became known as Judah and was comprised of the remaining two tribes of Israel; Judah being the dominant tribe. Rehoboam became the first king of Judah. Thus we have Israel divided into two Kingdoms:

1. The Northern Kingdom: Israel, or Ephraim
2. The Southern Kingdom: Judah

The prophet Ezekiel is told by God to take one stick and write upon it these words: "For Judah, and for the children of Israel, his companions." He was to take another stick and do the same, only write: "For Joseph, the stick of Ephraim, and for all the house of Israel, his companions." This was commanded in order to symbolize the two nations of Israel.

These were literal sticks, symbolizing the divided nation of Israel, the Kingdom of Israel, or Ephraim (the Northern Kingdom), and the Kingdom of Judah (the Southern Kingdom). The Lord then tells Ezekiel to take these two sticks and put them together as one in his hand. This symbolizes that the two nations would someday become one united nation of Israel, with one ruler or Shepherd, who is Jesus Christ.

If we look to the Bible to interpret itself, without the interpretation of man, we have no difficulty at all with this Scripture. The rest of the chapter is very clear. In verse eighteen (the next verse), the Lord tells Ezekiel, "When your countrymen ask you, 'Won't you tell us what you mean by this?' say to them, 'This is what the Sovereign LORD says...'" He continues on:

Say unto them, Thus saith the Lord GOD; Behold, I will take the stick of Joseph, which is in the hand of Ephraim, and the tribes of Israel his fellows, and will put them with him, even with the stick of Judah, and make them one stick, and they shall be one in mine hand.

—Ezekiel 37:19

Notice that the Lord includes the tribes of Israel associated with Ephraim (the entire Northern Kingdom) and says that He (the Lord), "will put them with him [with Judah] and they shall be one in mine hand."

As we keep reading we see that, in verse twenty, the LORD tells Ezekiel to hold before their eyes the sticks he has written on. Then the Lord gives the interpretation of what the sticks symbolize:

And the sticks whereon thou writest shall be in thine hand before their eyes. And say unto them, Thus saith the Lord GOD; Behold, I will take the children of Israel from among the heathen, whither they be gone, and will gather them on every side, and bring them into their own land: And I will make them one nation in the land upon the mountains of Israel; and one king shall be king to them all: and they shall be no more two nations, neither shall they be divided into two Kingdoms any more at all.

—Ezekiel 37:20–22

There is no ambiguity about the meaning of the two sticks. God gives the interpretation. At the time that God gives this prophecy through Ezekiel, the Israelites had already been taken captive. Ezekiel is one of those captives living in Babylon. God is making the promise to his chosen people, the Israelites, that even though they polluted themselves with the worship of false gods and pagan religions, He will someday gather them out of the nations to which they have been scattered because of their sins, and they will be brought back to their own land.

Furthermore, according to this prophecy, when God gathers them from the nations, they will no longer be two nations (not a divided Israel), but they will be one nation and He will be their King. As we finish reading the rest of the chapter, it is clear that this will happen in the day when they will accept Jesus Christ as their Messiah, the descendant of David, in whom David's throne will be realized (Luke 1:31–33). In the millennial Kingdom, Israel will be united and ruled by the True Shepherd, Jesus Christ. The Jewish nation will dwell in the land that God gave to Jacob, where all will live in peace. They will no longer defile themselves with idols. God will dwell among them, and He will be their God and they will be His people.

> Neither shall they defile themselves any more with their idols, nor with their detestable things, nor with any of their transgressions: but I will save them out of all their dwellingplaces, wherein they have sinned, and will cleanse them: so shall they be my people, and I will be their God. And David my servant shall be king over them; and they all shall have one shepherd: they shall also walk in my judgments, and observe my statutes, and do them. And they shall dwell in the land that I have given unto Jacob my servant, wherein your fathers have dwelt; and they shall dwell therein, even they, and their children, and their children's children for ever: and my servant David shall be their prince for ever. Moreover I will make a covenant of peace with them; it shall be an everlasting covenant with them: and I will place them, and multiply them, and will set my sanctuary in the midst of them forevermore. My tabernacle also shall be with them: yea, I will be their God, and they shall be my people. And the heathen shall know that I the LORD do sanctify Israel, when my sanctuary shall be in the midst of them for evermore.
> —Ezekiel 37:23–28

The two sticks represent the two nations of Israel that God would put together when Israel would again become one nation. That is the simple explanation of "the two sticks" that God Himself gives of this passage.

• An End-Times Prophecy

This is an extremely important prophecy that God gave through Ezekiel approximately 2500 years ago, and it is particularly exciting because the fulfillment of this prophecy is happening in our generation. On May 15, 1948, Israel was given its own land and made an independent nation. This had never happened over the 2500 years since Ezekiel made this promise! Israel had been scattered since the captivity of the Northern Kingdom of Israel by the King of Assyria in 722 B.C. (2 Kings 17:6) and the captivity of the Southern Kingdom of Judah by Nebuchadnezzar in 586 B.C. (Daniel 1:1). (The Babylonian siege of Jerusalem started in 605 B.C. At that time some Jews were taken captive to Babylon. Then in 597 B.C. more captives were taken including their king. In 586 B.C. Jerusalem and the temple were destroyed.)

After the Jews were in Babylon seventy years, King Cyrus of Persia made a proclamation allowing the Jews to return to Israel to rebuild the temple (Ezra 1:1–3). However, most of the Jews chose to remain in Babylon. Later, the walls were rebuilt to fortify Jerusalem in 445 B.C. under the leadership of Nehemiah (Nehemiah 2:1). Yet in spite of the remnant returning to their land, the Israelites have remained scattered throughout the nations after their captivity. Also, even though there has always been a remnant of Jews in the land, they did not have their independence; but they were ruled by various nations. The Roman Empire was reigning during the time of Jesus and the last empire to rule over Israel. In 70 A.D. Jerusalem was destroyed by the Romans and after that Israel did not exist as a nation—that is until its miraculous rebirth in 1948.

Since then thousands of Jews have returned to the Holy Land. Over one-half million Russian Jews have left Russia to join their brothers in the Promised Land. The return of the Jews from all the lands of the dispersion to their own nation, in their homeland, is the fulfillment of Ezekiel's prophecy in our day. Israel has not been one united, independent nation since King Solomon's reign, about 3000 years ago until 1948. That is not only amazing, but pretty exciting, as it means we are getting close to the Second Coming of Jesus. We are literally seeing the fulfillment of Ezekiel's prophecy of the two sticks and God's promise to Israel:

> And say unto them, Thus saith the Lord GOD; Behold, I will take the children of Israel from among the heathen, whither they be gone, and will gather them on every side, and bring them into their own land: And I will make them one nation in the land upon the mountains of Israel; and one king shall be king to them all: and they shall be no more two nations, neither shall they be divided into two Kingdoms any more at all.
>
> —Ezekiel 37:21–22

• Three Ways to Test Interpretations

If you are still not convinced what is meant by Ezekiel's sticks, let's look at three ways to test different interpretations of the Bible:

1. Look at the original language and the meaning used in the original text.
2. See which interpretation fits what the rest of the Bible says on the subject.
3. Put the Scripture in context.

Let's do a brief study following the above three suggestions. Suppose we wanted to know more about the prophecy of the two sticks. Where would one start?

Well, what is the original Hebrew word used by Ezekiel for stick? Does it literally mean "stick" or does it mean "book?"

The word that is translated *stick* and is used in Ezekiel 37:15–20, is *ets* in the Hebrew manuscripts. What do key sources say about this word?

> **ets** ates; a tree (from its firmness); hence wood (plur. sticks):+ carpenter, gallows, helve, + plus pine, plank, staff, stalk, stick stock, timber, tree, wood. (*Strong's Exhaustive Concordance of the Bible*, #6086 of the *Hebrew* and *Chaldee Dictionary*, p. 90)

There is another Hebrew word that means book or scroll. It is *ciphrah*.

> **ciphrah**; writing (the art or a document); by impl. a book; bill, book, evidence, x learn[-ed] (-ing), letter, register, scroll. (*Strong's Exhaustive Concordance of the Bible*, #5612 of the *Hebrew* and *Chaldee Dictionary*, p. 84)

These two Hebrew words (*ets* and *ciphrah*) are not related and they look very different; therefore they would not have been confused by translators. If Ezekiel were referring to books or scrolls, then why didn't he use the Hebrew word *ciphrah* for *book*? It is noteworthy that he does use this word ciphrah in the first part of his book when he refers to "a roll of a book." (See Ezekiel 2:9, 3:1.) He apparently knew the difference and correctly used *ciphrah* for book and *ets* for stick of wood.

Now, which interpretation fits into the rest of the Bible? The interpretation that the divided Israel would be reunited into one nation is supported many places in the Bible, as well as in history. Other prophecies stating that hostility between the two kingdoms would cease are Isaiah 11:13 and Jeremiah 31:6. Many Old Testament prophets prophesied of the reuniting of Israel and the gathering into its own land: Jeremiah 31:18–20, 23–25, 50:19; Ezekiel 37:16–19, Zechariah 10:7; and Hosea 11:11, 14:8. I'll include just two here:

> Behold, I will bring them from the north country, and gather them from the coasts of the earth, and with them the blind and the lame, the woman with child and her that travaileth with child together: a great company shall return thither.
>
> —Jeremiah 31:8

> Therefore, behold, the days come, saith the LORD, that it shall no more be said, The LORD liveth, that brought up the children of Israel out of the land of Egypt; But, The LORD liveth, that brought up the children of Israel from the land of the north, and from all the lands whither he had driven them: and I will bring them again into their land that I gave unto their fathers.
>
> —Jeremiah 16:14–15

We have already thoroughly discussed the surrounding Scriptures about Ezekiel's sticks, showing how they do state the meaning of the sticks to be the divided nations of Israel becoming united into one nation. We can also look at more context, as well. In the first half of Ezekiel 37, for instance, Ezekiel is given a vision of dry bones that come to life. This also symbolizes the rebirth of the nation of Israel.

As we study the entire book of Ezekiel we notice that he uses many visual demonstrations in order to get the Israelites' attention when warning them of the coming destruction and the days of their captivity. When we put Ezekiel 37:16–20 in context with the rest of the book, it is easy to see why he would hold up two sticks, symbolizing the two kingdoms, then hold them as one in his hand, symbolizing the one nation of Israel that exists today. This becomes even less surprising and more meaningful when we understand that the Israelites often used sticks symbolically to represent themselves and their tribes.

Even the LDS scholar Hugh Nibley acknowledges the use of a staff or sticks by the Israelites to identify tribes for formal occasions:

> Every man who came to the great gathering of the nation at the New Year was required to bring with him a staff with his name on it. For the same occasion the leader of every tribe had to present a tribal staff with official marks of identification on it; the twelve tribal staves were then bound together in a ritual bundle and laid up in the Ark of the Covenant as representing the united force of the nation.
>
> —*An Approach to The Book of Mormon*, Nibley, p. 278

Although Nibley does not accept a biblical interpretation of the literal sticks representing the two nations of Israel, his above description of the use of sticks in representing these tribes certainly verifies and fits the biblical, Christian interpretation, not his own Mormon interpretation; i.e. that the sticks represent the Bible and the Book of Mormon.

In the same book Hugh Nibley states that Bible scholars have no explanation for the verses of Scripture discussed in this article, saying:

> No passage in Ezekiel is more variously and more fancifully explained than the mysterious account of the stick of Joseph and the stick of Judah. . . . The wild and contradictory guesses of the ablest scholars on this passage demonstrate beyond a doubt that Ezekiel is here talking about a matter which, however familiar it may have been to his ancient audience, lies wholly outside the scope of conventional Bible scholarship.
>
> —*ibid.*, p. 272, 273

I think it has been well demonstrated that the Ezekiel 37:15–20 is not at all beyond biblical scholarship. In fact, this is such a clear prophecy concerning the rebirth of Israel prior to Christ's return and that we could recognize Christ's coming to be close when this occurs, that it is no wonder Satan would want to cloud its real interpretation with a clever, false one.

Please do not allow yourself to be deceived. If we open our hearts to God's Word and are willing to rid ourselves of our preconceived, determined opinions, there is no question about the meaning of Ezekiel 37. God's interpretation is clear. As Jesus said, "He that hath ears to hear, let him hear" (Matthew 11:15).

III. Three Degrees of Glory

"There are also celestial bodies, and bodies terrestrial: but the glory of the celestial is one, and the glory of the terrestrial is another. There is one glory of the sun, and another glory of the moon, and another glory of the stars; for one star differeth from another star in glory. So also is the resurrection of the dead."
—1 Corinthians 15:40–42

The Mormon Interpretation

The above Scripture embodies the biblical support for the Mormon doctrine of heaven as revealed in a vision to Joseph Smith and recorded in the Doctrine & Covenants, Section 76. The revelation sets forth that there are three main degrees of heaven: the Celestial, the Terrestrial, and the Telestial Kingdoms. Verses ninety-six through ninety-eight of section seventy-six sound very similar to the above Scripture in 1 Corinthians, reading:

> And the glory of the celestial is one, even as the glory of the sun is one. And the glory of the terrestrial is one, even as the glory of the moon is one. And the glory of the telestial is one, even as the glory of the stars is one; for as one star differs from another star in glory, even so differs one from another in glory in the telestial world.
> —D&C 76:96–98

According to Mormon theology, the Celestial Kingdom is the highest degree and is divided into three kingdoms. The top division of this glory or kingdom is where those who attain to godhood will dwell.

> Wherefore, as it is written, they are gods, even the sons of God.
> —D&C 76:58

The Celestial Kingdom is symbolized by the sun:

> These are they whose bodies are celestial, whose glory is that of the sun, even the glory of God, the highest of all, whose glory the sun of the firmament is written of as being typical.
>
> —D&C 76:70

The Terrestrial Kingdom is symbolized by the moon and is as different from the Celestial Kingdom as the sun is from the moon. This kingdom of glory is for those who died without law (D&C 76:72) and the, "honorable men of the earth, who were blinded by the craftiness of men" (D&C 76:75).

The Telestial Kingdom is symbolized by the stars. This is the lesser kingdom of glory for those, ". . . who are thrust down to hell" (ibid, vs. 84). "These are they who are liars, and sorcerers, and adulterers, and whoremongers, and whosoever loves and makes a lie" (vs. 103). "These are they who suffer the vengeance of eternal fire" (vs. 105), but are eventually redeemed from a temporary hell (also called spirit prison) at the last resurrection. (D&C 76:85, 106, 42, 43)

In the Mormon view of salvation, as described above, all are saved in a degree of glory—the just and the unjust, the righteous and the wicked. Joseph Smith said that even the Telestial Degree of Glory, where the wicked will dwell, is so glorious that if we could get one little glimpse of the Telestial glory, "we would be tempted to commit suicide to get there." (BYU Speeches, March 10, 1964, p. 4) The only individuals who will not be saved somewhere in the above kingdoms of glory are the so-called "sons of perdition, who deny the Son after the Father has revealed him. Wherefore, he saves all except them . . ." (ibid, vv. 43, 44). In LDS theology, very, very few people can fit this category because one has to literally know that Jesus is the Christ, the Son of God, and then defy and deny Him.

The LDS plan of salvation and interpretation of 1 Corinthians 15:40–42 appeals to human nature, which desires to believe in a loving, merciful God who will reward all men according to their works in the flesh and who would not condemn anyone to an eternal hell. Let's now compare this view with the Christian interpretation of Paul's message to the Corinthians.

The Biblical Christian Interpretation

In the fifteenth chapter of 1 Corinthians, Paul is writing to the gentile converts in Corinth who were influenced by their Greek background, which was a belief in the immortality of the soul but not in a resurrected body. Some of these new believers were saying that there was no resurrection (vs. 12), and Paul is convincing them that to deny our resurrection would be to deny Christ's resurrection and would render their faith useless.

Starting with verse thirty-five, Paul discusses the nature of the resurrected body:

> But someone may ask, "How are the dead raised? With what kind of body will they come?"
>
> —1 Corinthians 15:35 NIV

He then uses an example of a seed that is sown. It must first die. Then the plant that comes from the seed will be different from the seed, but will be the same kind of plant as the seed. He explains that there are different kinds of seeds and also different kinds of flesh; i.e. human, animal, fish, and birds. In the resurrection, our new bodies may resemble our human body, but they will be different and will no longer be earthly bodies. They will be spiritual bodies. In verse forty, Paul teaches the fact that, "There are also heavenly bodies and there are earthly bodies; but the splendor of the heavenly bodies is one kind, and the splendor of the earthly bodies is another" (NIV).

He uses another analogy of the sun, moon, and stars to demonstrate different kinds of splendor, in making his point that our heavenly bodies will be much greater in splendor than our earthly bodies. He clarifies this point in the verses that follow, and it would be helpful for readers to read through verse fifty in order to grasp Paul's meaning:

> The body that is sown is perishable, it is raised imperishable; it is sown in dishonor, it is raised in glory; it is sown in weakness, it is raised in power; it is sown a natural body, it is raised a spiritual body.
>
> —vv. 43, 44

> And just as we have borne the likeness of the earthly man, so shall

we bear the likeness of the man from heaven.

—vs. 49

Notice that Paul is making a clear distinction between two bodies— our present, earthly, physical, perishable body and our future heavenly, spiritual, imperishable body.

Three Ways to Test These Interpretations

1. By putting verses 40–42 in context with the verses surrounding them we see that Paul is not discussing three levels of heaven, but instead is stating that at the resurrection we will come forth with resurrected bodies that will be far superior to the mortal bodies we now have. Whenever there is a difference of interpreting a Bible passage, it is very important to read the passage in context in order to get the true meaning (as done above), rather than interpreting the passage according to what we want it to say. It is important that we be fair and not read into the passage an idea that isn't there.

2. A second way to verify the correct interpretation of Scripture is to go to the original Greek words and look up their definitions. The two words celestial and terrestrial, as found in the King James Translation, verse forty, according to the Greek Dictionary of the New Testament, are translated from the two Greek words listed below:

    "celestial #2032 : epouranios: above the sky: -celestial, (in) heaven (-ly), high.

    "terrestrial #1919 : *epigelos*: worldly (phys. or mor.): -earthly, in earth, *terrestrial."*

These definitions confirm that in the original Greek transcripts, both the King James and the New International translations are correct because *celestial* means, "of heaven," while *terrestrial* means, "of the earth." The NIV translation is easier to understand.

There are also heavenly bodies and there are earthly bodies; but the splendor of the heavenly bodies is one kind, and the splendor of the earthly bodies is another.

—1 Corinthians 15:40 NIV

The King James translators just chose to use the word *celestial* in place of heavenly and *terrestrial* in place of earthly. There are also *celestial* bodies, and bodies *terrestrial*: but the glory of the *celestial* is one, and the glory of the *terrestrial* is another.

3. A third way to verify that we are making a correct interpretation of Scripture is to put the Scripture or Scripture passage in question in context with the rest of the Bible. What do other verses say on the subject? If the interpretation disagrees with other clear passages, then it would be the wrong interpretation. On the other hand, a correct interpretation would be in agreement with other passages in the Bible.

Since the Mormon interpretation of the Scripture being discussed explains their idea of the plan of salvation, let's see what the rest of the New Testament says about this subject. We find that there is no mention of "three degrees of glory" in heaven anywhere, but that there are varying levels of rewards for believers that get into the Kingdom of Heaven (1 Corinthians 3:8, 14; Colossians 3:24, Revelation 22:12). Throughout the New Testament there are not three divisions of judgment, but only two. In other words, you are either in the Kingdom or out of it. You either have *eternal life* or *eternal condemnation*.

Christ spoke of men receiving *life* or *destruction*. (same Greek word for *perdition*). The Mormon plan of salvation is universal—seeing everyone in the Kingdom of Heaven in one of the three degrees of glory, except a few sons of perdition. (Introduction to the 76 Section of the D&C indicates that these kingdoms, as described in Joseph Smith's revelation, comprise heaven.) The Bible is very clear that not everyone will enter the

Kingdom of Heaven; only those who have been *born again* and confessed Jesus as Lord and trusted in Him alone for salvation will dwell there. John 3:16 says: "That whosoever believeth in him should not perish, but have everlasting life."

We see here the two possible destinies— to perish or to have everlasting life, and that life is based on a personal belief in Jesus Christ as the substitutionary Lamb of God, whose offering of Himself paid the full price for our sins. According to the words of Jesus and the other writers of the New Testament, everlasting life is not automatically given to everyone.

The reward of heaven is for believers— those who have gained eternal life through faith in Jesus Christ and his finished work on the cross. The words we find in the New Testament to describe the fate of nonbelievers are: death, destruction, perish, eternal damnation, cast out with the devil and his angels. (Matthew 5:29, Luke 13:3, John 3:16, John 10:28, 2 Thessalonians 2:10, 2 Peter 2:12, 3:9; Luke 16:23, and many others.) Be sure your faith is saving faith that matches the teaching of God's Word and meets the test of faithful interpretation!

IV. The Holy Bible: God's Double-Edged Sword

"The grass withers, the flower fades, but the word of our God stands forever."
—Isaiah 40:8

A major teaching of Mormonism is that the Bible is not trustworthy as the definitive source of God's Word to mankind. Nevertheless, the Bible declares over 3800 times that, "God said," or states, "Thus saith the LORD . . ." Thus, based on its own claim, the Bible is either the Word of God or it lies in making the claim that it is and could not be God's trustworthy Word.

Jesus Endorsed the Old Testament

The fact that Jesus quoted from the Old Testament gives us confidence that it was accurate in His day. Following are some examples of Jesus affirming the Old Testament:

In Mark 12:36, Jesus is quoting Psalm 110:1 and He validates David's writings as inspired by saying: "For David himself said by the Holy Ghost . . . ."

In Matthew 19:4–6, Jesus quotes Genesis 1:27 and Genesis 2:24 as if it is the spoken Word of God: "And he answered and said unto them, Have ye not read . . . ."

In Mark 7:9, 10, Jesus affirms that Moses' writings were the commands of God.

In Mark 7:13, Jesus again establishes Moses' writings as the Word of God and, as such, as more authoritative than tradition: "Making the word of God of none effect through your tradition, which ye have delivered:

and many such like things do ye." (See also verse 8.)

Jesus quotes from the Book of Isaiah in Mark 7:6, 7. Many more examples could be given wherein Jesus validated the Old Testament as God's Word. Christ said, in John 10:35, that, "Scripture cannot be broken." He confirmed His own words to be God's words in John 12:48, 49. He also quoted Scripture in answering his critics in Matthew 22:32 (quoting Exodus 3:6, 15) and Matthew 22:42–44 (quoting Psalm 110:1).

When tempted by the powers of Satan, Jesus used the Word of God— Old Testament Scripture—to overcome the enemy, thus demonstrating the Scripture's power over the clever and powerful attacks of the destroyer. To answer his temptations, Jesus quotes Deuteronomy 8:31, Deuteronomy 6:16, and Deuteronomy 6:13:

> But he answered and said, It is written, Man shall not live by bread alone, but by every word that proceedeth out of the mouth of God.
> —Matthew 4:4

> Jesus said unto him, It is written again, Thou shalt not tempt the Lord thy God.
> —Matthew 4:7

> Then saith Jesus unto him, Get thee hence, Satan: for it is written, Thou shalt worship the Lord thy God, and him only shalt thou serve.
> —Matthew 4:10

Notice that Jesus' reply to Satan is prefaced each time by the words, "It is written . . . ." How amazing! Think about how significant this is. The very Creator of the universe, the omniscient Christ, did not engage in a debate or use His own wisdom to reason with Satan. He simply used God's established, revealed Word. This demonstrates how powerful the Scripture was for Him, and thus it is for us, also. Do we use the Word of God to combat Satan's temptations and clever deceptions, as Jesus did? If not, we may be in serious trouble.

Notice how effectively Satan also quotes Scripture to validate himself. [In Matthew 4:6, Satan is quoting Psalm 91:11, 12.] Because of Jesus' complete and accurate knowledge of the message of Scripture, He is able to see through Satan's misuse of the Word. What an example for us this is! *Is Satan misleading the human race today by using this same tactic of quoting Scripture out of context to sincere people who do not know the Scripture well enough and consequently cannot detect the error?*

Christ did not waste time arguing with Satan, nor did He try to reason with the enemy by using logic. Rather, Jesus turned to the authority of the Scripture to confront the "Father of Lies." In doing so, Jesus vindicated the written Scriptures as accurate and trustworthy. He confirmed the power and authority of Scripture and set the correct standard for us to use when confronted with untruths and temptations of the devil.

The Book of Mormon states that when Jesus visited the Nephites in America He made sure their Scriptures contained what He wanted them to teach and told them to add certain things they had not included in their records (3 Nephi 23:6–14). Surely Jesus would have done the same for the Jews. I can't imagine Jesus quoting from an erroneous translation of God's Word without correcting it.

Jesus confirmed the authority and accuracy of the Old Testament after His resurrection when He said, in Luke 24:44, "And he said unto them, These are the words which I spake unto you, while I was yet with you, that all things must be fulfilled, which were written in the law of Moses, and in the prophets, and in the psalms, concerning me." Here Jesus mentions the three categories of writings that are contained in the Old Testament: 1) the writings of Moses (the first five books of the Bible, known as the *Pentateuch*), 2) the writings of the prophets, and 3) the Psalms:

> Then he said unto them, O fools, and slow of heart to believe all that the prophets have spoken…
>
> —Luke 24:25

Notice He said, "all that the prophets have spoken," thus validating the existent Jewish books of the prophets.

Manuscript Evidence for the Old Testament

One of the most exciting discoveries of modern times was that of the Dead Sea Scrolls in 1947, which was extremely significant in confirming the accuracy of the Old Testament. In an amazing, accidental discovery, hundreds of scrolls were found in a dozen different caves. The scrolls had been placed there by a Jewish sect called the Essenes. There they lay undisturbed for almost 1,900 years.[30]

These scrolls contained fragments from every book in the Old Testament, except Esther. They contained the complete Book of Isaiah. This provided us a remarkable comparison of manuscripts of the Old Testament currently in use to manuscripts of it that had been buried for about 1900 years, untouched and uncorrupted by men. Just how much error occurred in copies and translations during that time? Scholars compared them and made their conclusions:

> After comparing the entire Isaiah manuscript from Qumran with the present Hebrew text of Isaiah, Old Testament scholar Gleason L. Archer concluded that the Dead Sea Scrolls proved to be word for word identical with our standard Hebrew Bible in more than 95 percent of the text. The 5 percent of variation consisted chiefly of obvious slips of the pen and variations in spelling.[31]

Since Jesus gave no indication in His time that the Old Testament needed correcting, but did show support of it, as noted above, it becomes important to realize that these Dead Sea Scrolls were contemporary with Christ. Since the Dead Sea Scrolls agree with our present-day Old Testament and Christ validated the Old Testament of His time, what further evidence would we need for the trustworthiness of the Old Testament?

The Dead Sea Scrolls do not stand alone in Old Testament textual criticism. The Masoretic Text, from which our King James Old Testament and other Old Testament versions were translated, dated back to 900 A.D. Until the last century we did not have a lot to compare to these manuscripts. Now we have much older manuscripts, including the Dead Sea Scrolls, all independent of each other and found in different places that go back another one thousand years and confirm the accuracy of the Masoretic Text. A comparison of these manuscripts gives us overwhelming evidence that the Old Testament has been meticulously, or should we say miraculously, preserved. God has not only kept His Word pure but He has brought forth overwhelming evidence to disprove any false claims that would discredit its accuracy!

The Jews' reverence and care for copying their sacred Scriptures is well–attested–to by Flavius Josephus, the first-century Jewish historian:

> We have given practical proof of our reverence for our own Scriptures. For, although such long ages have now passed, no one has ventured either to add, or to remove, or to alter a syllable; and it is an instinct with every Jew, from the day of his birth, to regard them as the decrees of God, to abide by them, and, if need be, cheerfully die for them. Time and again ere now the sight has been witnessed of prisoners enduring tortures and death in every form in the theaters, rather than utter a single word against the laws and the allied documents.[32]

Manuscript Evidence for the New Testament

The evidence for the New Testament is even more overwhelming and convincing. There are more than four thousand manuscripts of the Greek New Testament available for comparison. Some were written in the second and third centuries. Over two hundred manuscripts date back to the fourth and eighth century. The most famous are:

1. **The Sinaitic Codex.** Discovered in 1859, it contains all of the New Testament. It dates back to the fourth century.
2. **The Vatican Codex.** Also from the fourth century, it contains almost the entire New Testament.
3. **The Alexandrian Codex.** From the fifth century, it contains almost all of both the Old and New Testaments.
4. **The Ephraim Codex.** From the fifth century, it contains much of the Old and New Testaments.

In all there are more than 2,400 original Bible manuscripts, in cursive writing, from the ninth to the sixteenth centuries. There are also more than 1,600 lectionaries, containing choice texts for the public reading of the New Testament.

In addition, there are in existence about 1,000 old manuscripts of numerous translations of the New Testament; and besides these, there are at least 8,000 manuscripts of the Latin Vulgate alone.[33]

No other works of antiquity can even come close to the abundance of manuscripts and the short time span between the original and the oldest copies, yet no one questions them. The following chart[34] demonstrates this:

COMPARISON OF ANCIENT TEXT VS. MODERN VERSION IN USE TODAY

Work	Date Written	Earliest Copy Existent	Time Span	Number of Ancient Copies Existent Today
Euripides	480–406 BC	AD 1100	1,500 years	9
Sophocles	496–406 BC	AD 1000	1,400 years	193
Catullus	54 BC	AD 1550	1,600 years	3
Aristophanes	450–385 BC	AD 900	1,200 years	10
Homer (*The* Iliad)	900 BC	400 BC	500 years	643
New Testament	AD 40–100	AD 125	50 years	Over 24,000

The shorter the time span between the date the work was completed and the earliest copy existent, the less time there was for error to creep in. Also, the more manuscripts available today, the better comparison of the modern-day to the original version we have. As the chart demonstrates, evidence for the validity of the New Testament dwarfs that of other ancient writings. More examples could be given of ancient histories of Rome, Caesar's *Gallic Wars* and other works, but none of them comes even close to the number of manuscripts we have of the ancient New Testament. Of all the writings of antiquity, *The Iliad* comes closest to the New Testament in manuscript authority. Yet the New Testament far surpasses *The Iliad* in manuscript evidence, as the above chart demonstrates.[35]

Writings of Early Church Fathers

Another source of comparison to test New Testament reliability is the writings of the early Christian church fathers. These men quoted the New Testament so much that one could almost reconstruct the New Testament from their writings. This provides another rich source of evidence that our New Testament has been transmitted to us accurately. One historian comments on this:

> Sir David Dalrymple was wondering about the preponderance of Scripture in early writing when someone asked him. "Suppose that the New Testament had been destroyed, and every copy of it lost by the end of the third century, could it have been collected together again from the writings of the Fathers of the second and third centuries?" After a great deal of investigation Dalrymple concluded: "Look at those books. You remember the question about the New Testament and the Fathers? That question roused my curiosity and as I possessed all the existing works of the Fathers of the second and third centuries, I commenced to search and up to this time I have found the entire New Testament, except eleven verses."[36]

David Dalrymple lived in the nineteenth century. Wow! What amazing evidence to show accurate transmission of the sacred writings. Think about it. Dalrymple's research shows that the New Testament was accurately preserved and translated for over 1,600 years (within 100 to 200 years of the original writings of the New Testament books, until 1800 A.D.).

Translation Errors in the Bible?

Translation error is a very broad term that could refer to an insignificant variation, such as a spelling or grammar change, or a significant change of the text that profoundly affects the message. Because I had always trusted my church so much and I had been taught that the Bible had many translation errors, I verbalized my belief in the untrustworthiness of the present Bible translation in use without having any knowledge of what I was talking about. Obviously there are variances in the copies and translations of Scripture from antiquity until present times, but according to textual critics these variance do not change the message of the text and are rather insignificant.

What about the variants of the Old Testament?

A *variant* is when two manuscripts differ on a particular word or phrase in the text. These are usually differences in spelling, word order, or words employed. Concerning the variants found in comparing early to later manuscripts of Bible texts, one scholar comments:

> It is to be expected that scholars would seek to compare, if possible, all the ancient documents on the Old Testament at their disposal. Herculean efforts have been expended in recent centuries to bring to light all the variations which may have crept into the manuscripts of the Scriptures: the oldest versions (The Septuagint, the Jewish Targums, the Syriac Version, the Peshitta and the Latin Vulgate) and the innumerable Biblical citations made by all the church fathers, along with the allusions in the Jewish commentaries (the Talmud).

> The famous B. Kennicott based his critical edition of the Hebrew Bible on the study of 581 manuscripts. Professor Rossi examined about 680. J. H. Michaelis spent thirty years of his life making a similar study. Professor R. D. Wilson declared that in the texts studied by Kennicott there are about 280 million letters. Of this total, there are about 900,000 variants, of which 750,000 are nothing but insignificant changes of v and of i. Taking the largest figure, one arrives at one variant for 316 letters. Laying aside the unimportant changes of v and i, one finds only one variant for 1,580 letters. Add to this the fact that most of the variants are found in only a few manuscripts or even in just one. Very few variants occur in more than one of the 200–400 manuscripts of each book of the Old Testament.[37]

What about Joseph Smith's Translation of the Bible?

I've included the above quotation to show the abundance of manuscripts available and how meticulously they have been scrutinized for comparisons. Whatever mistakes of men were made, it is clear that they were minute and that they in no way affected the Holy Bible's message. It would certainly be very obvious to see great alterations and/or omissions in the text if there were any—especially omissions of complete thoughts, phrases, or even verses. These were the kinds of additions Joseph Smith made in various places in the Bible. Following are a few examples from Genesis:

- In Genesis, chapter fourteen, he added sixteen complete verses.
- In Genesis, chapter fifteen, he added three complete verses and changed one.
- In Genesis, chapter seventeen, he added six complete verses and changed one.
- In Genesis, chapter nineteen, he added four complete verses and changed two.
- In Genesis, chapter forty-eight, he added five complete verses and changed two.
- In Genesis, chapter fifty, he added sixteen complete verses (one verse alone contained one hundred words.)

There is no evidence of error in Bible transmission or translations that would justify or support such vast additions to Scripture made by Joseph Smith.

What about the variants in the New Testament?

It is often charged by those opposed to Christianity that the variant readings in the manuscripts undermine the reliability of the text. These people point to some 200,000 variants in the existing manuscripts and contend that it is impossible to recover the New Testament's exact text and message. Nothing could be further from the truth!

It must be remembered that some 25,000 manuscripts of the New Testament exist in either Greek or one of the many other language versions. Every time one word or letter is different in a manuscript, it is counted as a variant. For example, if a word is misspelled in 2,000 manuscripts, it is counted as 2,000 variants. Most of the variants found in comparing New Testament manuscripts are of this variety and are only incidental to the meaning of the text. Here are some further examples:

- In Luke 4:23, along with other places, there is a variation in the spelling of the name Capernaum. It is sometimes spelled Capharnaum. Every time this occurs, it is counted as a variant.
- In Mark 7:24, some manuscripts read "Tyre and Sidon." Others read "Tyre." Every time they differ, it is counted as a variant.
- In John 19:7, some manuscripts read "our law." Others read "the law." Every time they differ, it is counted as a variant.

As stated, most of the variants do not materially affect the meaning of the text. At the turn of the century, B.B. Warfield observed that the New Testament, "has been transmitted to us with no, or next to no, variation; and even in the most corrupt form in which it has ever appeared, to use the oft-quoted words of Richard Bentley: 'The real text of the sacred writers is competently exact.' Further, because we possess so many manuscripts, we can be assured of preserving the original text."[38]

Here is another example of some variants from over 140 manuscripts of the Epistle to the Romans. This is a comparison of the first eight verses of Chapter 1, as compared by the scholar Griesbach.

GRISEBACH'S COMPARISON OF ROMANS 1:1-8

textus receptus (Elzevir, 1624)	variants from all the Greek manuscripts
1: no difference	
2: by his prophets	by the prophets (in only one manuscript, that of Paris)
3: born of the posterity (seed)	begotten (in the Upsal manuscript only, and this is but a change in two letters)
4: no difference	
5: Jesus Christ, our Lord	Jesus Christ, our God (in the Vienna manuscript only)
6: no difference	

7. that are in Rome, beloved of God, called from God our Father	who are in the love of God, called (only one manuscript, an uncial, of Dresden); who are at Rome, called (only two manuscripts, the uncial of St. Germaine and the minuscule at Rome) from God, the Father, (only the Upsal manuscript)
8: first for you all	first (a difference impossible to put down; it exists in only one manuscript) in regard to you all (in twelve manuscripts).

About this comparison, one scholar says this:

The true result is a demonstration of the admirable integrity of the epistle to the Romans. We chose this letter as an example because of its length and its importance. But the rest of the New Testament fully confirms like conclusions. According to Gaussen, scarcely ten verses out of 7,959 contain differences of any gravity.[39]

Additions or Deletions?

In testing the validity of the LDS claim of Bible error, another important observation needs to be considered. When a significant textual difference does exist, it is considered to be an addition to the text, not a deletion. The earliest and most reliable manuscripts do not have Mark 16:9–20 or John 7:53–8:11. For this and other reasons, scholars believe these two passages were added and were not in the original gospels. This is the opposite of the Book of Mormon claim "that there are many plain and precious things taken away from the book, which is the book of the Lamb of God." (1 Nephi 13:28b)

Notice that the addition of these verses does not change any message or meaning of the Bible. It could not be classified as an *error* of the Bible.

Who Changed the Text of the Bible?

When Mormons use the term "translation errors," they mean

343

something much different than the variances found in textual criticism. According to the LDS Church, translation errors are significant changes in the meaning of the text. *The Joseph Smith Translation* demonstrates some of these changes.

King James Translation	Joseph Smith Translation
John 1:1 In the beginning was the Word, and the Word was with God, and the Word was God. (KJV)	John 1:1 In the beginning was the gospel preached through the Son. And the gospel was the word, and the word was with the Son, and the Son was with God, and the Son was of God.
John 1:7 The same came for a wit- ness, to bear witness of the light, that all men through him might believe. (KJV)	John 1:7 The same came into the world for a witness, to bear witness of the light, to bear record of the gospel through the Son, unto all, that through him men might believe.
John 1:17–19 For the law was given by Moses, but grace and truth came by Jesus Christ. No man hath seen God at any time; the only begotten Son, which is in the bosom of the Father, he hath declared him. And this is the record of John, when the Jews sent priests and Levites from Jerusalem to ask him, Who art thou? (KJV)	John 1:17–19 For the law was given through Moses, but life and truth came through Jesus Christ. For the law was after a carnal command- ment, to the administration of death; but the gospel was after the power of an endless life, through Jesus Christ, the Only Begotten Son, who is in the bosom of the Father. And no man hath seen God at any time, except he hath borne record of the Son; for ex- cept it is through him no man can be saved. And this is the record of John, when the Jews sent priests and Lev- ites from Jerusalem, to ask him; Who art thou?

Hebrews 7:3 Without father, without mother, without descent, having neither beginning of days, nor end of life; but made like unto the Son of God; abideth a priest continually. (KJV)	Hebrews 7:3 For this Melchizedek was ordained a priest after the order of the Son of God, which order was without father, without mother, without descent, having neither beginning of days, nor end of life. And all those who are ordained unto this priesthood are made like unto the Son of God, abiding a priest continually.
Luke 16:17–18 And it is easier for heaven and earth to pass, than one tittle of the law to fail. Whosoever putteth away his wife, and marrieth another, committeth adultery: and whosoever marrieth her that is put away from her husband committeth adultery. (kjv)	Luke 16:18–23 And it is easier for heaven and earth to pass, than for one tittle of the law to fail. And why teach ye the law, and deny that which is written; and condemn him whom the Father hath sent to fulfill the law, that ye might all be redeemed? O fools! for you have said in your hearts, There is no God. And you per- vert the right way; and the Kingdom of heaven suffereth violence of you; and you persecute the meek; and in your violence you seek to destroy the Kingdom; and ye take the children of the Kingdom by force. Woe unto you, ye adulterers! And they reviled him again, being angry for the saying, that they were adulterers. But he contin- ued, saying, Whosoever putteth away his wife, and marrieth another, committeth adultery; and whosoever marrieth her who is put away from her husband, committeth adultery

Does manuscript evidence support The Joseph Smith Translation? No. These changes are not small variances but are very obvious changes in which many words are added, sometimes even entire verses that give a very different meaning to the text. Textual criticism has demonstrated that none of the changes to the text of the Bible that Joseph Smith made are valid. There is no evidence to support such "translation errors." On the contrary, it is easy work to research the studies done by experts in the field of textual criticism to see just what and where the variances lie.

The changes Joseph Smith made to the Holy Bible are glaring evidences that he is a false prophet. Surprisingly, I had found an answer to my question, "Who changed the Bible?" It wasn't "the great and abominable church," as the Book of Mormon said, which I had been raised to believe was the Catholic Church. Who'd changed the Bible? *Joseph Smith had!*

Two key Scriptures come to mind on the subject:

"Every word of God is pure: he is a shield unto them that put their trust in him. Add thou not unto his words, lest he reprove thee, and thou be found a liar."
—Proverbs 30:5–6

"To the law and to the testimony: if they speak not according to this word, it is because there is no light in them."
—Isaiah 8:20

God has brought forth overwhelming evidence that leaves no doubt that His hand has preserved his Word and kept it from corruption. Many of these manuscripts have been discovered in the twentieth century, long after Joseph Smith made his changes to God's Word. Little did Joseph Smith know that these manuscripts proving the inerrancy of the Bible were hidden in the ground, just waiting for God's time to bring them forth to prove wrong those who would try to discredit His Word.

In short, there is plenty of evidence for accurate Bible transmission if one wants to seek the truth with an open heart and mind. God's Word, the Bible, is a faithful measuring rod to detect false prophets and false doctrines, but if we don't use it we are likely to get fooled. God has kept His Word pure for us—just as He promised He would:

The grass withereth, the flower fadeth: but the word of our God shall stand for ever.
—Isaiah 40:8

Forever, O LORD, thy word is settled in heaven.

—Psalm 119:89

Concerning thy testimonies, I have known of old that thou hast founded them forever.

—Psalm 119:152

For verily I say unto you, Till heaven and earth pass, one jot or one tittle shall in no wise pass from the law, till all be fulfilled.

—Matthew 5:18

Heaven and earth shall pass away, but my words shall not pass away.

—Matthew 24:35

Key Reference Books for Further Information

Ten Reasons to Trust the Bible, Don Stewart, ETW (Educating the World)

Family Handbook of Christian Knowledge: The Bible, Don Stewart and Josh McDowell, Here's Life Publishers, Inc.

You Can Trust the Bible, John MacArthur, Jr., Moody Press

Evidence That Demands a Verdict, Josh McDowell

A Ready Defense: The Best of Josh McDowell, Compiled by Bill Wilson, Here's Life Publishers

Records of the Past Illuminate the Bible, Siegfried H. Horn, Review and Herald Publishing Association

A General Introduction to the Bible, Norman L. Geisler and William E. Nix, Moody Press

V. Discussing the Aaronic Priesthood with Dad

Bible Interpretation

As I mentioned before in this book, Dad insisted that I didn't believe in the Bible anymore because I didn't believe in the apostasy and restoration, and the necessity of the LDS Priesthood. As we turned to Bible Scriptures concerning these subjects, I tried to show him that my interpretation fit the context of the Bible more than his interpretation did.

Dad responded in a strong, very annoyed voice.

"You don't '*interpret*' the Bible. I don't like the word interpret! You just read it and accept what it says! Of course, you need the Holy Ghost to help you."

I answered rather timidly.

"Well, others think they are just reading it and accepting what it says, too. But they get a different interpretation than the Mormons do, and they also think they have the Holy Ghost."

"Well, that's the problem," Dad said. "They don't have the gift of the Holy Ghost! Now people in other churches are sometimes influenced by the Holy Ghost, but they don't have the gift of the Holy Ghost because they don't have the Priesthood to give them the gift of the Holy Ghost."

Priesthood Authority

The subject of priesthood came up frequently with Dad. Authority is definitely very important to a member of the church and it is definitely a stronghold. Priesthood was one of Dad's strong foundations.

"No other church has the Priesthood. No other church even claims to have the Melchizedek Priesthood," he said.

Then he repeated one of his favorite Scriptures: "No man taketh this honour unto himself, but he that is called of God, as was Aaron" (Hebrews 5:4).

Dad was on a roll. He went on.

"And how was Aaron called? He was called by the Prophet Moses! Moses laid his hands upon Aaron to ordain him and give him the Priesthood. Now all the preachers, evangelists, or whatever else they are called, are not called by God because they have not been called by a prophet, nor have they been ordained and given the Priesthood by one who has that authority. A policeman doesn't just make himself a policeman. He has to be given that authority to function as a policeman through the proper channels. It is the same with God and his church. Joseph Smith got the Priesthood from John the Baptist, Peter, James, and John and they got it from Christ by the laying on of hands. Every Priesthood-holder can trace his line of authority back to Joseph Smith. I have my ordination card at home that says who I received the Priesthood from and who he received it from—all the way back to Joseph Smith!

"Now, all these preachers in other denominations have just decided they want to preach, but they have not been called by God or properly ordained to do so! One can only get the Priesthood by the laying on of hands by one who already has the Priesthood. That is what Hebrews 5:4 is all about. It says, 'no man taketh this honour unto himself!'"

Wow, he was really wound up. I was not surprised, however. He felt very strongly about the subject of authority. What was interesting, though, was that Dad was demonstrating that he didn't just read the Bible, but that he indeed *interpreted* it. Hebrews 5:4 was a great example. Dad had just given quite an interpretation to "called of God, as was Aaron." I remembered studying this before and now I could hardly wait to follow through on this verse Dad had mentioned.

Aaron's Ordination to the Priesthood

"Why don't we read in the Old Testament how Aaron was ordained," I suggested.

Dad agreed. We found the chapters in Exodus that described Aaron's ordination, as well as his sons' (Exodus 28 and 29). Chapter twenty-eight goes into great detail about the special clothing they were to wear. Chapter twenty-nine goes into detail about the animals that were to be burnt on the altar and what was to be done with their blood.

Instructions are given in verses twelve to twenty-one to kill one bullock and two rams. Before burning the animals on the altar, some of the blood was put on the altar then the rest of the blood was poured at the bottom of the altar. The blood of the second ram was to be put on the tip of Aaron's right ear, the thumb of his right hand, and the big toe of his right foot. The same was to be done for Aaron's sons. Then they took blood from the altar, along with anointing oil, and sprinkled it on Aaron and his sons and their special anointing clothes that they wore.

I looked at Dad and responded.

"That would have been quite a sight. After they got dressed in all those fancy clothes, they had blood everywhere. Imagine what they looked and smelled like!"

Dad didn't like all that talk about the blood. He was checking out to see if this really was the way they were called to be priests. There was no question about that. The first verse of chapter twenty-nine says: "And this is the thing that thou shalt do unto them to hallow them, to minister unto me in the priest's office: Take one young bullock, and two rams without blemish."

Verse thirty-five(b) says, "seven days shalt thou consecrate them." This was quite an ordeal. There was no denying that the ordination of Aaron and his sons to the priesthood was not even remotely connected to any ordination to the Priesthood in the Mormon Church!

I wasn't finished yet.

"There's still more," I said. "We haven't read the part I really want you to see. Each time before they killed the bull and the two rams, they did something I think you will find significant."

We started with verse ten: "You shall also have the bull brought before the tabernacle of meeting, and Aaron and his sons shall put their hands on the head of the bull."

"Now that is interesting," I said. "Instead of Moses laying his hands on the heads of Aaron and his sons to ordain them to the priesthood, Aaron and his sons put their hands on the head of the bull before they killed it."

351

Verse fifteen continues: "You shall also take one ram, and Aaron and his sons shall put their hands on the head of the ram."

One more time in Verse nineteen: "You shall also take the other ram, and Aaron and his sons shall put their hands on the head of the ram."

I couldn't resist commenting.

"I'm sure they were not giving the animals the Priesthood."

I was surprised at my boldness. Half-sarcastically and half-jokingly, Dad responded, "Well, I guess I don't have the Priesthood, after all!"

I was very relieved and taken back at his unexpected response. Then he had a lot more to say.

"Now, Carma! I'm not really concerned what the Old Testament has to say about the priesthood. Christ ordained His twelve apostles and gave them the priesthood! That same priesthood was restored to the earth through the Prophet Joseph Smith. I know that more than I know anything! All this that we've been reading about the blood just doesn't matter anymore. The LDS Church is the only church with the Aaronic and Melchizedek Priesthoods. We have to go through the proper channels that God has ordained. Man cannot just take the authority of God upon himself! He must be ordained by one who holds the Priesthood that is found only in the Mormon Church!"

Dad was starting to get louder and more intense. I knew it was time to be quiet.

Why the Laying on of Hands?

I also knew it was time for me to learn more about "the laying on of hands." Why did God specifically command the Israelites to lay hands on the heads of the animals to be slain? I resolved that when I went home I would continue to research this subject.

I learned that the laying on of hands was symbolic of being identified with someone or something. The Jewish priests had laid hands on the animals' heads before sacrificing them in order to symbolically identify the animal with the sins for which they were being sacrificed. It was symbolic of a transfer, but not literally transferring something.

The instructions to lay hands on the animals' heads before sacrificing them and sprinkling their blood on Aaron and his sons were repeated in

Leviticus chapter eight. This was something they did routinely.

Also, Numbers chapter eight gives instructions for the cleansing of all the Levite priests for their service. The Levites were to be sprinkled with water and were to shave all the hair off their bodies (v. 7). Then they were to bring burnt offerings of grain, and sin offerings (vv. 8, 12).

I found Numbers 8:10 to be very interesting: "And thou shalt bring the Levites before the LORD: and the children of Israel shall put their hands upon the Levites." Wait a minute? Wasn't that backwards? Why would the children of Israel (who did not have the priesthood) lay their hands on the Levites as part of their cleansing for the Levites priestly service? The Israelites certainly were not giving the Levites the Priesthood since they didn't have it. It was only the tribe of Levi that God called to be priests. So why did the other Israelites lay their hands on the Levites?

I eventually learned the answer. The children of Israel laid hands on the Levites to identify the Levites as substitutes for the firstborn of Israel whom God had separated for himself when they left Israel. This commandment of God to have the Israelites lay hands on the Levites was symbolic—showing that the Levites were now separated by God to be His own and to do the service at the tabernacle as the representatives of the whole congregation of Israel.

> Thus you shall separate the Levites from among the sons of Israel, and the Levites shall be Mine . . . I have taken them for Myself instead of every first issue of the womb, the firstborn of all the sons of Israel. For every firstborn among the sons of Israel is Mine . . . on the day that I struck down all the firstborn in the land of Egypt I sanctified them for Myself. But I have taken the Levites instead of every firstborn among the sons of Israel. I have given the Levites as a gift to Aaron and to his sons from among the sons of Israel, to perform the service of the sons of Israel at the tent of meeting and to make atonement on behalf of the sons of Israel, so that there will be no plague among the sons of Israel by their coming near to the sanctuary.
>
> —Numbers 8:14–19 NASB

The Laying on of hands definitely did not transfer any power, especially a priesthood power in the Old Testament. The Levites were

353

the tribe called and set apart by God to be His, and to serve at the temple. No special power was needed to do the work at the sanctuary (tabernacle, later the temple). It was their service to God and the Israelites.

The priesthood in the Old Testament was not a power transferred from man to man by the laying on of hands as Mormon's think of it today. Neither was the priesthood transferred from man to man in the New Testament by the laying on of hands. Neither Jesus, nor his apostles, ever mentioned the need for priesthood. Jesus did ordain His apostles (Mark 3:14) and He gave them power; but that power was in His name—through faith in Him. Also, the word used in Mark 3:14 for "ordained" is translated from the Greek word "poleo" which means "appoint." This Greek word has a long definition; but does not mention "priesthood," "power," or "the laying on of hands." (See Chapter 13's "What Does Ordain Mean?" section)

I found it interesting that Hebrews 9:6 (King James translation), states that the things in the tabernacle (candlestick, shewbread, ark of the covenant, etc.) were *ordained*.

About a year later, I attended a series of lectures (at a Seventh-day Adventist Church) on the Old Testament tabernacle and the High Priest. I was amazed to learn how every detail of the tabernacle was significant and how it fulfilled a purpose in foreshadowing the ultimate sacrifice of our Lord Jesus Christ, who is our High Priest. He fulfilled the role of the Old Testament High Priest and is the only one "after the order of Melchizedek." (To learn more, please see Vol. Two, Ch. 22, *Jesus, Our High Priest Foreve*r, p. 223.)

I had learned that the concept of priesthood in the LDS Church could not be substantiated by the Bible.

ENDNOTES

1. *Jesus the Christ, Thirty-Second Edition* by James E. Talmage, one of the twelve apostles of the Church of Jesus Christ of Latter-day Saints, Deseret Book Company, Salt Lake City, Utah, 1962, p. 489 and 501. Following are two quotes from *Jesus the Christ* concerning John 10:34: "They angrily retorted: 'For a good work we stone thee not; but for blasphemy; and because that thou, being a man, makest thyself God.' Plainly they had found no ambiguity in His words. He then cited to them the Scriptures, wherein **even judges empowered by divine authority are called gods**, and asked: 'Is it not written in your law, I said, Ye are gods? If he called them gods, unto whom the word of God came, and the Scripture cannot be broken: say ye of him, whom the Father hath sanctified, and sent into the world, Thou blasphemest; because I said, I am the Son of God?' Then, reverting to the first avouchment that His own commission was of the Father, who is greater than all, He added: 'If I do not the works of my Father, believe me not. But if I do, though ye believe not me, believe the works: that ye may know, and believe that the Father is in me, and I in him.' Again the Jews sought to take Him, but were foiled by means not stated; He passed from their reach and departed from the temple." (p. 489, bold emphasis mine)

   At the end of the chapter James Talmage explains that the term "gods," as used by Jesus in John 10:34 (when He was quoting Psalm 82:6), refers to *human judges* of Israel: "8. Divinely Appointed Judges, Called 'gods'—In Psalm 82:6, judges invested by divine appointment are called 'gods.' To this Scripture the Savior referred in His reply to the Jews in Solomon's Porch. Judges so authorized officiated as the representatives of God and are honored by the exalted title 'gods.' Compare the similar appellation applied to Moses (Exodus 4:16, 7:1). Jesus Christ possessed divine authorization, not through the word of God transmitted to Him by man, but as an inherent attribute. The inconsistency of calling human judges 'gods,' and of ascribing blasphemy to the Christ who called Himself the Son of God, would have been apparent to the Jews but for their sin-darkened minds." (p. 501, emphasis his)

2. *Harper's Bible Dictionary*, Paul H. Achtemeier, Editor; Harper & Row Publishers, San Francisco, 1985, p. 510.

3. *Mormon Doctrine*, Bruce R. McConkie, Bookcraft, Inc., Salt Lake City, Utah, 1958, p. 359. Note: Mormons do not believe in the Trinity. They believe that Jesus is Jehovah and Father in Heaven is Eloheim. These two are separate persons and two separate gods. On the other hand, the Bible teaches that there is only one God manifested in three persons. Since there is only one God who is

plural in nature, the name "Jehovah" can refer to the Father, or to Jesus the Son, or to both of them, as a family name would refer to different members of one family. Neither Jehovah's Witnesses nor Mormons believe in the Trinity. However, Jehovah's Witnesses believe that the name "Jehovah" refers only to God the Father, while Mormons believe "Jehovah" refers to Jesus.

4. Ibid, p. 359.

5. Isaiah 26:8 and all the other verses here demonstrate that this chapter is a prayer to Jehovah: "Yea, in the way of thy judgments, O LORD, have we waited for thee; the desire of our soul is to thy name, and to the remembrance of thee."

6. Isaiah 26:19, New International Version reads: "But your dead will live; their bodies will rise. You who dwell in the dust, wake up and shout for joy." This passage is clearly speaking of earth's dead being resurrected and not Jehovah's body being resurrected (as the LDS Apostle Bruce R. McConkie makes it appear.)

7. *How We Got The Bible*, Lenet Hadley Read, (Deseret Book Company: Salt Lake City, Utah, 1985) p. 14.

8. Ibid, p. 47.

9. Ibid, p. 55.

10. Ibid, p. 56.

11. Ibid, p. 59–61.

12. Ibid, p. 68.

13. Ibid, p. 70.

14. Ibid, p. 71.

15. Ibid, p. 72.

16. Ibid, p. 73, 74.

17. Ibid, p. 59.

18. *The Holy Bible*, Published by The Church of Jesus Christ of Latter-day Saints, Salt Lake City, Utah, USA, 1979; p. 654, 655.

19. *Family Handbook of Christian Knowledge: THE BIBLE*, Josh McDowell and Don Stewart, Here's Life Publishers, Inc., San Bernardino, CA. 1983, p. 51.

20. *Journal of Discourses*, Vol. 7, page 289. "No man or woman in this dispensation will ever enter into the Celestial Kingdom of God without the consent of Joseph Smith . . . Every man and woman must have the certificate of Joseph Smith, junior, as a passport to their entrance into the mansion where God and Christ are—. . . He reigns there as supreme a being in his sphere, capacity, and calling, as God does in heaven."

21. Webster's New World Dictionary of American English, Third College Edition, Copyright 1988 by Simon & Schuster, Inc., page 1293.

22. *Journal of Discourses*, vol. 19, p. 229.

23. *Teachings of the Prophet Joseph Smith*, p. 356.

24. Joseph Smith was referring to Paul's statement (or whoever wrote the book of Hebrews) in Hebrews 11:40. This chapter is sometimes referred to as "the faith hall of fame" because it mentions many of the great prophets and leaders of the Old Testament who accomplished great things because of their faith. The preceding verse (Hebrews 11:39) states that even though all these great people obtained a good report through faith, they did not receive the promise. What was the promise? That they would be made perfect through Jesus Christ. They did not receive this promise through the law of Moses, but the promise of eternal life is realized for us as well as them only through the new covenant of Jesus Christ. Joseph Smith's misuse of this Scripture shows that he did not understand salvation by grace through faith in Jesus.

25. *Webster's New World Dictionary*, Third College Edition; p. 906.

26. The Book of Mormon contradicts the following statement made by Joseph Smith that the Father, Son, and Holy Ghost are three gods. "I have always declared God to be a distinct personage, Jesus Christ a separate and distinct personage from God, the Father, and the Holy Ghost was a distinct personage and a spirit: and these three constitute three distinct personages and three Gods. If this is in accordance with the New Testament, lo and behold! We have three Gods anyhow, and they are plural; and who can contradict it?" (*Teachings of the Prophet Joseph Smith*; p. 370)

Yet, the Book of Mormon says the three are one God.

"And the honor be to the Father, and to the Son, and to the Holy Ghost, which is one God. Amen." (The ending to the testimony of the three witnesses in the introduction to the Book of Mormon.)

"And now, behold, my beloved brethren, this is the way; and there is none other way nor name given under heaven whereby man can be saved in the Kingdom of God. And now, behold, this is the doctrine of Christ, and the only and true doctrine of the Father, and of the Son, and of the Holy Ghost, which is one God, without end. Amen" (2 Nephi 31:21).

". . . and shall be brought and be arraigned before the bar of Christ the Son, and God, the Father,, and the Holy Spirit, which is one Eternal God, to be judged according to their works, whether they be good or whether they be evil" (Alma 11:44).

"And he hath brought to pass the redemption of the world, whereby he that is found guiltless before him at the judgment day hath it given unto him to dwell in the presence of God in his Kingdom, to sing ceaseless praises with the choirs above, unto the Father, and unto the Son, and unto the Holy Ghost, which are one God, in a state of happiness which hath no end" (Mormon 7:7).

27.   "And this is according to the oath and covenant which belongeth to the priesthood. Therefore, all those who receive the priesthood, receive this oath and covenant of my Father, which he cannot break, neither can it be moved. But whoso breaketh this covenant after he hath received it, and altogether turneth therefrom, shall not have forgiveness of sins in this world nor in the world to come" (Doctrine & Covenants 84:39–41).

The next verse gives strength to the power of the oath and covenant of the priesthood by claiming to be given by a voice out of the heavens. "And woe unto all those who come not unto this priesthood which ye have received, which I now confirm upon you who are present this day, by mine own voice out of the heavens; and even I have given the heavenly hosts and mine angels charge concerning you" (Doctrine & Covenants 84:42).

28.   For more information about the Pearl of Great Price and the Egyptian papyri, a good book is *By His Own Hand Upon Papyri*.

29.   *Webster's New World Dictionary, Second Concise Edition*; Copyright 1975, The Southwestern Company, Nashville, Tennessee, p. 408.

30.   *Family Handbook of Christian Knowledge: THE BIBLE*, Josh McDowell and Don Stewart, Here's Life Publishers, Inc., San Bernardino, CA. 1983, p. 51.

31.   Ibid. p. 52.

32.   *Family Handbook of Christian Knowledge: THE BIBLE*, Josh McDowell and Don Stewart, Here's Life Publishers, Inc., San Bernardino, CA, 1983, p. 48.

33.   *The Inspiration and Authority of Scripture*, Rene Pache, Moody Press, Chicago, 1969, p. 191.

34.   *Family Handbook of Christian Knowledge: THE BIBLE*, Josh McDowell and Don Stewart, Here's Life Publishers, Inc., San Bernardino, CA. 1983, p. 61.

35.   Ibid. p. 62.

36.   Ibid. p. 65.

37.   *The Inspiration and Authority of Scripture*, Rene Pache, Moody Press, Chicago, 1969, p. 190.

38.   *Family Handbook of Christian Knowledge: THE BIBLE*, Josh McDowell and Don Stewart, Here's Life Publishers, Inc., San Bernardino, CA. 1983, p. 68

39.   The Inspiration and Authority of Scripture, Rene Pache, Moody Press, Chicago, 1969, p. 194–196.

TOPICAL INDEX

Carma Naylor

Descendant of Mormon pioneers, Mormonism was more than a religion to Carma Naylor; it was her connection with God. She fully believed that it was the only true church of Jesus Christ on earth, and she was committed to being a faithful servant to Him through serving in the LDS religion and obeying its laws and ordinances. Beyond its place as a religious ideal, Mormonism was also her identity as a person, encompassing every aspect of her life. It was her lifestyle, culture, and heritage.

Carma's forefathers were a part of the Martin Handcart Company who trekked on foot from Iowa to Utah in 1856, pushing their belongings in wooden handcarts. Some members of her family died of hunger and freezing temperatures in the Rocky Mountains on that arduous journey. True to his Mormon beliefs, her great-great-grandfather became a polygamist.

Carma was born in Ogden, Utah, daughter of a Mormon Bishop, who taught her what he believed was true, Mormon doctrine. She loved having theological discussions with him, and she believed he had every book ever published by the Mormon Church in the vast library that filled an entire room in their home.

Carma graduated from the LDS seminary program in high school, fulfilled a full-time mission to New Zealand, and attended Brigham Young University where she met her husband. They were married in the Salt Lake Temple and Carma faithfully attended the temple for nineteen years. She served in music, teaching, and leadership positions, never expecting to be anything but a faithful Latter-day Saint.

She was forty when she became a born-again Christian, and she wrote of that experience in A Mormon's Unexpected Journey, published in two volumes. Carma and her husband reside in Southern California. They have five sons, three daughters, thirty-three grandchildren, five great grandchildren and counting.

Mormonism to Grace

Visit Carma's website for even more information, including interviews, photos, and articles: **mormonismtograce.com**

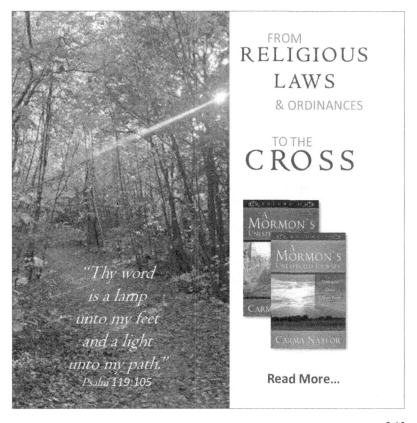